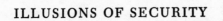

ILLUSIONS OF SECURITY

MICHAEL G. FRY

Illusions of Security
North Atlantic Diplomacy
1918-22

UNIVERSITY OF TORONTO PRESS

© University of Toronto Press 1972
Toronto and Buffalo
Printed in Canada
ISBN 0-8020-1774-6
Microfiche ISBN 0-8020-0084-3
LC 74-163814

Frontispiece
Clemenceau, Lloyd George, Bonar Law, and Lord Birkenhead
at the Peace Conference 1919

To my mother and the memory of my father

Contents

ILLUSTRATIONS

Preface

Amid the seminal themes of wartime diplomacy none surpasses in significance that of the debate within the victorious alliance as its members individually and collectively seek to imprint their version of justice on the future peace. Idealism and crusading zeal, realism and the logic of their separate histories tend to transform this debate into an internecine struggle, often intense and bitter in tone. During the mid and late stages of the two world wars of the twentieth century this interallied contest centred on three issues: national interests, expressed in economic, political, and strategic terms as the allies sought to establish their postwar world positions; ideological and philosophical confrontations; and differences over racial problems. In the prolonged process of peacemaking the debate matured.

Statesmen, experiencing the prospect of victory simultaneously with the frustrations caused by the disintegration of their wartime co-operation, sensed the magnitude of the task. History would condemn a false step, accuse them of sterility, or indict them for setting the world on the wrong path. Indeed many analysts of the tragedies of the interwar years base their mansion of logic on the single premise of the frailties of the 1919 peace settlement. The policy-makers sought new formulae to avoid the egregious errors of the past, to surmount current problems, to set the world on a peaceful course, and to secure their place in history. Yet, curiously but understandably, these were sanguine years; to Lord Curzon, soon to become British foreign secretary and citing the Hellas chorus to the House of Lords, the golden age would return. Military success combined with diplomatic ingenuity would induce reconstruction.

While the Second World War led to the creation of the United

Nations, eventually to the North Atlantic Treaty Organisation and other international systems, the first great conflict bred or accelerated the birth of the League of Nations and various ephemeral concepts and schemes. Less frail than most, although for lengthy periods seeming to survive *in absentia*, was the theme of Atlanticism, rooted deeply enough in the pre-1914 era and yet frequently obscured by more dramatic theses. Under the impact of the entry of the United States into the war in April 1917 and despite the legacy of deeply-felt fissures in Anglo-American relations created by such problems as that of the blockade, Atlanticism took on greater attraction and even fascination for a section of the elite of the British empire. These seemingly inspired men were the Atlanticists and they viewed the future of world peace and civilising progress as intimately bound up with the sustained co-operation of the British empire and the United States. In the eyes of the most optimistic, Atlanticism was a panacea for all problems; others, however, were more cynical and even antagonistic.

In a complex yet logical fashion the Atlanticists, after frequent disappointments and even disillusionment, turned to Pacific and Far Eastern problems. Specifically, the question of whether or not to renew the Anglo-Japanese alliance, which raised the vital issues of imperial defence and the empire's relations with the United States, provided both the vehicle and the test case. Anglo-American co-operation might be forged, the Atlanticists felt, out of the debates on the future of the twenty-year-old alliance. Their hopes were raised by the Imperial Conference held in London in the summer of 1921 and by the Washington Conference, deliberating from November 1921 to February 1922, only to be disappointed by subsequent developments in 1922 and beyond. Optimism in fact had bred illusion and resulted virtually in despair. Apostasy was then possible.

The three North Atlantic powers, Canada, Great Britain, and the United States, along with the other dominions, participated at the centre of this debate. Atlanticism quite naturally was their preserve. This study, abstaining from lengthy observations on domestic politics, is of those members of the elites who helped formulate the foreign policies of the North Atlantic powers. Based primarily on official and private archives in London, Ottawa, and Washington, it attempts to investigate the fortunes of Atlanticism in the immediate postbellum period up to 1922.

Acknowledgments

A North Atlantic Treaty Organisation fellowship enabled me to complete this study. I am also grateful for support from the Research and Publication Fund of Carleton University and for a grant in aid of publication from the Social Science Research Council of Canada, using funds provided by the Canada Council.

Anyone familiar with his work will appreciate my debt to D.C. Watt, reader in international history at the London School of Economics. Over a longer period, I am one of those students fortunate enough to have received the assistance and encouragement of Professor W.N. Medlicott, former holder of the Stevenson Chair of International History and now senior editor of *Documents on British Foreign Policy, 1919–1939*. Professor Roger Graham, of Queen's University, gave me help and guidance, and D.M.L. Farr, professor of history and dean of arts at Carleton University, provided continuous support.

The staffs of the Public Record Office, the British Museum, the Birmingham University library, the Scottish Record Office, Queen's University library, the Public Archives of Canada, the Library of Congress, the Massachusetts Historical Association, the Houghton Library at Harvard, the Burton Historical Division of the Detroit Public Library, and especially of the Beaverbrook Memorial Library were unfailingly helpful. I am indebted to them all in varying degrees. I also appreciate the assistance of my typists, M. Clark and H. Zourdoumis.

I am grateful for permission to use and to quote from the following sources: the Beaverbrook Newspapers Ltd for the Lloyd George

Papers; the Controller of HMSO for crown copyright material in the Public Record Office; the Trustees of the British Museum for the Balfour Papers; and Professor A.K.S. Lambton and Francis Noel-Baker for the Cecil Papers.

M.G. FRY
Ottawa 1970

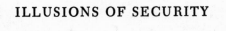

ILLUSIONS OF SECURITY

ONE

The Atlanticists Prospects and Problems 1919-21

As the great war drew to a close in the fall of 1918 and the dream of victory over the Central Powers became a sudden reality, the allied leaders sought to ensure that ingenious diplomacy would consummate military achievement. The democratic powers, shorn of ideologically embarrassing allies, could delude themselves into thinking that they had reached the pinnacle of success and they sought to seize the opportunities apparently created. They must make peace with Germany and her satellites, settle European, Middle Eastern, and even Far Eastern frontiers, begin to resurrect the world economy, and provide global security.

In broad terms this gigantic task presented itself in triple form. First, and traditionally, France, Italy, the members of the emerging British commonwealth, the United States, and Japan would demand that their national interests, legitimate, justifiable, moral, and defensive be met. Clemenceau must seek a new order in the Rhineland and in Eastern Europe and ensure France's economic and financial rehabilitation, and Orlando must attempt to secure for Italy extended frontiers, control of the Adriatic, and new influence in North Africa and Asia Minor. Lloyd George must ensure the destruction of German naval and colonial power and resurrect Britain's world economic position, while the dominions sought to confirm their authority in Africa, in the Pacific, and in the Atlantic. President Woodrow Wilson must defeat proposals which threatened his perception of world order and at the same time strengthen America's commercial, financial, and maritime position. He would, therefore, deprecate either Japanese attempts to consolidate her position in the northwest Pacific, in Shantung, and in Manchuria or the renewal of commercial imperialism by the European powers.

The second dimension of the problem of peacemaking arose because of the single fact of the Bolshevik seizure of power in Russia which enveloped and impregnated those material issues.[1] The global threat of Bolshevism had emerged and although the democratic elite differed in their assessment both of the nature of the problem and on what would be the most efficacious solution, they sensed its significance and felt the magnitude and urgency of the threat. In London no one surpassed Winston Churchill, soon to inherit the War Office, and Sir Maurice Hankey, head of the cabinet secretariat, in their concern.[2] Political leaders looked for signs of domestic malaise and internationally they feared a new terror. Dangerous forces were abroad, men sought inspiration across national frontiers, and liberal-democracy seemed to some degree vulnerable despite the victory over German militarism. Perhaps the war's total rhythms had unleashed irresistible social and political forces which would sweep across Europe. This was the great dilemma, for if victory was not to be a cruel illusion the allies must find an answer, whether economic, political, or military, which was an expression of the combined will of a league of ideologically acceptable powers. Indeed, narrow national interests might be forfeited consciously to meet this challenge from Bolshevik Russia, for what value was the left bank of the Rhine to France if communism overtook Germany or a formidable Russo-German combination emerged; and what if Japan joined Russia and Germany in a menacing triplice?

The victorious allies were also imperial powers and in their midst stood Japan, China, and India, symbols of the third dimension of the overall problem. The war had ushered in a new phase in the history of imperialism, the slogans and rallying cries of liberal-democracy were not applicable exclusively to Anglo-Saxon communities, and, however muted and incipient, equality, justice, and national self-determination were phrases with appeal in Afro-Asia. Japan's demand that the Allies insert a statement on racial equality into the preamble of the Covenant of the League of Nations was neither an empty gesture nor a mere tactical move. The demand was both real and symbolic, sounding the challenge to all facets of imperialism and to

1 For the various dimensions of this problem, see Mayer, *Politics and Diplomacy of Peacemaking*, Thompson, *Russia, Bolshevism and the Versailles Peace*, and Ullman, *Britain and the Russian Civil War*.

2 Fry, 'Britain, the Allies and the Problem of Russia'; Hankey memoranda, 19 March 1919, Cab 1/27, and 17 July 1919, Cab 21/159

parts of the very foundations of western society. Consequently, devotees of the emerging British commonwealth could envisage one of its primary goals as that of building a bridge between East and West and of reducing racial divisions lest they become irrevocable. At the same time many felt the need to create the unity and confirm the prestige of the Anglo-Saxon powers.

In terms of broad principles of policy, where did solutions apparently lie? How could the peacemakers serve immediate national interests in Europe and the Middle East primarily, meet the challenge of communism, and create the basis of a new rapport with non-white peoples? Orthodox realist opinion in France and Britain, as represented by Clemenceau and Curzon, sought the answer in traditional concepts associated with military alliances, naval hegemony, and the balance of power. Russia's defection complicated the situation but the realists sought to preserve the wartime coalition, reinterpret its function, and frame it in precise political terms. After all, such traditional methods had saved France and Europe. They were proven and vindicated, they demanded sustained allied co-operation, a reduced Germany, selective disarmament, a reorganised Eastern Europe, and, to counter both Germany and Bolshevik Russia, a strategic and ideological *cordon-sanitaire*. The degree of hostility toward and the extent of acceptance of an accommodation with Germany and Russia would be expressed through variables such as the establishment or not of *de facto* diplomatic relations and the continuation or termination of the economic blockade.

In contrast to those who advocated traditional solutions stood those, primarily in the United States and the British empire, who sought a powerful League of Nations. This concert would constitute a set of regulations and directives to govern the conduct of international affairs which would render obsolete much of the old diplomacy and be an expression of democratic statecraft. Only when these revised rules governing international relations were operative, they argued, would the world experience peace and justice.

Other members of the western elite, having discounted preventive war and military roll-back, saw salvation in part through changes within Russia itself. They hoped that the Bolshevik government would moderate its attitudes quite rapidly and return to sanity and decency, aided by commercial, cultural, and political contacts. Then a new Russia, federal and liberalised, would emerge cleansed and ready to play a stabilising role in European and world affairs.

Finally, in Britain, the dominions, and in the United States, Atlanticists advocated their solution, urging that the key to peace lay in the creation of a global hegemony enjoyed by the United States and the British empire, expressed in maritime and financial terms.[3] The Atlantic Powers, aided by the dominions, would police the seas, help pacify Europe, the Middle East, and Asia, stimulate economic reconstruction, wield the powers of trusteeship, and provide moral and philosophical leadership. In sum, Atlanticism meant drawing the United States into sustained and complete co-operation with the British empire as a panacea for the world's ills.

Who were the Atlanticists, on what assumptions was their credo based, and why had they any grounds for optimism in the face of alternative propositions and even fierce criticism? Although Atlanticist sentiments were expressed publicly by many who held high office throughout the world war, oratory, especially in the flush of victory, was an inadequate guide. Who could dismiss or discount with confidence the seemingly momentous potential of intimate rapport with the United States? The process of identifying the Atlanticists among the British and dominion statesmen must emerge from a study of the postures adopted in the British and the Imperial War Cabinets, in British Empire Delegation deliberations, and in other intergovernmental and private exchanges on relevant issues. Their differing motives should permit the historian to make general classifications and to note further important distinctions on the basis of dedication to the Atlanticist thesis. One must also note the criticisms levelled at the advocates of Anglo-American co-operation by proponents of alternative courses of action, in order to weigh the strength and credibility of the Atlanticists and to assess their prospects of success in postwar policy reviews.

Three groups are identifiable within the British and dominion elites: the Atlanticists with varying and usually diminishing degrees of dedication; the sceptics, whose disillusionment bred cynicism; and those who became frankly hostile. The levels of devotion among the Atlanticists tended to fluctuate more severely than those among the other two factions, but actual movement between the groups was rare. However, the profound sceptic could adopt a more hostile attitude on occasions, those who were hostile could appear to have moments of conversion, and the dedicated could justifiably lapse into

3 This study will view Atlanticism primarily from the standpoint of Britain and her dominions, although an investigation of Atlanticist elements within the United States is obviously needed.

despair. Unquestioning Atlanticists, embodying the traits of the convert, were rare, for the legacies of America's prolonged period of neutrality during the war, reinforced by postwar friction over naval, financial, and commercial problems, placed a severe and even intolerable burden on Atlanticist loyalties. Indeed, over certain issues Atlanticism seemed to survive despite the absence of Atlanticists.

Within the ranks of the Atlanticists stood groups, identifiable by the varied emphases in their motives, although certain stimuli were common to many of them. Edward Grey and Lord Haldane, respectively foreign secretary until December 1916 and lord chancellor until May 1915, but still participating marginally in the relevant policy debates of 1919, H.A.L. Fisher, minister of education and a successor in part to C.P. Scott as the custodian of Lloyd George's liberal conscience, and G.N. Barnes, Labour's renegade representative in Lloyd George's coalition, stood, on some questions, closer to the liberal-radical-left opposition than to the coalition Liberals, Conservatives, and apolitical adventurers around Lloyd George.[4] They were Atlanticists because they subscribed to an interpretation of the historical realities of the preceding quarter-century which insisted that the growth of American power was a complementary rather than a competitive factor. Moreover, they were attracted by the radical idealism which viewed the United States as a model of political organisation, social harmony, and economic progress and because they identified with the ideals of the Wilsonian peace programme as expounded by President Wilson's confidant, Colonel House. Indeed, Wilson embodied an Anglo-American radical-liberal programme of war aims which seemed to offer plausible guidelines for international behaviour and prospects for order, justice, and disarmament. Edward House provided a significant link, especially for Grey, who regarded their personal friendship as an expression of the common aims and

4 Grey, note, May 1917, Balfour Papers, 49738; Curzon to Lloyd George, 30 July and 6 Aug. 1919, Lloyd George Papers, F/12/1/30 and 35; Fisher Papers and Ogg, *Fisher*, 89, 95, 111–12. When discussing policy issues, prior to his accepting the special mission to Washington in 1919, Grey stressed how, before 1914, the Liberal government had unanimously agreed never to build naval forces against the United States. This decision recognised that the United States could always outbuild Britain in a race and that Britain must never risk war with her. Grey urged Lloyd George to remain true to this policy and never to allow false prophets to replace the old German menace with a supposed threat from the United States.

ideals of the two democracies. Grey, although ousted with Asquith, was therefore willing to represent Lloyd George's government in Washington in 1917 and again in 1919. Moreover, Grey, as early as 1916, had realistically viewed the creation of a League of Nations as a function of Atlanticism. In his view Britain must adopt the idea of a League both as a war measure to help draw the United States into the allied fold and as a method decisively to influence the peace. Anglo-American co-operation became, to Grey, vital during the war, a prerequisite of a just settlement, and, in full circle, fundamental to the health of the future League itself. Barnes, for his part, had been prominent in the leftwing League to Abolish War and had been Robert Cecil's only constant ally in the pre-armistice debates of the War Cabinet on the question of the League of Nations. Both had earned the contempt of the Foreign Office, the service departments, and many of their cabinet colleagues.[5]

Robert Cecil, most effective in the wartime Foreign Office and in control of blockade matters, head of the League of Nations section of the British delegation at Paris and a member of the Supreme Economic Council, and General Jan Smuts, most influential of the dominion leaders, were Atlanticists by acceptance of historical realities, but principally because of their concern for the League of Nations. Anglo-American co-operation was the pivot on which the League would turn and conversely the demise of Atlantic harmony would be the rock on which the League would founder. Cecil had been the most prominent supporter of the League idea in official circles since September 1916. With Smuts he enjoyed significant discretionary scope at the Peace Conference to handle the relevant negotiations and, co-operating more closely with President Wilson than with Lloyd George, Cecil had used his powers more effectively than wisely. The Covenant was an Anglo-American compromise, born of Cecil and Wilson, but not one which satisfied Cecil's principal colleagues or Lloyd George.[6]

In turn Cecil could not but regard the Premier, whose indifference and preoccupation elsewhere ironically had in part resulted in Cecil's discretionary powers at the Peace Conference, as a menace to the League and to Anglo-American accord. Cecil's devotion to Atlanticism faltered over only one issue, that of naval competition, and he warned House at the Peace Conference that he would spend his last

5 Imperial War Cabinet debates 13 Aug. and 2 Oct. 1918, Cab 23/7 and 8
6 Raffo, 'Robert Cecil and the League of Nations'

shilling to perpetuate Britain's naval authority. In contrast, Lloyd George seemed obsessed with tactical manoeuvring and indifferent to fundamental principles of policy. Cecil was convinced that his own approach was not only morally sound and represented the best of British opinion but also the most realistic, as Britain needed the support of the United States far more than the reverse. Attempts to impose terms on President Wilson or to complete tactical deals amounting to blackmail, such as Lloyd George had determined on during the momentous weekend at Fontainebleau between 22 and 26 March 1919 to secure a naval agreement, were both foolish and dangerous. In view of the resulting Anglo-American naval battle of Paris, Cecil's criticisms can hardly be dismissed and, considering the apparent power disparities, neither can one reject Cecil's view that the United States had followed Britain's lead to a surprising degree at the Peace Conference. This development, Cecil felt, showed that Britain retained the moral leadership and that her greatest asset, typified in Grey, was still her reputation for justice, magnanimity, and generosity. Full and frank co-operation between London and Washington and a process of mutual commitment above all to the League would ensure sustained harmony between the Atlantic Powers and were, in Cecil's opinion, the pillars on which to base world peace.[7]

Smuts could also qualify as an Atlanticist in part because he regarded the empire, based on the freedom and equality of all participant states, as the only successful experiment in international government and as a 'polity of many sovereignties and many cultures.' In his search for a solution to international anarchy, Smuts came to regard the empire as the embryo of the League which itself would bring a new degree of co-operation between Britain, the dominions, and the United States.[8] Before and during the Peace Conference, Smuts's position had not been free from embarrassment for he could not tolerate, even from the United States, opposition to South Africa's territorial claims on South West Africa. Moreover, although he agreed that Britain must encourage American international involvement, Smuts preferred to divert and restrict that involvement to the Middle East or even to a development board for tropical Africa. However,

7 Cecil to Smuts, 4 Dec. 1918, Cecil to Lloyd George, 27 May 1919, Cecil Papers, 51076; Cecil to Balfour, 5 April 1919, Cecil to House, 8 and 10 April 1919, ibid., 51094; Cecil to Drummond, 7 Oct. 1918, Balfour Papers, 49738; Cecil, *All The Way*; Cecil, *A Great Experiment*, I, 356

8 Hancock, *Smuts*, I, 429–67, 491–523 and *Smuts*, II, 17, 37–8, 129–30

his admiration for President Wilson and his personal rapport with other leading Americans such as Bernard Baruch reinforced Smuts's belief that Atlanticism would counter American isolationism, which in turn persisted as the chief obstacle to European recovery and to the success of the League.

Moreover, Smuts seemed utterly disillusioned with France in particular and with European entanglements in general, and Atlanticism was an avenue of escape or withdrawal from Europe. At the end of the war Smuts regarded international politics as a tripartite system involving France, the British empire, and the United States, and he advocated without reservation that the empire proceed in close harmony with America. Smuts denounced France as a bad neighbour historically, until thrashed by Germany in 1870, as likely to revert to her old arrogant diplomacy, as seeking to reduce Germany and become the mistress of Europe, and as an ambitious, militant, and unscrupulous imperialist power. Britain had, in Smuts's opinion, been excessively generous to France even to the point of stupidity in the Middle East, and only Anglo-American pressure could remove such iniquities. Britain must join with the United States, in so far as co-operation was consistent with the empire's interests, and link the two great democratic 'Commonwealths,' tied by language, interests, and ideals, in the pursuit of a common destiny. Whether Smuts looked to imperial security in the Pacific, to the Middle East, or to the threat of a revival of European militarism, the United States seemed the key consideration, and, therefore, 'All fundamental considerations of policy point to our having to co-operate with the United States in future world politics.'[9] The point of departure was obvious to Smuts and it also completed the circle: Britain must support Wilson's League as the 'reversionary' of the destroyed European empires, as the new foundation for European stability, as the solvent of global problems, and as a check on all vindictive powers. In this way the empire, the United States, and the League, in splendid harmony, would bring salvation.

Next to Smuts stood the Canadian prime minister and Conservative party leader, Sir Robert Borden, his successor Arthur Meighen, and their principal aide in foreign affairs, Loring C. Christie, legal adviser in the Department of External Affairs. They were Atlanticists at the same time as being nationalists, anglophiles, and devotees of a matur-

9 Smuts to Cecil, 3 Dec. 1918, and Smuts memorandum, 'Our policy at the Peace conference,' 3 Dec. 1918, Cecil Papers, 51076

ing commonwealth relationship, because the vital considerations of Canadian and imperial policy seemed realistically to permit no other posture.[10] Whatever dissenting voices in other parts of the country might think, Borden, viewing the situation from Ottawa, could not but advocate the closest possible relations between the British empire and the United States. The Canadian government, consuming the security provided by the Monroe Doctrine and British sea power, and tending toward postwar isolationism, sought the most economical and satisfying policy. In an Atlantic entente, Canada could play her role of persuasion in the formulation of British empire policy and function as a junior but vital partner in the North Atlantic Triangle. This was the summit of her expectations. When Borden argued that all other considerations were secondary to those concerning the United States and the British empire, he advanced the Atlanticist argument but little; when, however, he asserted with conviction that American isolationism was in decline and that the anticipated degree of American international involvement was sufficient to form the basis on which to secure peace, he broke vital ground. This latter view was the singular premise basic to the whole Atlanticist structure, and of course the premise proved to be unsound. While realism and yet excessive optimism were abundantly in evidence in Ottawa, Borden could also talk freely of a common ancestry, language, and culture, of Canada sharing the same democratic ideals as Great Britain and the United States, and of enjoying similar political institutions. For Borden and those politically vigorous sections of Canadian opinion who thought as he did, to work for a league of the great English-speaking communities was, therefore, natural, enlightened, and morally responsible.

Linked symbolically and intellectually with the South African

10 Borden, Meighen, and King Papers, records of the Imperial War Cabinet, the British Empire Delegations, and the Imperial Conferences, 1917–22, Cab. 23, 29, 30, 32; Borden, ed., *Robert Laird Borden*, 2 vols.; Graham, *Meighen*, 2 vols.; Wallace, *Memoirs of Sir George Foster*. Detailed references from these sources are in Fry, 'Anglo-American-Canadian Relations.' Christie, a product of Acadia and the Harvard Law School, a Canadian nationalist with strong American affiliations, earned the reputation of the brilliant young man and rapidly became the acknowledged expert on foreign policy. Confident and hard working, he possessed ideas, judgment, and a fluent pen, and accompanied Borden and then Meighen from the sessions of the Imperial War Cabinet in 1917 to the Washington Conference in 1921–22.

leader were Philip Kerr, Lloyd George's principal private secretary handling foreign affairs until May 1921, Edward Grigg, Kerr's successor and secretary of the Rhodes Trust, and their mentor and patron, Lord Milner, minister of war until the armistice, colonial secretary until his resignation in March 1921, and senior Rhodes Trustee from 1917. These elite publicists or *illuminati*, virtually apolitical in terms of party machinery and loyalties, were Atlanticists because all things imperial were their intellectual meat and drink.[11] Their milieu was the Round Table group in London, and their closest associates were Lionel Curtis, dubbed 'the Prophet,' fertile and productive but erratic, and an adviser to the British delegation at Paris; R.H. Brand, F.S. Oliver, L. Hichens, Waldorf Astor, also a member of Lloyd George's secretariat; and G. Dawson. These men of the Round Table were neither a homogeneous group slavishly tied to Milner, nor an uncomplicated conspiracy led by the proconsul. They shared, however, a radical, idealistic, moralistic view of the empire, they possessed a deep faith in the emerging commonwealth, they were Anglo-Saxon racists and elitists but accepted a missionary obligation to raise the lesser races to new heights of civilisation, and they remained devoted to their mentor.

Because of the changed circumstances produced by the war, such as the defeat of Germany, the threat of Bolshevism, the maturing of dominion nationalism, and problems associated with the third world and imperial defence, the Round Table movement faced a new era. In terms of their imperial preoccupations since 1910 they were floundering or awaiting introspective and reorientative study, but the principal members in London were heavily involved in the service of government, business, finance, and the press. Kerr and Curtis were no less fertile or confident, no less committed to imperial union and to a commonwealth based on the rule of law, order, good

11 Milner, Lothian, Grigg, and Garvin papers; Gollin, *Proconsul in Politics*, 17, 18, 45, 48, 123–32, 164–7; Wrench, *Milner*, 329–32, 354–5; Milner to Lloyd George, 9 June 1918, Lloyd George Papers, F/38/3/37; Butler, *Lothian*; and Smith, 'Lord Lothian and British Foreign Policy.' Kerr had been editor of the Round Table until December 1916, many of this group were active in the Rhodes Trust and the English-Speaking Union, and Curtis became deeply involved in the Royal Institute of International Affairs from 1920. Cecil had established some rapport with the Round Table group in 1910 and L.S. Amery, though a party political animal and qualifying as a sceptic, had enjoyed quite close links with them.

Lloyd George, Milner, and Philip Kerr on holiday in Wales

government, and freedom, but broader problems in international affairs, the League, and Anglo-American relations now confronted them. Milner was a tiring giant even as early as the spring of 1917 and lost influence perceptibly after the armistice, despite his contribution to the creation of the mandate system. Even Kerr declined somewhat in importance towards the end of 1920. But they enjoyed a significant period when they were rarely far from Lloyd George and the vital policy debates.

Kerr and his associates tended to view Lloyd George as a dynamic force, who brought almost total fluidity to politics and would be susceptible to their influence. The Premier's lack of intellectual commitment they regarded as an asset in their favour and they were confident they could defeat any competition for his mind. However, Lloyd George's very dynamism created the danger that he would break free from their influence.

Arthur Balfour, who vacated the Foreign Office in October 1919 but continued to enjoy influence and high position, was the outstanding representative of the Conservative Pan Anglo-Saxons, long convinced emotionally and intellectually, a conviction reinforced by realism, of the common heritage and the joint future of the English-speaking peoples.[12] The Pan Anglo-Saxons and the imperialists had much in common and both welcomed the radical idealist who had viewed the United States since the nineteenth century as a model of political virtue. Whether Balfour was writing to his friends in the Republican party in the early years of the century, speculating at the height of the world war, or eulogising as vice-president of the Anglo-American Society and as the British empire president of the English-Speaking Union, he lingered on the community of ideals and character and the joint mission enjoyed and inherited by the co-heirs of Anglo-Saxon civilisation. To Balfour, Anglo-American co-operation was not a mere temporary or tactical expedient but a fundamental policy

12 Balfour to J. Chaote, 1 June 1905, Balfour Papers, 49742; Balfour to Putnam, 27 Dec. 1917, ibid., 49865; Balfour to Cecil, 8 Oct. 1918, ibid., 49738; Balfour to Lord Weardale, 1919, ibid., 49749; Balfour to Bryce, 15 Aug. 1919, ibid., 49749; Balfour memorandum, GT 1138, 22 June 1917, 'Future Naval construction in the United States,' ibid., 49699; Balfour to Sir G. Trevelyan, 2 Jan. 1917, FO/800/211; Balfour to House, 5 July 1917, FO/800/209; Balfour to Lloyd George, 29 Nov. 1918, FO/800/199; Young, *Balfour*, 386, 419; Dugdale, *Balfour*, I, 226–31; II, 203–12, 300–3. Balfour was a close friend of Joseph Chaote and knew H.C. Lodge, H. White, and N.M. Butler.

contributing to an ultimate goal. It followed that war between Britain and the United States would be civil war. To some degree Balfour had shared the concern of Cecil and Smuts at the Peace Conference that Lloyd George's willingness and determination to co-operate with Wilson would waver, and he denounced as insane any attempt to side with the greedy and inflated French against the Americans. Yet while Balfour advocated the policy of encouraging United States participation in the League of Nations and in the troubled areas of the postwar world, he gave surprisingly little support to Cecil in the cabinet discussions and stood closer to Lloyd George than to Cecil and President Wilson on the question of the nature and extent of the League's powers. Moreover, although Balfour had been the principal British negotiator in the 1917 attempt to secure a defensive treaty and a naval agreement with the United States, his devotion to Atlanticism was also tempered by a determination to retain Britain's treaty links with Japan, perhaps in a triple alliance, and to ensure that Britain, while avoiding an arms race, would not fall behind Japan or the United States in postwar naval power. Balfour never deviated from his position on these two questions and, in the brief period of postwar disillusionment, one might even see Balfour lapsing into scepticism. And yet he typified those who could still view Anglo-American relations in terms of a partnership of strength between equals rather than a relationship in which the United States would bring aid to a wounded and venerable empire.

With Balfour were lesser men politically, including Lord Lee of Fareham, friend of Theodore Roosevelt, married to an American, one time professor at the Royal Military College of Canada, and rising with Lloyd George to become first lord of the Admiralty in February 1921.[13] On most matters Lee was a cypher, owing all to Lloyd George, but on questions relating to the United States he claimed special understanding and paraded his Republican connections, even his visits to the very nursery of Col. Theodore Roosevelt jr, Edwin Denby's assistant in the Navy Department during the Harding administration. Lee, tolerating no professional naval speculation on the possibility of war with the United States, and speaking of close Anglo-American relations as a function of civilisation, threatened to reject Lloyd George's offer of the Admiralty unless the government intended to

13 Lee to Lloyd George, 10 Feb., 19 March, and 16 July 1921, Lloyd George Papers F/31/2/50, 52 and 61; Young, *Powerful America*, 48–52; and Fry, 'Anglo-American-Canadian Relations,' 347–51, 358

seek an armaments agreement with Washington. Lee dismissed Ambassador Aukland Geddes's reports as the product of an overwrought, ill-informed, and panicky mind and he offered to go to Washington and re-open the negotiations. A naval race with the United States Lee denounced as ruinous, insane, and criminal, but, conscious of imperial security, even he agreed with the decision to lay down four capital ships in 1921 in order to avoid qualitative inferiority to Japan and the United States by 1925, and to enable Britain to negotiate from a position of strength. His support, however, was conditional on an attempt being made to resume negotiations with the United States, and he did not regard the replacement of obsolete ships as a breach of Atlantic co-operation. Significantly, Lee had extensive personal contacts with the United States; Balfour, aided by Lord Reading, lord chief justice and ambassador to the United States, and by Sir William Wiseman, wartime head of British Intelligence in the United States,[14] handled many of the negotiations with President Wilson; and, with the exception of Philip Kerr, they were the best travelled of the Atlanticists in terms of visits to America.

Finally, on specific issues relevant to this study, the Atlanticists received pragmatic and empirical support from various sources.[15] King George v, on naval and Far Eastern matters, urged co-operation with the United States, and the Foreign Office and the diplomatic service produced similar influences. Sir John Jordan, ambassador to China and acknowledged Far Eastern expert; Sir Beilby Alston, Jordan's successor; Sir Miles Lampson serving with Alston in Peking, Victor Wellesley, and possibly Sir William Tyrrell at the Foreign Office preached a policy of Anglo-American co-operation as a solution specifically to the problem of the Anglo-Japanese alliance and generally to a broad range of Asian questions, often in the face of direct criticism from their superiors. In addition, officials at the Board of Trade reached similar conclusions and participated in the policy review in opposition to the Admiralty and the War Office.

The intellectual and spiritual foundations of Atlanticism were ex-

14 Balfour to Wiseman, 24 Feb. 1919, Balfour Papers, 49741; Willert, *The Road to Safety*; Seymour, *Intimate Papers of Colonel House*. II, III, IV; Hyde, *Reading*, 213–41

15 Johnson, *George Harvey*, 323; Watt, *Personalities and Policies*, 13; Fry, 'Anglo-American-Canadian Relations,' 215; and below, chap. 2. Alston's Atlanticism grew and matured whereas Jordan could lapse into scepticism, but Wellesley seemed consistently dedicated.

pressed most articulately by the imperial *illuminati* and the Pan Anglo-Saxons. Of these, Philip Kerr, reinforced by Lionel Curtis, provides the most appropriate example as an intimate of Lloyd George and as a person who deviated little on this question until his death.[16] The future Lord Lothian, his complicated and sometimes bewilderingly inconsistent thought processes both illuminated and clouded by religious beliefs which changed from Roman Catholicism to Christian Science, worshipped a form of government based on the rule of law to protect civilisation and ensure peace. Any such form of government depended for its success on individuals within the state upholding basic religious values, being obedient to conscience, and agreeing to subordinate their wills to a central authority, the fountain of law. Subordination must replace anarchical competition, and the rule of law must oust brute force and ensure mutual service, general happiness, welfare, and justice. This thesis, which prevailed for any individual state, was equally relevant for a group of nations united in an imperial framework and for a global international system. Individuals, states, and ultimately all mankind must observe the code so that civilisation could prevail as the expression of Christian principles, of human love, of God's will, and of the reign of law. In sum, heaven on earth was attainable or at least should be pursued with dedication and optimism.

Such themes bear the unmistakable stamp of a missionary idealism which was relevant to the individual, the race, and the British empire. Whatever its constitutional future, whether organic union and imperial federation ensued; whatever relationships emerged between the white and other races of the empire; and even though constitutional reform languished and India and Ireland presented seemingly intractable problems, the empire was the vital model for the future. The emerging commonwealth, the greatest civilising force and the fullest expression of humane, efficient, and democratic government, bringing the rule of law to a broad and heterogeneous group of nations and races while securing common interests and denying no separate rights, provided the basis for a world commonwealth. In sum, the British empire offered an example of the most elevated, Christian, and hopeful form of internationalism, before which even the League of Nations paled. Within this imperial structure the English-speaking, white, advanced peoples controlled and guided the backward races toward higher values and ultimately self-govern-

16 Smith, 'Lothian,' 69–76; Butler, *Lothian*, 234, 253, 316

ment, and as the empire fulfilled this civilising role it became a free, enlightened, and great association of nations.[17] Once this mission was accomplished, the 'spiritual commonwealth' or world state should emerge logically from the British commonwealth, be self-enforcing and self-perpetuating, and bestow the blessings of peace on all mankind. To Kerr this was the imperialism of ideas and morality, religion and empire were one, and after the process of self-indoctrination came the phase of activism to convert others.

The strong elements of idealism in Milner, and Kerr's emphasis on the intangible rather than the material benefits of imperialism are undeniable. Other and not always consistent themes emerged, however, when Kerr insisted that the civilising task of imperialism, which was the hope of mankind and the embryo of utopia, was also the preserve of the white English-speaking races. The missionary was white and, indeed, a white elitist who alone possessed 'the majestic governing art,' scientific, orderly, and comprehensive. These elite missionaries were enlightened paternalists, detached experts, and, morally and intellectually unassailable, they alone could guide politicians and peoples. Politics, race, and culture were thus inextricably interwoven. Kerr asserted that the process of civilisation which would eventually elevate the non-white races to new heights of achievement was not that of compromise between cultural concepts, but the dissemination of superior Anglo-Saxon political and spiritual ideals. Clearly, therefore, the cultural heritage of the Anglo-Saxons demanded that they take up the task and shoulder the supreme burden. Kerr's frailties and arrogance are undeniable and examples in his writings abound:

I think it is true that there has never yet been a successful democracy outside the Christian World, and that the most successful ones have been predominantly Protestant. Democracy is much more than a question of political machinery. It requires an intelligent, educated electorate, a considerable degree of public spirit, an interest in public affairs in the people, and a readiness to understand, support, and fight, sometimes physically, for the right – for law and for freedom, as against corruption, oppression and lawlessness. The whole story of democracy is one of struggle and

17 Milner, in the late stages of the war, urged Lloyd George to send Smuts to the United States to demonstrate Britain's dedication to the liberty and freedom of young nations, and as an object lesson of how the empire promoted the extension of self-determination and democracy (Milner to Lloyd George, 21 Oct. 1918, Lloyd George Papers, F/38/4/22).

sacrifice for right ideas on the part of large numbers of people. I often wonder whether the dominant religions of Asia – Mohammedanism, Hinduism, Buddhism, Confucianism – are capable of giving to their adherents that energy, fidelity to the right, brotherhood, public spirit, and devotion to duty and the rule of law without which democratic institutions simply give rise to a more subtle and veiled form of tyranny.[18]

These imperial *illuminati* tended to make a fictional utopia of the late nineteenth century, regarding that period as a golden age of expanding democracy, growing prosperity, and peace under the Pax Britannica. The world war, however, had brought new crises and the sadly constrained British empire, still lacking organic unity, could no longer stand alone. Fortunately, however, even divinely fashioned, the other great experiment of the nineteenth century, the United States, stood ready to assist. As part of the English-speaking world, the United States shared the same language and spiritual values, an Anglo-Saxon cultural heritage flourished, and, as Balfour would agree, the United States experienced the same inspirational ideals. A broader English-speaking union could emerge and Britain, the dominions, and the United States, wielding vast resources and possessing moral fibre and a sense of common destiny, must co-operate to police the seas and restore the Pax Britannica. Only an Anglo-American global hegemony would secure the peace and induce solutions to the world's problems, and Britain should not fear the growth of American power for that process was necessary, inevitable, and innocuous. Philip Kerr,[19] frequent visitor to the United States from his youth and at ease with Americans, would argue, as Milner before him,[20] that while the empire was still Britain's destiny and her

18 Kerr, 'World Problems of Today,' in Kerr et al., *Approaches to World Problems*, 92–3

19 Kerr, 'The Harvest of the War'; Kerr, 'The Harvest of Victory'; and Kerr, 'Walter Page'; Kerr, in discussing prospects for Anglo-American co-operation or even union, could range from loose co-operative schemes to the idea of an 'Amphictyonic Council.'

20 At the height of the military crisis in June 1918, Milner saw salvation only in the closer co-operation between and the willingness to make the maximum sacrifice by Britain, the dominions, and the United States. He called for a gigantic effort on the part of the 'only remaining free peoples of the world' to defeat the bid for world hegemony by the Central Powers. President Wilson, as part of this effort, must drop his aloofness and co-belligerency, or 'whatever

source of power and prestige, she could no longer stand alone. The solution, intuitive, intellectually sound, and morally defensible, lay in the closest co-operation with the United States. None could deny the urgency and magnitude of the problems facing the postwar world and, according to Kerr, should Atlanticism fail then the only barrier to the triumph of irrational and immoral ideologies would collapse, and heaven on earth would be lost forever. The fact that Milner was never an admirer of Woodrow Wilson and that Kerr described the Fourteen Points as mostly verbiage so as to calm Premier Hughes of Australia was not pivotal, for the task of civilising was not a party political matter and the problems involved in securing American co-operation did not deter the Atlanticists, even though Kerr himself was at times driven to soul-searching almost to the point of despair.[21] What mattered most at the end of the war was that the United States, led by Wilson, seemed ready to accept broad involvement and even commitment and she was demonstrably the most suitable and attractive partner.

If the Atlanticists needed confirmation that the United States was the ideal partner for the British empire they found it in their faith in the historic special relationship between Britain and the United States.[22] The Atlanticist could elevate this special relationship often in fine disregard of such facts as British appeasement of the United

half way house he loved to shelter in.' Milner to Lloyd George, 9 June 1918, Lloyd George Papers, F/38/3/37

21 Kerr did not close his eyes to the dangers involved in the sustained force of American isolationism, nor did he ignore the various problems involved in securing American co-operation in the postwar world. He wrote in 1915, and his words were relevant in 1919, 'By breaking her long-established national tradition and assuming common responsibilities for maintaining right and justice throughout the world she can probably save the world from another Armageddon. By clinging to the policy of isolation she can condemn mankind to another era of estrangement and war' (Kerr, 'The Harvest of the War'). In 1918 Kerr noted the problems involved in securing United States willingness to shoulder the burden, for the Americans had 'a childlike faith in the nature of democracy and laisser-faire,' and regarded paternal guidance of the backward peoples as 'iniquitous imperialism' (Kerr to Curtis, Oct. 1918, Butler, Lothian, 68–9). Amery would have applauded such sentiments.

22 A recent attempt to analyse this phenomenon is Max Beloff, 'The Special Relationship: An Anglo-American Myth,' in Gilbert, ed., A Century of Conflict, 151–71.

States begun by Lord Salisbury and the fundamental divisions, principally over maritime questions so recently elevated by the world war. They seemed able to mask deep-felt antagonisms, disguise serious differences by resorting to phrases in praise of racial similarities, and dismiss divergencies of view and even confrontations as errors and aberrations or merely American gaucheries. After all, an Atlanticist could argue, the United States had neither joined any European coalition hostile to Britain nor courted Britain's imperial enemies, and Britain had not attempted to mount a coalition to offset the rise of American power. Neither of them really threatened the other's vital interests, a growing intimacy was natural, and problems of leadership and power disparities were ephemeral. Indeed, one must assume that London and Washington would walk in step and act in unison. Moreover, with patronising comfort, the Atlanticist expected the American elite to recognise the implicit values and the moral content of British ideals and aims, to learn from Britain, to follow her lead, not to act the parvenu, and to overcome any rash feelings of irritation. In addition, and almost without exception, Atlanticists tended to regard anglophobia in the United States as the preserve of the lower classes, of vulgar chauvinists, of the ill-bred masses, and of the racially divergent.[23] They would thus lament on the results of misguided immigration laws and fervently hope that Anglo-Saxon Americans would retain their authority. The sceptics in England also tended to accept this interpretation of America's racial decline and were less sanguine about the future, while the more hostile had already written off America as beyond salvation.

Embedded in the idealism and the sanguine themes of the special relationship were obvious elements of realism as Britain, burdened with obligations and hampered by overtaxed resources, invited the United States to share the responsibilities and benefits of world leadership. At one level, and a viewpoint dear to American isolationists, the British invitation could be interpreted as a crude attempt to ensnare the United States in under-writing Britain's imperial in-

23 Geddes to Curzon, 2 Dec. 1920, FO/371/4548. House, Geddes reported, had
  spoken of the struggle of Anglo-Saxon Americans to retain power in the face
  of 'undignified swarms of immigrants' of a bad type who must be 'Ameri-
  canised.' Tyrrell, at the Foreign Office, minuted that the Anglo-Saxon stock
  were a diminishing quantity, watered down by foreign elements, as the United
  States produced a new race essentially American and hardly Anglo-Saxon,
  and nationalist if not chauvinist. Curzon and Crowe did not dissent.

terests. At its most elevated the process was moral leadership, demanding joint involvment in world affairs and ultimately detachment and even escape when all was secure. Meanwhile, Britain's national interests and those of her empire would be safeguarded in defiance of the dislocation produced by the war. Disarmament and lower taxes would go hand in hand with peace and prosperity, British and dominion public opinion would enjoy new levels of emotional satisfaction and economic prosperity, and the statesmen would receive their applause.

In the heat of war and under the threat of a military collapse in France in June 1918, Milner had advocated a new and closer relationship between the Atlantic powers and Japan.[24] This proposal was not free from contradiction although it might aid the empire in its task of forging links between the world's races and between East and West. Milner's proposal was clearly, however, a temporary and emergency measure and hardly deviated from the more fundamental proposition that Atlanticism was the basis on which to erect world peace.

The most revealing issue and the most appropriate *entrée* to the critics of Atlanticism, notwithstanding the fact that it ranged Kerr, the Round Table group, and Balfour to some degree against Cecil, Smuts, and President Wilson, and alongside Lloyd George and Hankey, was the debate within the Imperial War Cabinet and the British Empire Delegation before and during the Peace Conference on the League of Nations. The question of more lenient treatment of Germany was similarly instructive. In the first place, Kerr and the *Round Table* could not view the League in isolation from their aspirations for a British commonwealth and ultimately for a world commonwealth.[25] In their view, the Allies led by Britain and the

24 Milner, when demanding co-operation between Britain, the United States, and the dominions as the key to victory, also pressed for a new and less grudging attitude toward Japan and for accepting her as a full and equal partner, in order to tie Japan securely to their side (Milner to Lloyd George, 9 June 1918, Lloyd George Papers, F/38/3/37). The difficult question of the precise relationship between the Atlantic powers and France or Japan was often discussed in terms of an ideal tripartite arrangement.

25 Kerr's articles 'The Foundations of Peace,' 'The End of War,' 'The War for Public Right,' 'The Principle of Peace,' 'The Making of Peace,' 'The British Empire.' Also Curtis, 'Windows of Freedom,' and anon., 'The Victory that will end the war'

United States, having destroyed Prussian militarism, must negotiate a moderate and just peace, foster democratic government and national self-determination, erect a league or concert of nations in the short run, and pursue the ultimate civilising world commonwealth. The league or concert would serve two interim purposes for Kerr; it would protect the peace treaty which, however just and moderate, could hardly be self-enforcing, and, by substituting international law for anarchy and worship of the balance of power, by enforcing new regulations for international behaviour, and by providing an effective consultative body in which all the great powers would meet regularly, deal with controversial questions and remove antagonisms, it woud help preserve general peace until a world community had evolved. Kerr's concert would be in fact a voluntary association in which the member states would lose none of their sovereign independence but would act in unison for the welfare of the whole and as their national and imperial interests dictated. The league could help prevent war but it could not ensure permanent peace. It was not even a substitute for all the traditional safeguards for British and imperial security and, as Lloyd George would agree, the league must reflect pragmatism not wild idealism and embody what was possible and desirable. For Lloyd George a sensible group of great powers, led by a realistic Welshman, would suffice.

To Philip Kerr, in the hierarchy of moral internationalism, the League of Nations must in fact reinforce the British commonwealth and help hold the line until a civilised, peaceful, legal, global order ensued. This view of the League set the Round Table group somewhat apart from the liberal-radical-left, and from Cecil, Smuts, and President Wilson, but it did not undermine their devotion to Atlanticism. At every stage in Kerr's argument, the need for a just peace, the desirability of a realistic league based on wartime allied and British empire practices, and the pursuit of a world order, he returned to the crucial theme: the intimate co-operation of Britain, the dominions, and the United States.

The related question of mandates evoked a similar analysis. The Round Table group and their American confidant, G.L. Beer, were convinced that a system of trusteeship would help prevent the exploitation of less civilised races, establish a new level of contact between East and West, and help the white man fulfil his obligation to raise backward peoples up to higher levels of civilisation. These unfortunate races were unable to civilise themselves and were vulnerable to oppressive influences but, with humane and responsible guidance, they could probably achieve self-government, enjoy law, liberty, and freedom, and ultimately even participate in the British and then the world commonwealth. Mandates would, therefore, Kerr argued, express the most suitable relationship between the lesser races and white administrations and between these governments and the rest of the civilised world. Germany and Turkey were unworthy of trusteeship and predictably Britain, the dominions, and the United States, and perhaps even France, must turn to this glorious task. The United States must accept its responsibilities, probably in tropical Africa or the Near East, and furnish the most practical and the most significant example of functional Atlanticism, joint co-operation in the highest form of imperialism. The fundamental problem was of course as obvious to Kerr as to anyone.[26] The conscience of the United States seemed immune to such theory and indifferent to these prospects, and naïve American leaders, suspicious of British and dominion aspirations, harboured fears of iniquitous imperialism. The critics of Atlanticism could not but be impressed with such attitudes.

When the British and dominion leaders deliberated on the nature of the League, weighing its practicability, potential for success, its likely contribution to imperial interests and security, and how far its powers should impinge on national sovereignty, virtually everyone had agreed that Britain must support some form of association because public opinion and the United States government expected or demanded it.[27] A league clearly had electoral and international value. Moreover, in so far as the Imperial War Cabinet opted for co-operation with the United States rather than with France, it viewed acceptance of the League in part as a way to help ensure Wilson's support of the empire's interests, and to secure United States co-operation in economic and political reconstruction and in the contest with Bolshevism. Wilson's devotion to the League was demonstrably confirmed by late December 1918, the British delegation at Paris would hopefully exercise significant influence on the actual negotiations to settle the terms of the Covenant, and consequently they could permit Wilson to have a league. Fundamental to this decision, and subsequently proven false at the Peace Confer-

26 See note 21.

27 Imperial War Cabinet debates, 26 Nov., 24, 30, and 31 Dec. 1916, Cab 23/42

ence, was the assumption that Cecil would adopt that version of a league, limiting its powers and functions, favoured by Lloyd George, Hankey, and Kerr.

A direct if complex correlation between attitudes toward the League, mandates, and Atlanticism was therefore established. Cecil, Smuts, and Barnes supported a league with the most extensive powers and duties possible. Borden felt obliged to oppose specific articles in the final Covenant negotiated by Cecil and Wilson, but his concern lest the empire embark on annexationist imperialism caused him to insist that the United States be unreservedly involved in the trusteeship system. All four in their own way, therefore, sought the closest possible co-operation with the United States. Lloyd George, Bonar Law, Churchill, Austen Chamberlain, Hankey, and, on this issue if not for identical motives, Balfour and Kerr, did not regard the League with such gravity. A postwar concert was not a substitute for traditional policies or the empire, it had a lower priority, and must be functional, and realistically limited in scope. Moreover, the League, like so many other questions, was in part a tactical consideration which must help service other vital interests and still, hopefully, induce Anglo-American accord. A certain scepticism about the League matched a similar attitude toward Atlanticism, and while Balfour and Kerr shared the former they could avoid the latter for other and to them more vital reasons. More cynical and even hostile toward the League and Atlanticism were Curzon, Field Marshal Sir Henry Wilson, the chief of the imperial general staff, the representatives of the Admiralty, and Prime Minister Hughes of Australia, who were most reluctant to compromise on matters pertaining to the balance of power and naval hegemony. In any case the debate did not fully mature until the Senate rebuffed Wilson's League and the American electorate demonstrated indifference rather than regret.

Personally the Atlanticists were impressive enough, their views initially had a sufficient measure of idealism and realism to merit close consideration and the cabinet could hardly rebuff them abruptly. Both domestic and international considerations dictated that the British government test the validity of Atlanticism. As the glow of victory receded, however, sterner examinations presented themselves. The Atlanticists were not united on every issue, empiricists searched out their intellectual weaknesses, the response of the United States was progressively hardly encouraging, and realism seemed to become overshadowed by a more frail idealism. All too rapidly the Atlanticists' expectations seemed ridiculously exaggerated. Moreover, Lloyd George's coalition was not a stable group and its power structure fluctuated. Milner lost ground, so to a lesser degree did Balfour, Kerr gradually became emotionally exhausted, Cecil and Grey eclipsed themselves, and Smuts and Borden returned home. Given these developments and the failure to maintain a close Anglo-American dialogue, with both London and Washington at fault, the task of the Atlanticists became almost intolerably difficult. They were never impotent, however, and the debate continued, but the Atlanticists seemed to face progressive disillusionment.

The sceptic often indulged in oratorical Atlanticism, but, lacking the basic convictions of the Atlanticists, he was increasingly difficult to convince. The sceptic was somewhat attracted by the possible advantages offered by Atlanticism, but that policy was at best one of several. David Lloyd George, as prime minister, was both the pivot of scepticism and the most important voice in the policy debate among the British elite.[28] In some of his rare speeches on foreign policy before 1914 Lloyd George had accepted the special relationship theme, applauding Anglo-American co-operation and stating that war between them was unthinkable. During the world war, however, he had shared the anger and despair felt in Britain at the policies adopted by President Wilson in the period of American neutrality and particularly Wilson's attempts to secure a negotiated peace. At the same time Lloyd George's premiership coincided with the high period of Anglo-American wartime co-operation. Despite the British government's reservation on the freedom of the seas and the problem of naval hegemony[29] there was much in the Wilsonian peace programme that Lloyd George could applaud and their rapport at the Paris Peace Conference was as impressive as was the extent of their differences.[30] Lloyd George was certainly influenced

28 In a recent attempt to classify Lloyd George, D.C. Watt, pointing to the Premier's contempt for idealism, his chauvinistic patriotism, and his delight in the exercise of power, called him an 'irresponsible' (Watt, *Personalities and Politics*, 33).

29 Fry, 'Imperial War Cabinet'

30 Walter Long, first lord of the Admiralty, warned Lloyd George of damaging rumours that he was so committed to the League of Nations and a peace policy that he would cut the navy drastically and accept United States control of the seas. Long also expressed fears that Lloyd George's loyalty to President Wilson could endanger his influence in Britain (Long to Lloyd George, 8 May 1919, Lloyd George Papers, F/33/2/42 and 43).

by Kerr, Milner, and Smuts; his position on the question of whether the United States should become a mandatory power in the Middle East and Africa was close to that of Milner, and, indeed, on occasions the Premier could exaggerate the significance of the Round Table group, observing on one occasion: 'It is a very powerful combination and in its way perhaps the most powerful in the country. Each member of the group brings to its deliberations certain definite and important qualities; and behind the scenes they have much power and influence.'[31]

However, Lloyd George's somewhat cavalier treatment of what he regarded as an excessively narrow institution, the Foreign Office,[32] his impulsive and creative virtuosity, his nerve, energy, and imagination, his tactical unorthodoxy, his realism and patriotism, rather than any sheer irresponsible opportunism, led him to explore all avenues and test all shades of opinion. His skill in debate and in verbal transactions and his lesser facility on paper led him to encourage sustained discussion on policy as he sought to discover the political and social realities of the day. The clues to Lloyd George, therefore, are found more in conference minutes than in personal memoranda, and in letters received rather than in letters despatched. The Atlanticists' arguments must survive by their intellectual content, their realism, their timing, their repetition in the fluctuation of debate, and whether they stood the test of empiricism. Lloyd George would weigh them along with other views, less as philosophical or idealistic arguments and more as pragmatic answers to current problems.

Lloyd George could write and speak about the great postwar role which the United States could play and about the need for Anglo-American co-operation as the surest basis on which to secure peace, and these views became an oft repeated statement of regret as he became more disenchanted with French policy.[33] On specific issues, such as the disposal of Germany's colonies, Lloyd George agreed

31 Riddell diary, entry of 23 Oct 1921, Riddell, *Intimate Diary*, 329–30
32 This view of Lloyd George's relationship with Balfour and especially with Curzon is as widely accepted as it is exaggerated.
33 Draft of interview between Lloyd George and W.W. Hawkins (United Press), June 1921, Lloyd George Papers, F/86/1/4; Lloyd George, *Where Are We Going*, 108–9, 115. In a different vein he would applaud those who engineered prohibition in the United States as 'of our own race and kind, bred in the Puritan tradition that came originally from our shores' (ibid., 350).

that Britain should work with the United States as far as their co-operation was in harmony with the vital interests of the empire, but he never accepted the basic assumption of inevitable compatibility of interests. If Britain's interests were endangered Lloyd George, very reluctantly, would attempt to co-operate with France.[34]

As early as November 1919 Lloyd George, Hankey, Kerr, and others, never happy about President Wilson's Covenant, were even more dubious.[35] Precisely that aspect of the League which they valued most, United States involvement and co-operation, was obviously in jeopardy from the Senate. Should the United States refuse to ratify the peace treaty, the League could become a divisive factor in Anglo-American relations and place intolerable burdens and unacceptable obligations on Britain. To some members of the British government such an outcome would be a prime example of how the unreliable and even treacherous Americans urged one on and then left one in the lurch, a sentiment which died hard in the interwar years. Moreover, and a cause dear enough to Lloyd George, in all probability the prospects for disarmament would languish. In Kerr's opinion, the League could not be effective without the United States, in any case it was secondary to imperial considerations, it was obviously forfeit to nationalist policies, and served narrow European interests. Therefore, Kerr looked even more urgently for direct co-operation between the empire and the United States, with revision of the Covenant a desirable but secondary problem. Ironically, both Lloyd George and Kerr could have pointed out to Cecil that their more limited view of a concert would have been more attractive to the United States than was Wilson's Covenant. Lloyd George shared many of Kerr's views and expressed doubts as to whether devotion to the Covenant could persist as a basic principle of British foreign policy. While his secretary denounced the results of the League's inadequacies, however, Lloyd George emphasised their principal cause, the defection of the haphazard and 'comet-like' United States.[36]

34 Imperial War Cabinet, 47th and 48th meetings, 30 and 31 Dec. 1918, Borden Papers, Memoir Notes, 5, 1917–18, and Cab 23/42

35 Curzon to Lloyd George, 7 Nov. 1919; Kerr to R.H. Campbell (Foreign Office), 30 Oct. 1919; Hurst to Campbell, 4 Nov. 1919; Hurst to Lord Hardinge, 5 Nov. 1919, Lloyd George Papers, F/12/2/3; Kerr memorandum, 10 Nov. 1919, Lothian Papers, GD/40/17/62 and Kerr, 'The British Empire'

36 Lloyd George, Where Are We Going, 74–5

Kerr would regard Atlanticism as an alternative to the League but he met the growing disillusionment of his chief. Lloyd George also regarded the absence of the United States from the Reparations Commission as its basic and crippling defect and his concern and anger mounted as political, strategic, and financial problems unfolded.[37] Such considerations could not but sway even the dedicated Atlanticist and clearly the sceptics would be impressed to the point of asking whether one could be an Atlanticist without appearing somewhat naïve and even ridiculous.

Beneath Lloyd George stood other sceptics of varying intensity. Bonar Law, Conservative party leader, high in temperature and low in spirits, declining in health and influence, and just as elusive in the archives as the Premier, was not excessively concerned with foreign policy but he qualified as a sceptic.[38] On the crucial question of naval construction, Bonar Law, agreeing with Lloyd George, accepted Grey's plan of avoiding any challenge to the United States in order to produce a reciprocal response. Equally so, however, Bonar Law accepted the fact that they must regard the absence of any such response from Washington as clear evidence that global co-operation with the United States could not be achieved.[39] Sir Maurice Hankey, the only member of the cabinet secretariat to outrank Kerr, seemed willing to pursue and test Atlanticist policies, but only in an empirical fashion and never with total dedication. During the war Hankey had expressed doubts about compulsory arbitration coupled with sanctions machinery as a way of preventing war, damning the proposal as dangerous because of the differing national characters of the great powers.[40] Britain, in Hankey's view, was thoroughly honourable, Germany and Russia could neither be trusted nor coerced, and the United States 'as likely as not will be on the eve of a Presidential election and unwilling to take a hand.' Moreover, the United States was simply unreliable and 'so cosmopolitan and wedded to the almighty dollar that they cannot be judged even

37 Ibid., 143
38 Bonar Law Papers, and Blake, *The Unknown Prime Minister*. This otherwise
   excellent study says relatively little on foreign policy. Lloyd George offered
   Bonar Law the Foreign Office in January 1922, but he declined (ibid., 437).
39 Fry, 'Anglo-American-Canadian Relations,' 234–5
40 Hankey to Balfour, 5 May 1916, 29 June and 11 Nov. 1927, Balfour Papers,
   49704

by the comparatively low standard of other nations in regard to matters of national honour.' Hankey wrote in the atmosphere of bitter
disillusionment so prevalent in 1916 but his scepticism prevailed. In
1927, at the height of Anglo-American cruiser controversy, he recalled
how Britain, under the misguided impression that she could earn
American goodwill by a policy of concessions, had reaped only scorn
and abuse as the United States interpreted concessions as weakness.
Hankey advised, therefore, that Britain should stand on her rights,
ward off a conspiracy hatched by Aukland Geddes, Esme Howard,
the *Manchester Guardian,* and an embittered Colonel House, and
refuse to be blackmailed or browbeaten even at the risk of controversy and cruel phrases aimed at the United States 'which will be
none the less palatable because they are true.'

Reading, lord chief justice and ambassador to the United States
from September 1917 to May 1919, intermittently spoke and behaved
like an Atlanticist, particularly in the course of contacts with United
States leaders such as Colonel House.[41] But Reading was Lloyd
George's man, tied to his political fortunes, luxuriating in office and
power, and one must conclude that an opportunistic realism dominated his views. In brief, Reading was dedicated to little in any
permanent way. Sir Aukland Geddes, apolitical ambassador to the
United States from early 1920, and adding fuel to the debate of
varying quality and persuasion, revealed the complicated traits of
the sceptic willing to be convinced, but went further than anyone
in proposing retaliatory measures aimed at the United States to meet
commercial competition.[42] By the mid-1920s he had something of a
reputation as an Atlanticist but he was a late convert. Austen Chamberlain, as chancellor of the Exchequer and prominent in the war
debts negotiations, also qualified as a sceptic; and Churchill, war
minister and then colonial secretary, impressed with the dangers of
permitting the United States to become a mandatory power in the
Middle East and of stimulating her naval power in the Mediterranean, must, by his contribution to the debate on naval construction, qualify as a sceptic at best.[43]

41 Hyde, *Reading,* 314
42 Geddes to Curzon, 11 June 1920, FO/414/246 and Geddes, *Forging of a
Family.* Both the Geddes brothers were very much Lloyd George's creatures.
43 Chamberlain, *Down The Years,* 231–8. Chamberlain's public posture seemed
to identify him as an Atlanticist but his record points elsewhere; Hall, 'British

So must Leo Amery, holding secondary military and political positions but highly regarded by Lloyd George, even though he was still close enough to the imperialists around Milner virtually to be one of them. Amery agreed that intimate Anglo-American co-operation was the most vital asset which the empire could secure from the war, but he was a Conservative imperialist, most unimpressed with the League, involved in material matters of security, naval power, and imperial preference, and prone to question the compatibility of close Anglo-American with strong imperial family ties. Frequently, inconsistencies and confusion emerged when imperialists investigated the precise relationship between these two desiderata and clearly the imperialist mind must 'take off' into the more rarified atmosphere of interlocking relationships or close itself, as in the case of Philip Kerr on occasions, in order to preserve dedication to Atlanticism.

Amery could not complete either of these manœuvres. He told Lloyd George in August 1918 that while he agreed with the policy of inducing the United States to accept postwar responsibilities, the process must be a natural one and confined to areas of special interest to America.[44] He warned both that the United States would not welcome the offer of an 'undigested lump' of unfamiliar problems at the other end of the world, and that 'To dump Americans with their vigorous and crude ideas down into the middle of complicated Middle Eastern problems in Palestine would lead to endless complications in Egypt, Arabia and Mesopotamia.' He urged the establishment of a series of Monroe Doctrines, with Britain's spheres of control clearly marked, and, to reduce friction with the United States, Britain should relinquish one of her several possessions such as Guiana, Honduras, Gambia, or even Gibraltar and accept American control of the Congo, Angola, or Mexico. Amery advocated only selective American involvement, adjusted so as to leave the empire's interests untouched and the imperial and naval aspirations of the United States dormant.

Commonwealth,' in Bourne and Watt, eds., Studies in International History, 349–50. Sir Robert Horne, Sir Laming Worthington-Evans, and Edwin Montagu probably qualify as passive sceptics but the evidence is insufficient.

44 Amery memorandum, 15 June 1918, 'War Aims and Military Policy'; Amery memorandum, 20 Dec. 1918, 'United States and the Occupied Enemy Territories'; Amery to Lloyd George, 16 Aug. 1918, Lloyd George Papers, F/2/1/25, F/23/3/82, and F/2/1/29; Amery to Balfour, 21 Dec. 1918, FO/800/209; Amery, My Political Life, II, 81, 98–100, 210

Specific areas of Turkey, West Africa, Armenia, and Central and South America were all expendable spheres and he rejected Churchill's fears that a selective American mandate in the Middle East would dangerously stimulate her naval construction. Only a conflict of interest or policy would induce the United States to launch a naval race, Amery felt, and he did not regard an American mandate for Armenia or Constantinople as giving rise to any such conflict. However, should such a conflict arise, Amery saw great strategic advantages in Britain holding the Atlantic, keeping the American fleet 'bottled up' in the Mediterranean. His strategic reasoning was undeniably wild but such speculation tended to remove him from the ranks of the Atlanticists.

Behind the sceptics were ranged those who were even hostile and who, while often genuflecting to Washington in public, regarded Americans as a foreign species rather than brothers or even cousins. In the forefront were Lord Curzon, foreign secretary in succession to Balfour, and Field Marshal Sir Henry Wilson, supported by Lord Birkenhead, the lord chancellor,[45] Eric Geddes, when first lord of the Admiralty, Walter Long, Geddes's successor at the Admiralty, First Sea Lords Admirals Wemyss and Beatty,[46] and important Foreign Office officials such as Sir Eyre Crowe,[47] Lord Hardinge,[48]

45 Birkenhead, damned by his Ulster record and disliking idealists and 'doctrinaire perfectionists,' seemed utterly insensitive to American public and official feelings even in wartime (Murray to Drummond, 25 Jan. 1918, FO/800/329; Earl of Birkenhead, *Life of F.E. Smith*, 487–93; Callwell, *Sir Henry Wilson*, II).

46 Long, *Memoirs*; Petrie, *Walter Long*; Chalmers, *Earl Beatty*; Wemyss, *Wester Wemyss*; Roskill, *Naval Policy Between the Wars*, I, 105, 214–16, 220.
Jellicoe is rumoured to have told Admiral Kingsmill, wartime head of the Canadian naval service, that he was under orders at Jutland to bring the capital ship fleet back intact because, among other considerations, Britain might have to defend herself against the United States. In the postwar period, although the Admiralty accepted the one power standard in the face of political and economic considerations and did not seek to challenge the United States in a naval race, professional hostility toward America was very apparent.

47 Crowe minute, on Alston's memorandum, 1 Aug. 1920, 'Respecting suggestions for an Anglo-Saxon policy for the Far East,' Woodward, Butler, and Bury, *Documents on British Foreign Policy* 1919–1939 (hereafter cited as BD), 1st ser., XIV, no 80, 86. Crowe noted, 'I wish I could share Sir B. Alston's

and Sir Cecil Hurst.[49] Significantly these pillars of the Foreign Office and the service departments seemed convinced that Atlanticism was already found wanting and did not provide a basic principle of British foreign policy in the postwar period. In the name of realism and rejecting missionary idealism, they demanded a foreign policy based on proven principles and methods. To Curzon, Beatty, and Henry Wilson the securing of Britain's national and imperial interests was a function of sea power, of military, economic, and financial strength, all measured unilaterally, of intuitive and realistic diplomacy, and of international credit and prestige. In contrast, Atlanticism seemed to be mere sanguine and idealistic rhetoric.

Entrenched in key positions, these opponents of Atlanticism were extremely powerful and, but for Lloyd George and the sceptics, may well have proved irresistible especially as they also received crucial reinforcement from the dominions. 'Billy' Hughes, premier of Australia, with a New Zealand echo in Premier Massey, could match anyone on the public platform on the need for cordial Anglo-American relations.[50] But in imperial councils Hughes's antagonism toward Atlanticism was unmistakable and sustained, expressed in December 1918 as a denunciation of President Wilson over the question of the disposal of former German colonies in the south Pacific and in his

robust faith in American "co-operation" in China or elsewhere. But I see no objection to making further efforts to gain it.' The second sentence might qualify Crowe as a sceptic, but he viewed Atlanticism partly as a facet of the struggle between the Foreign Office and Downing Street for the control of foreign policy and he favoured both traditional policies and methods.

48 Hardinge, having served in India, as had Curzon, seemed to prefer co-operation with Japan rather than the United States and was utterly pessimistic about the future of Anglo-American relations; Hardinge, record of conversation with the Japanese Ambassador, 18 Aug. 1920, ibid., no 92, 95; Hardinge, minute, on Geddes to Curzon, despatch, 30 April 1920, FO/371/5359; Hardinge, Old Diplomacy, 231–2, 244

49 Hurst memorandum, 18 Nov. 1919, 'American Reservations to the Peace Treaty,' BD, 1st ser., v, no 399, 1024–8. Hurst, with Curzon in agreement, analysed the impact of the proposed American reservations to the League Covenant on British and imperial interests and on the League itself, and the tone was decidedly unsympathetic toward the United States. Hurst was chief legal adviser to the Foreign Office.

50 Hughes, Splendid Adventure; Fry, 'Anglo-American-Canadian Relations,' 93–106, 114–26; Hall, 'British Commonwealth,' 349–64

demand that Britain renew the Anglo-Japanese alliance in June 1921. Whether Hughes was denying the significance of the American war effort in 1918 or insisting on the unreliability of the United States in 1921, his words were scathing and undeniably critical.

Clearly those who were sceptical, cynical, and hostile were a formidable group, growing in conviction and authority, while the Atlanticists were increasingly in disarray, retaining their faith apparently in defiance of the tide of events. These trends were the result of four interrelated factors. First, and as already suggested above, the Atlanticist credo was not without its weaknesses and contradictions. Second, Wilson's personal and political collapse, the demise of House's influence, and the inability of secretaries of state R. Lansing and B. Colby to initiate high policy, meant that the United States government lacked directing leadership, and this loss was expressed in a partial withdrawal from international affairs. Third, a decline in bilateral Anglo-American co-operation occurred, accompanied by a loss of rapport between London and Washington. Finally, the unfinished business of the peace conference left menacing problems and, elevating the question of British naval power and imperial defence, touched on the rawest nerves. All four factors operated to the detriment of the Atlanticist cause before 1921.

The Atlanticist thesis contained certain demonstrable contradictions and illusions and laid them open to attack. United States resources were not being matched by sustained and congenial executive control; Wilson had become an inaccessible and mysterious invalid; a rump administration could scarcely rule amidst its own death throes; and Edward Grey, Britain's special representative in 1919, and his successor could not even secure a meeting with the President.[51] Thus the idea of a reliable, trustworthy, and willing United States, anxious for co-operation, became difficult to sustain and the question of whether American isolationism was in retreat became at best a finely balanced one. Rather than being 'ready aye ready' to follow Britain's lead, the United States could appear incurably and unrepentantly isolationist, ignorant, stubborn, and naïve,

---

51 Geddes to Lloyd George, 4 and 8 June 1920, Lloyd George Papers, F/60/4/1 and 2; Lindsay to Curzon, 10 Feb. 1920, FO/414/246. Lindsay described Washington as full of rumour, like an oriental bazaar. The vacuum suited the Republicans who refrained from criticism so as to avoid making a martyr of Wilson, while the Democrats remained silent to preserve party unity.

bordering on political and moral collapse and unaware of or unimpressed by her responsibilities. Sceptics doubted whether Britain could guide the United States and teach her new lessons and attitudes, and, indeed, the United States seemed excessively suspicious of British motives especially as politicians pandered to anglophobe sentiments.[52] Many in Washington, for example, agreed that the offer of a mandate to the United States was a clever move to enable Britain to secure disguised annexations elsewhere, and others viewed proposals of Anglo-American co-operation as attempts to entangle the United States, to destroy the basic principles of her foreign policy, and to enmesh her in underwriting the security of the British empire. Such views, not devoid of substance but often expressed irresponsibly in the press, in public, and in private, tended to undermine the Atlanticists' theories, defy their predictions of American behaviour, and obscure the sympathy still felt for Britain in certain sections of the United States. Viewed in reverse, of course, Americans could justifiably complain of both the public and official hostility toward the United States harboured in Britain, and Horatio Bottomley in *John Bull* was certainly a match for William R. Hearst.

These problems revealed that the critics of Atlanticism, while unwilling to jettison all hopes of co-operation, were impressed by the problems of leadership in any Anglo-American combination and by the power disparities favouring the United States, which all recognised to be immediate and irrevocable. The Atlanticists assumed that the rise of United States power was not detrimental to the British empire and that the question of leadership was less of an issue, but others were unsure. Could Britain view the advent of United States naval, commercial, and financial power as a simple process of adjustment, containing no challenge to Britain and her empire? Indeed United States opposition to imperial preference, her opposition to the empire's six votes in the League, and her professed ideological dislike of imperialism suggested that the United States would favour the disintegration of the empire rather than its rejuvenation by way of a commonwealth. The compatibility of Atlanticism with Britain's national and imperial interests was consequently a constant source of doubt and concern.

52 Lindsay to Curzon, 5 March 1920, FO/414/246. Lindsay interpreted Colby's appointment to the State Department as a move to placate Irish opinion and he regarded Admiral Benson's elevation to chairman of the Shipping Board as an anti-British gesture.

Any discussion of wartime differences, when the United States had seemed unable to appreciate that Britain fought to destroy militarism and to safeguard civilisation, carried with it disturbing recollections that Wilson's political intimacies were shared with the liberal-radical Left in Britain, with the political opponents of the Lloyd George coalition. While Lloyd George had no wish to challenge the opposition on questions such as disarmament, domestic political considerations and foreign policy were in conflict to some degree and many members of the coalition government rapidly lost whatever sympathy they had for Wilson and the Democratic party. Tactical considerations were also involved, made more sensitive and delicate by the fact that 1920 was a presidential election year in the United States. How could the British government approach Washington and yet avoid any suggestion of appearing to lead or ensnare her in nefarious schemes? How could Britain convince the United States that she was not an iniquitous imperial and naval power? Such tactical problems were urgent and the Atlanticist would merely seem naïve to ignore them.

Consequently all critics of Atlanticism, with varying degrees of intensity, experienced similar feelings; disillusionment with Wilson's administration, concern that the United States understood neither the empire and its mission nor Europe and its security problems, a growing conviction that the United States was both unreliable and irresponsible, some apprehension about the possible impact of American power and potential and anger at the moralising, idealistic tone of United States diplomacy. Perhaps tried and traditional policies were preferable to ventures in new diplomacy and, in the final analysis, the British elite waited for a grand gesture from Washington on naval problems or war debts, and they waited in vain.[53] The United States never made the gesture and, although Anglo-American relations did not deteriorate to a dangerous level, there occurred a cumulative loss of confidence, mutual irritation, and abrasive exchanges.

The crucial themes in Anglo-American relations were maritime, financial, and commercial, with naval supremacy, imperial security particularly in the Pacific, war debts, and economic reconstruction at the core.[54] Although in retrospect Anglo-American naval rivalry,

53 Geddes to Lloyd George, 8 June 1920, Lloyd George Papers, F/60/4/2;
   Geddes wrote that Colby realised that Britain was 'holding on' again as she
   had in the war, waiting for another round of help from the United States.
54 Hankey to Lloyd George, 17 March 1920, ibid., F/24/2/18

bearing little relation to strategic requirements, appears to be the artificial creation of admirals in search of a prospective foe for politico-financial reasons and arriving by default at each other, the controversy was real enough.[55] Naval power was a superb vehicle for the anglophobe in the United States and control of the seas could call forth emotional slogans in Britain. The United States, viewed from London, could replace Germany, as the 'oily' secretary of the navy, Josephus Daniels, a resurrected Tirpitz, seemed bent on launching a naval programme sufficient to give the United States qualitative superiority in capital ships by 1925. Britain, as seen from Washington, could inherit Germany's role, for was not navalism the partner and heir of Prussian militarism?[56] Moreover, unsettling technical and financial problems associated with the development of submarine and air power, the future of the capital ship, the lessons of Jutland, and the changeover from coal to oil had emerged. The problems were as urgent as they were fundamental and an unsound decision could be disastrous.

Related to the naval controversy were the problems of merchant marine strength and postwar commercial competition. During the war Balfour had proposed to upgrade Britain's diplomatic representation in South America and send a mission, led by Sir M. de Bunsen, to demonstrate Britain's determination to expand her economic and political position despite American and German competition. The mission could not escape Washington's scrutiny, indeed Balfour suggested that the Chilean government welcomed it as a check on American domination and a competitive response from the United States seemed inevitable.[57] The Shipping Ministry, under J.P. Maclay, also planned to counter Japanese and American designs on Britain's prewar maritime interests and the problem of the disposal of the captured German merchant fleet, debated at the Peace Conference and subsequently in the Supreme Council, kept the

55 Notes of a talk with Daniels and Benson, 29 March 1919, ibid., F/192/1/4 (the author was either Long or Admiral Wemyss); Fry, 'Anglo-American-Canadian Relations,' 66–77

56 United States Naval Advisory Staff, memorandum, 13 March 1919, 'Disposition of German and Austrian Vessels of War'; Admiral Benson to Wilson, 9 April 1919, enclosing Naval Advisory Staff memorandum, 'United States Naval Policy,' Baker, *Woodrow Wilson*, III, docs 22, 23, 197–205, and 206–17; Geddes to Curzon, 21 May 1920, FO/414/246

57 Balfour memorandum, GT 4253, 16 April 1918, Balfour Papers, 49699.

question alive. By 1920 the Jones Shipping bill, then before Congress and regarded as discriminatory and prejudicial to Canadian trade, followed in 1921 by the Panama Canal tolls question, reactivated the dispute, although the Board of Trade dismissed Geddes's retaliatory schemes as folly.[58]

These questions were associated with the freedom of the seas controversy which, in the post-armistice negotiations, had revealed that the United States did not appreciate the blessings of British seapower. President Wilson threatened a naval race to force Lloyd George's compliance with his policies, just as he threatened the United States electorate with large naval estimates unless they adopted the League, but the freedom of the seas issue dissipated itself in the negotiations over the Covenant. Lloyd George, however, in March 1919 demanded an agreement, limiting naval construction and confirming British supremacy as the price of his accepting the Monroe Doctrine amendment to the League Covenant, and a provisional arrangement on naval construction was arrived at in April 1919. However, despite this success for Lloyd George's diplomacy, which Cecil had viewed as alarmingly irresponsible, the Admiralty were determined to retain the blockade weapon, the postwar naval balance was still unsettled, the atmosphere was bitter enough, and much of the talk was less than responsible.[59] Clearly the United States Navy Department would support multilateral disarmament only if its construction programmes were left intact sufficiently to ensure at least qualitative superiority over Britain. The Admiralty, for its part, would support a process of disarmament only if British

58 Maclay to Cecil, 8 July 1918, Cecil Papers, 51093; Geddes to Curzon, 12 May 1920, FO/414/246; Board of Trade to Foreign Office, 26 July 1920, FO/414/246; Maclay to Lloyd George and Curzon, 30 June 1921, Lloyd George Papers, F/35/3/58

59 Admiralty memorandum, 'Freedom of the Seas,' 21 Dec. 1918 and confirmed on 6 March 1920, CID paper 239-B, Cab. 4/7; Fry, 'Imperial War Cabinet'; Fry, 'Anglo-American-Canadian Relations,' 66–77. Daniels referred to the British attitude as 'the impudence of impotence and the impotence of impudence.' The naval agreement, not entirely satisfactory to Britain, stated that the United States would 'abandon or modify' only her new 1918 naval programme not yet authorised by Congress and would be willing to consult with Britain on future building programmes. This agreement meant, however, that the United States would most probably complete its 1916 programme and future administrations need not honour House's signature.

naval power were left supreme. In fact, recoiling from the cost of recreating global naval power, Britain, from a position of current superiority, trod the path of selective contraction, cited the abandonment of inflated wartime programmes as disarmament, and invited her competitors to follow her lead. Irritation on the part of the United States naval professionals was inevitable, and the General Board of the Navy called for 'equality with the strongest' or a 'navy second to none' with new base facilities particularly in the Pacific. They used strategic, political, prestige, and commercial arguments to justify their demands, the Hearst press supported them, and the whole preparedness campaign took on an anti-Japanese and anglophobe tone. President Wilson, backed by Daniels, could in turn pose as a saviour and act like an admiral, reconciling his demands for a 'league of peace' and a 'big navy,' and British reactions inevitably mixed bewilderment with apprehension and determination with anger.[60]

The situation, when viewed from London with less heat and emotion, was tolerable at least until 1921. Britain had a comfortable margin in capital ships and in most other classes; the weaknesses of the United States in capital ships and personnel, the result of a keen Congressional financial axe, were actual and Congress seemed unlikely to repent. But Britain wanted more, for the United States could realise her potential by 1925 at the latest. She sought, therefore, the security of a comprehensive naval agreement to reinforce the interim arrangement of April 1919, which bound only the Wilson administration. Grey's mission, however, proved utterly barren[61] and the subsequent conversations between Lloyd George and Senator J. Medill McCormick produced no response.[62] From December 1920

60 Admiralty to cabinet, memorandum, wp 73, 7 Nov. 1918, 'United States Naval Policy,' Lloyd George Papers, f/163/4/7; Long to Lloyd George, 16 Feb. and 7 March 1919, ibid., f/33/2/13 and f/33/2/22. The Admiralty memorandum, signed by Eric Geddes, was extremely hostile to Wilson and concluded that he aimed to reduce comparatively the preponderance in sea power of the British Empire. Walter Long was somewhat less hostile but he clearly saw a naval 'menace' from the United States, distrusted Wilson, and urged Lloyd George to strike hard for British interests.

61 bd, 1st ser., v, chap. 2, 980–1065

62 Lloyd George regarded McCormick as President-elect Harding's personal envoy. McCormick to Lodge, 22 Dec. 1920, Henry Cabot Lodge Papers, File 1921, Sept. to Dec. (mis-filed); Geddes to Kerr, 3 Jan. 1921, Lloyd George

to March 1921, therefore, the Committee of Imperial Defence (CID), under revived pressure from the Admiralty for a renewal of capital ship construction and with the controversy over the value of the capital ship reopened in *The Times*, turned to the question.[63]

The CID assembled on 14 December 1920 and listened to Lloyd George state the problem.[64] They must decide what type of navy was necessary to ensure imperial security and lines of communication, what construction might be required, and how to balance political and naval considerations. Initially, Lloyd George suggested, they must decide which power they should regard as the 'probable enemy.' They could eliminate the European powers but 'There were, however, two formidable new Powers in the world, formidable today and possibly overwhelmingly so in a few years time. Both at present were friendly nations, and they were Japan and the United States of America.' The Premier dismissed the possibility that Britain might face a hostile combination of the United States and Japan but their individual naval strengths presented problems. Before 1914 Britain had ignored the United States when calculating her naval requirements and Lloyd George felt that the economic and strategic grounds for that decision were still valid. Moreover, a decision to enter into naval competition with the United States would be of greater significance even than that of deciding to enter the war in 1914. A naval race would eventually ruin Britain and as she owed the United States a debt of £1000 million, Washington could demand immediate cash payment. The whole affair would perforce be debated publicly and, reminiscent of Anglo-German relations, the press and public opinion would begin 'snarling.' In cold hard

Papers, F/60/4/11; for a less flattering view, Dressel (US chargé d'affaires, Berlin) to W.H. Buckler (US Embassy, London), 30 Dec. 1920, Buckler to Dressel, 15 Dec. 1920, Dressel to W.C. Castle (US State Department), 29 Dec. 1920, and Castle to Dressel, 17 Jan. 1921, E.L. Dressel Papers, b, MS Am., 1549, box 2

63 Hankey note, 13 Dec. 1920, CID paper 263-B, 'Naval Shipbuilding Policy,' Cab. 4/7; Roskill, *Naval Policy Between the Wars*, I, 220–1

64 Minutes of 134th meeting of CID, 14 Dec. 1920, Cab. 2/3 and Lloyd George Papers, F/192/1/5; Lloyd George to Long, 14 Dec. 1920, Lloyd George Papers, F/34/1/56. Present, and all were either sceptics or hostile, were Lloyd George, Bonar Law, Curzon, Austen Chamberlain, Churchill, Eric Geddes, Beatty, Henry Wilson, Brock, Trenchard, Chatfield, and Hankey. Walter Long, close to resignation, was absent owing to ill health.

terms the cost to Britain, Lloyd George stated, would be the £1000 million plus at least £100 million for actual naval construction, and a comparison of Britain's national debt and population figures with those of the United States and Japan showed that Britain faced the greatest resources in the world from a seriously disadvantageous position. As Lloyd George pointed out, the task was gigantic, the significance of any decision was momentous, and they could not commit Britain to a possibly disastrous naval rivalry except for the most urgent and convincing reasons. 'The decision was of such moment that he would suggest that it might be fatal to enter into competition with the United States until every means of amicable arrangement had been exhausted.'

Lloyd George, however, saw certain encouraging signs. High taxation was unpopular in the United States and the incoming Republican administration was as hostile to the Daniels naval programme as it was to the League. Moreover, the Republicans seemed ready for a settlement with Britain and he personally favoured negotiations, after consultation with Ambassador Geddes, on the following lines:

... to say, that we had no intention of embarking on a rivalry in respect of general supremacy at sea, but that we propose that each nation should be superior in her own seas. We, for instance, in the North Sea, the Mediterranean, the Indian Seas, etc., while the United States should be conceded unchallenged superiority in her special seas. This was not challenging American supremacy. If, on the other hand, Great Britain claimed complete supremacy in *all* seas, the United States would undoubtedly accept the challenge, and this would eventually lead to a fight. This was one of the political considerations to be borne in mind.

Should a building programme be necessary, the committee must consider technical matters and seek expert advice, and Lloyd George summarised the whole task as first deciding on the potential enemy and then deliberating on the best method of combatting that enemy by land, sea, and air.[65]

65 In his letter to Long, Lloyd George wrote that he hoped to establish two sub-committees, one under Balfour to 'choose' the potential enemy, and a second to consider technical problems. In reply, Long affirmed that on all political issues the Admiralty agreed with the cabinet, but that their main concern was to retain the supremacy of the seas. He felt that this problem outweighed all political, diplomatic, and economic considerations, for Britain must retain

Churchill, not particularly impressed with the Premier's views, responded in characteristic fashion. Britain must retain supremacy of the seas as the very basis of the life of the nation, of its culture and its prosperity, and should plan in general terms to ensure supremacy rather than first identifying a specific enemy. Churchill could see no reason why the United States should object, he opposed the idea of an Anglo-American division of the seas, and seemed unmoved by the view that the great distances between Britain and the United States provided a measure of security. Churchill then warned against calculating naval power solely in post-Jutland dreadnoughts and, broadening the debate, urged that they consider all relevant naval and political factors, such as Britain's alliance with Japan. He personally favoured the link with Japan, but Britain could amend the alliance and, to avoid a naval race, she must not renew it until discussions on naval policy had been held with the new United States administration.

Lloyd George regarded the curtailing of the use of American naval forces, compelling the United States to maintain a large part of her fleet in the Pacific, as an advantage gained from the Anglo-Japanese alliance, and both Chamberlain and Curzon welcomed signs that some elements of United States opinion opposed naval preparedness. However, after these diversions and speculations, Beatty brought the meeting back to the central theme. The Admiralty had already stated that unless Britain reached an agreement with the United States they must decide on a building programme within one year from October 1919, in order to secure equality in sea power with the next strongest nation. The Admiralty, after a study of the lessons of the war, was not tied exclusively to battleships as a yardstick of strength and would accept having three less of such ships in comparison with the next fleet, but, to ensure equality with the second strongest power, construction must commence soon or Britain would lose her facilities for the production of armour plate.[66] Austen Chamberlain dismissed both war as a solution to a naval race and naval competition with the United States as a solution to Britain's predicament, unless she could utilise dominion resources, and he received the support of Henry Wilson who preferred alliances to adjust the balance of power in

naval supremacy, and he personally could not support a policy which permitted Britain to fall into second or third place among the naval powers (Long to Lloyd George, 17 Dec. 1920, Lloyd George Papers, F/34/1/57).

66 Admiralty memorandum, 10 Dec. 1920, CID papers 261-B, Cab. 4/7

Britain's favour.[67] Bonar Law virtually concluded the debate, repeating the view he held on the eve of Grey's departure for Washington in September 1919 that only a direct challenge from Britain would arouse the United States and provide justification for her naval programme. Britain should accept the attendant risk, refrain from competitive building, and avoid antagonising the United States. War with the United States was not probable in the next five years and the new Republican administration most likely would be unwilling to support the aspirations of the Navy Board. Beatty, however, was emphatic in his response. The race was already on, the Republicans would complete the current naval construction programme, and Britain must act.

The remaining discussion was cyclical, argumentative, and not particularly elevated. Lloyd George clearly leaned toward the idea of using Japan as a counterweight to and a lever on the United States, even speculating on Japan's naval value in an Anglo-American war.[68] He met with Churchill's opposition, denouncing the idea of basing naval policy on possible co-operation with Japan against the United States. The Premier, however, preferred that policy to one which left Britain at the mercy of the United States. Supported by Bonar Law, Austen Chamberlain, and Curzon, Lloyd George repeated his idea of opening negotiations with the American government, after consultation with Aukland Geddes, to prevent a capital ship race with Japan and the United States. The meeting then decided that Curzon should recall Geddes, after the ambassador had sounded out the Harding administration but disguised the reason for his recall, and that Beatty should report to Lloyd George on possible economies in other categories of warships if the government decided to build new capital ships.

The CID debate on 23 December was much narrower in scope.[69] Despite the Admiralty's recommendations for a capital ship building

67 Collier, *Brasshat*, 320–1. Collier wrote that Henry Wilson urged an alignment with European powers against the United States, but that Lloyd George rejected the proposal.

68 Incongruously but characteristically Lloyd George actually quoted his Rumanian confidant, Také Jonescu, to the effect that Japan was preparing for war with the United States.

69 Minutes of 135th meeting of CID, 23 Dec. 1920, Cab. 2/3 and Lloyd George Papers, F/192/1/5; Curzon and Chatfield were absent and Balfour was in attendance.

programme and Beatty's protests, Lloyd George, backed by Churchill and Chamberlain, insisted on a comprehensive and expert re-examination of all relevant financial and technical considerations. All agreed, with Churchill most reluctant, that the one power standard was an acceptable one, meaning the retention of a fleet equal to that of any other single power, and the committee decided to create a sub-committee under Bonar Law to report on the capital ship question, and, further, to ask for an Admiralty study of auxiliary services necessary to supplement their proposed capital ship programme. This sub-committee was in addition to the one to be chaired by Balfour to study the probable conditions resulting from war between the empire, with or without allies, and various powers or groups of powers, in the light of their relative armed and economic strengths.[70] Clearly Lloyd George had carried the meeting. Negotiations with the United States would await Geddes's personal report, experts would comment on the value of the capital ship, and, should negotiations with the United States prove fruitless, the cabinet would know what type of naval programme would best fulfil Britain's needs.

In pursuance of these decisions, Aukland Geddes was recalled to London in January and, leaving R.L. Craigie in charge of the embassy, brought information both extremely disturbing and only faintly hopeful.[71] On the one hand he feared an increase in American naval estimates, as the General Board of the Navy pressed for a new three-year programme to ensure American naval equality with or even superiority by 1927 over the combined fleets of Britain and Japan. Moreover, even the 1916 programme would produce sixteen post-Jutland capital ships by 1925 and the Hearst press denounced all disarmament plans as subservience to Britain, France, and Japan. In addition, Senators Lodge and Knox and elder statesman Elihu Root demanded that policy decisions wait on Harding's assumption of office and that the United States negotiate a multilateral disarmament agreement only from a position of strength. The appeal

70 I have found no further evidence of this sub-committee and possibly it never met. The reference may have been to the Standing Defence Sub-Committee.

71 Curzon to Geddes, 12 Jan. 1921, FO/371/5667; Geddes to Curzon, 29 Dec. 1920 and 7 Jan. 1921, and Craigie to Curzon, 28 Jan. and 11 Feb. 1921, FO/414/247; Geddes to Kerr, 3 Jan. 1921, Lloyd George Papers, F/60/4/11; Riddell diary, entries, 18 Dec. 1920, 1 and 26 Jan. 1921, Riddell, *Intimate Diary*, 255, 259–60, and 271–3; Riddell noted Lloyd George's reaction as one of disbelief mingled with depression.

of naval preparedness was not easily dissipated from the public and the professional mind.[72] American resources were, in Geddes's opinion, limitless and were matched by high levels of anglophobia. Yet, congressional pressures for arms limitation, led by Senator Borah, received widespread press support and, having forced Daniels on the defensive, ensured that completion of the 1916 programme would be the limit of his achievement. Consequently, Geddes offered some faint hope for an Anglo-American naval agreement.

Study of the capital ship question in London progressed into the early months of 1921 but the sub-committee's reports, reflecting the evidence and debate, were divided both on the value of the capital ship and especially on the need for new construction.[73] Beatty and Churchill, advocates of the capital ship and an immediate construction programme, wanted four capital ships per year for four or five years, followed by arms limitation negotiations with the United States and Japan. Bonar Law and the other members, however, were more impressed with political and economic considerations and these differences of opinion resulted in divided counsel and compromise. Partly as a result of this compromise the British government's decisions were plural and even somewhat ambiguous. Lord Lee, now first lord of the Admiralty, would initiate appropriate informal moves and public gestures to secure a naval agreement with the Harding administration. However, as announced in the naval estimates for

72 American sources confirm that Lodge and President Harding supported only multilateral disarmament negotiated from a position of strength, and regarded Borah's efforts as premature, politically dangerous, and pursuing false economies. In addition, Lodge saw the value of the navy as a lever on Japan to ensure that Asian problems were settled in America's favour. Borah was thus an acute embarrassment to both the retiring and the incoming executives from December 1920 to July 1921, although Secretary of State Hughes saw the value of his campaign as a defensive manoeuvre if Borah's proposals could be adopted at the most suitable moment (Harding to Lodge, 20 Feb. 1921, Lodge to Harding, 25 Feb. 1921, Lodge Papers, file 1921; Col. Theo. Roosevelt Jr. to Denby, 8 Aug. 1921, Edwin Denby Papers, file 1918–21, Aug. 1921).

73 Roskill, *Naval Policy Between the Wars*, I, 221–7; Fry, 'Anglo-American-Canadian Relations,' 245–7; Churchill to Balfour, 26 Feb. 1921, Young, *Balfour*, 419; Bonar Law, Beatty, Long, Horne, and Eric Geddes comprised the sub-committee.

1921–2, Britain would design and plan to lay down before the end of 1921 four new 'super-Hoods' at a preliminary cost of £ 2½ million, in order to modernise her battle fleet, replace obsolete vessels, and build to the one power standard.[74]

Next in importance to naval matters stood the question of war debts, hardly less pressing and embarrassing and equally frustrating. Britain, as part of a mutual cancellation of interallied debts, hoped to be relieved of her specific debt to the United States and, as a suppliant, was again dependent on a gesture of understanding from Washington. However, the United States made no such gesture and the general tone of the negotiations was less than cordial, as shown in the exchanges between Austen Chamberlain and the secretary of the Treasury, D.F. Houston.[75] Chamberlain, applauded by Bonar Law, stated that he regarded the debate on a multilateral cancellation of debts as closed. Britain had made a proposal, the United States had rejected it, and Britain would not repeat the suggestion. Moreover, denouncing Houston's inference that the United States had gained nothing from the war whereas Britain and her allies had made significant economic and territorial advances, Chamberlain insisted that Britain's war effort had been a gigantic strain and had merely produced new responsibilities. In contrast, the Chancellor of the Exchequer asserted, the United States had refused to meet her obligations and, on the question of the Turkish mandate, had actually accused Britain of attempting to entangle her. Surely if a mandate were a source of economic benefit the United States would accept a friendly British offer to share in the advantages, but if a mandate were a burdensome ensnarement then the United States should recognise what Britain had gallantly undertaken. Chamberlain, in typical sceptic style, then concluded by assuring Houston that he hoped for cordial Anglo-American relations, but that the United States must be fair and just.

Once the Spa Conference was concluded, Lloyd George made a personal appeal to President Wilson, in an attempt to revive their

74 Craig (Lee's deputy), statement, House of Commons, 17 March 1921, 139, *Debates*, 5 ser., Cols. 1763–78; Statement of the First Lord of the Admiralty, explanatory of the naval estimates, 1921–2, Cmd. 1191; Fry, 'Anglo-American-Canadian Relations,' 347–51; Young, *Powerful America*, 48–52

75 Chamberlain to Houston, 12 March 1920, in reply to Houston's telegram, 5 March 1920, Lloyd George Papers, F/31/1/18

Peace Conference dialogue on financial matters and secure a responsible United States policy.[76] He asked Wilson for a new round of Anglo-American co-operation to cure Europe's ills and to diffuse the responsibility. More specifically, Lloyd George stated that a moderate reparation settlement depended to a great extent on a multilateral cancellation of interallied war debts and that the funding of Britain's debt to the United States was delayed because of the interrelationship of all war debts. Lloyd George's appeal brought no early response, however, and on 3 November 1920 the British cabinet met to discuss the debt question without the benefit of Wilson's reply.[77] They concluded that the outlook seemed bleak, United States opinion appeared to regard Britain's policy as a selfish attempt to avoid paying her debts, the presidential election campaign had bred confusion, and the United States could demand immediate payment of the interest due. The cabinet were not united in their views about the respective Democratic and Republican attitudes on the debt question, but, as Harding's anticipated victory could perhaps be regarded as a defeat for anglophobe elements in the United States, Britain would not resume negotiations until Harding took office. In the meantime, Geddes should try and find out whether Wilson had ever received Lloyd George's letter.

In fact Wilson's reply was sent that same day but, predictably, it offered little.[78] He could not act without congressional approval and Congress would never accept the cancellation of Britain's debt in return for Britain remitting allied debts owed to her. The United States would never remit any other allied debts either, nor would she concede any connection between reparations and debts. Delays, Wilson wrote, were merely embarrassing and dangerous because ultimately the United States would have to collect both accumulated and current interest. Wilson suggested, therefore, that Britain send a special representative to Washington to open negotiations to convert her demand debts into longterm obligations. Other than that, United States policy must wait on the election results, though Wilson expressed his personal hope that ultimately the United States would co-operate unselfishly.

76 Lloyd George to Geddes, 15 July 1920, ibid., F/60/4/6, and Lloyd George to Wilson, 5 Aug. 1920, ibid., F/60/1/28

77 Conclusions of cabinet meeting, 3 Nov. 1920, Cab. 23/23

78 Wilson to Lloyd George, 3 Nov. 1920, Lloyd George Papers, F/60/1/31

Reports from Washington confirmed Wilson's assessment[79] and emphasized the widespread opposition to cancellation, the mounting charges of fraudulent behaviour against Britain, and the tendency to link the debts question with the campaign to reduce taxes. Geddes felt that domestic economic problems would increase the clamour for payment by Britain rather than force cancellation and, moreover, he felt that Britain would merely secure worse terms by delaying a settlement.

Cold comfort indeed, and the final cabinet debate of 1920 on this question understandably instituted rather gloomy proceedings.[80] Chamberlain pointed out that by refusing to convert her sight debt into a longterm debt Britain had ignored her obligations, and, while the United States was unlikely to demand payment of the whole sum, Geddes had warned of possible renewed demands that Britain fund her debt and pay the accrued interest at a cost of £80 million. In the ensuing debate some members of the cabinet strongly denounced the United States for taking unfair advantage of Britain's strained economy and for jeopardizing her naval position. Others feared that if Britain admitted the principle of an obligation to pay her war debts she would place herself at the mercy of the United States. The general feeling at one stage in the debate was that Britain should deny that her debt was an ordinary commercial one and should refuse to pay.[81] Finally, however, the cabinet agreed that although the United States was selfishly undermining Britain's trade, she could not repudiate her debts and must send an expert representative to open negotiations in Washington.

By early May, however, the cabinet, wary of gestures from A.W. Mellon, Houston's successor at the United States Treasury, was still debating whether they could expect more sympathy and understanding from Harding's administration. Further delay was inconsistent with national dignity, damaged the nation's credit, and continued to injure Anglo-American relations, but the government decided in fact against reopening negotiations at that time, and on

79 Geddes to Curzon, 2 Dec. 1920, FO/371/4548; Craigie to Curzon, 17 Feb. 1921, FO/371/5667

80 Conclusions of cabinet meeting, 17 Dec. 1920, Cab. 23/23

81 Only Lord Inverforth and Sir A. Mond argued firmly against default and for funding the debt, although Curzon warned that the Republican administration would be harsher than its predecessor and advised against delay.

this second fundamental question there seemed little sustenance for the Atlanticists.[82]

Other problems, while of perhaps less direct importance, were almost equally distressing. With some rationalisation, Britain could view the debris and the unfinished European and Middle Eastern business of the Peace Conference as a direct result of the lack of United States co-operation. The Reparations Commission had become a monument to French extremism and Lloyd George cited the absence of a United States representative to support moderate policies as the principal reason. The Adriatic confrontation between Italy and Yugoslavia simmered and boiled and United States obstructions and delays seemed responsible in part.[83] The Middle East presented a triple problem. First, as Curzon told Grey,[84] the entire area was in turmoil owing to delays in drawing up the Turkish peace treaty, the chief obstacles being Wilson's illness and the resulting uncertainty about United States policy. Second, the Middle Eastern mandates question was further disturbed by United States accusations of crude imperialism coupled with her own refusal to accept a mandate.[85] She seemed unable to decide whether the mandates were terrible burdens which she must avoid, or lucrative assets seized by Britain, but, demanding equal treatment for the interests and nationals of all states in the mandate areas, the United States favoured the latter assessment. Finally, and at the core of the mandates question, oil rivalries were involved with the Standard Oil Company pressing Washington to protect its exploration and exploitation rights, which they felt were threatened by British oil interests. Geddes, noting the intimate relationship between Wilson's administration, the Standard Oil Company, the Navy Department, and the press, forecast aggressive American policies to secure cancellation of pre-

82 Conclusions of cabinet meeting, 10 May 1921, Cab. 23/25

83 Lloyd George and Clemenceau to Wilson, 16 Feb. 1920, and J.W. Davis to Curzon, 25 Feb. 1920, Lloyd George Papers, F/60/1/24, and 25

84 Foreign Office to Grey, 22 Oct. 1919, ibid., F/60/3/11. Grey, however, was more concerned than Curzon about possible United States hostility to the Anglo-Persian treaty (Grey to Curzon, 17 Oct. 1919 and Curzon to Lloyd George, 9 Nov. 1919, ibid., F/12/2/4).

85 Churchill to Lloyd George, 9 June 1921, Lloyd George to Churchill, 11 June 1921, ibid., F/9/3/51 and 54; Grey to Curzon, 29 Oct. 1919, ibid., F/60/3/15; J.W. Davis to Curzon, 12 May and 28 July 1920. FO/414/246

war arrangements and to force new concessions from Britain in Mesopotamia. Furthermore, Geddes warned that these policies would be accompanied by a propaganda campaign to arouse fears about the exhaustion of domestic American resources and the dangers of future dependence on reserves under British control. Inevitably this campaign would be anglophobe in tone and Geddes offered little hope either that the influence of the oil companies would decline or that the policy of the new Republican administration would be different from that of its predecessor. Geddes suggested counter-propaganda and even economic ripostes, and Curzon, while avoiding such extremism, lectured the American ambassador on the legality and the morality of Britain's policies, and on the frailties of the American case. Of course the links between the British government, the Admiralty, and the oil companies were just as close as those of their American counterparts, and the exchanges were almost as acri-monious as the stakes involved were high.[86] Clearly also, on these questions, the Atlanticist case seemed transparently frail.

Beneath these major issues were more minor irritants which, in a cumulative way, also helped undermine what mutual confidence and cordiality remained in Anglo-American relations. London and Wash-ington differed over the status of the island of Yap, a focal point in the trans-Pacific cable system, as the State Department demanded international control while the Foreign Office insisted that the Coun-cil of Four at the Peace Conference had accepted the inclusion of Yap in Japan's mandate area. This problem, focussing on the question of whether Wilson had made a specific reservation on Yap in the Council of Four and projected into the debate within the United States on the ratification of the peace treaty, was an extremely deli-cate one, for both the veracity of the participants and the accuracy of Hankey's secretariat were involved.[87] Charges of British deceit were not really far from the surface and the question of whether Balfour or others had fully revealed the wartime secret treaties to Wilson and to members of his administration, a question perpetuated

---

86 Geddes to Curzon, 29 July, 24 Sept., 26 Nov., and 9 Dec. 1920, and Curzon to J.W. Davis, 9 Aug. 1920, FO/414/246; Rowland and Cadman, *Ambassador for Oil*

87 S.P. Waterlow (Foreign Office) to Kerr, 3 Dec. 1920, Lloyd George Papers, F/13/1/36. This letter is an effective summary of the nature of the contro-versy.

by the Shantung controversy and by Wilson's defence of the peace treaty, pointed in the same direction.[88] In a similar vain complaints from the United States of British interference with the trans-Atlantic cable system to the detriment of United States commercial and political interests and the round of abrasive negotiations in Washington toward the end of 1920 on the whole question of trans-Atlantic cable facilities did little to improve the tone of Anglo-American relations.[89] Indeed, Geddes reported that Wilson regarded the cables problem as a test of British good faith, as a measurement of London's willingness to co-operate with Washington rather than with Paris, and as the final opportunity to influence the United States decision on League membership. In addition, the State Department threatened a press campaign against Britain or the closure of her cable facilities in the United States should Britain fail to support America's claims. The only comforting sign on this issue lay in the fact that Wilson seemed even more upset with France and might appeal to Lloyd George for Anglo-American co-operation.

Two other problems, widely different and ebbing and flowing in their significance, seemed to defy solution. First stood the perennial Irish question, its hysteria and fanaticism fanned by the war and the Peace Conference, rekindled by the heat of the United States elections of 1920, and gratefully utilised by convinced anglophobes and anxious politicians of both parties. Wiseman, for instance, suggested that the potent Irish weapon was the only one left to Britain's enemies and that Lodge, ashamed but determined, was bidding for Irish support. Geddes interpreted J.M. Cox's nomination by the Democratic party convention as the work of Tammany Hall, the Irish bosses, and the east coast factions, and as revenge for the failure to insert an Irish plank in the platform and for the rejection of Al Smith. They rejected N.H. Davis because he was Wilson's man and because they regarded him as an anglophil.[90] Grey, reporting on the strength of anglophobia in the United States, told Curzon that Irishmen were

88 A significant ramification also emerged when Britain argued, not altogether consistently or convincingly in American eyes, that while she must honour her wartime secret treaty commitments to Japan, she was in no sense committed by the Anglo-Japanese alliance to adopt a hostile attitude toward the United States in the event of a confrontation between Washington and Tokyo.

89 Geddes to Curzon, 3 and 29 Nov. 1920, FO/414/246; Fry, 'Anglo-American-Canadian Relations,' 133–4

90 J. Macpherson (Irish Office) to Lloyd George, 7 July 1919, Wiseman to Ian

everywhere and that the antagonism of the Irish was at the root of all Britain's troubles with the United States.[91] Grey's analysis was orthodox enough and his solution was the familiarly elusive one of some policy of self-government for Ireland, but broader and even more dangerous considerations were involved. In June 1919 the British Consul-General in Chicago reported that, amidst the usual screaming about the 'plunder of Ireland' at a three-thousand strong rally, he heard demands for the freedom of India, Egypt, and South Africa.[92] Sir Aukland Geddes, in October 1920, ascribed 'an hysteria of hatred' against England 'to the influence of the Irish, Indian seditionists, and German groups, and all those political factions in the United States whose world activities are hindered by the machinery of law and order maintained by the British Empire,'[93] and, in January 1921, he reported on plans to weaken or destroy the British empire:

The support that Ireland has been receiving is part of the general plan, so is the welcome given to revolutionary Indians and Egyptians. Imperium Britannicum delendum est. England I suppose ultimately is to be purchased and kept as an interesting museum – The Old Home Land – a sort of glorified Mount Vernon managed by a committee of the Daughters of the American Revolution.[94]

By September 1921 Philip Kerr seemed convinced of the existence of links between the American Sinn Fein and certain Indian, Egyptian, and Bolshevik groups and all those in France and Germany who hated Britain.[95] He saw an international conspiracy led by Irish-Americans seeking to smash the British empire on the rocks of nationalist republicanism in Ireland, India, and Egypt while Britain lay exhausted and impotent because of the war. Kerr's answer, typically, was to unite Ireland with the empire and to show the Irish that others sought to use and manipulate them for sinister purposes. Clearly then the Irish question was not a narrow or limited one, but

Malcolm, 1 July 1919, and S. Watt (Dublin) to Davies, 23 July 1919, Lloyd George Papers F/46/1/8 and 9; Geddes to Curzon, 8 July 1920, FO/414/246

91 Grey to Curzon, 29 Sept. 1919, and Grey to Lloyd George, 6 Oct. 1919, Lloyd George Papers, F/60/3/6 and 7

92 British Consulate General (Chicago) to chargé d'affaires (Washington Embassy), 9 June 1919, ibid., F/46/1/8

93 Geddes to Curzon, 18 Oct. 1920, ibid., F/60/4/8

94 Geddes to Kerr, 3 Jan. 1921, ibid., F/60/4/11

95 Kerr to Lloyd George, 14 Sept. 1921, ibid., F/34/2/7

was an issue that could affect the future of the whole empire and, in any case, while 'Cromwell remained in Hell' Ireland would bedevil Anglo-American relations.

More difficult to assess and evaluate was the question of diplomatic representation in London and Washington respectively. In recognition of the significance and peculiarities of the Washington embassy, the Lloyd George government rid themselves of the orthodox and tragic Sir Cecil Spring-Rice in January 1918 and opted for special representation.[96] This decision, prefaced in the discussions of May 1917 on the respective merits of Grey, Lord Northcliffe, and Austen Chamberlain,[97] and in the special missions headed by Balfour, Northcliffe, and Lord Reading, turned the Washington embassy into something of a revolving door. Meanwhile, Sir William Wiseman and Frederick Dixon, editor of the Boston *Christian Science Monitor*, provided quite brilliant, unorthodox, and indispensable continuity until the fall of 1919, usually by way of personal contacts with Colonel House and others.[98] Lord Reading performed successfully though intermittently as ambassador until May 1919,[99] and Sir C. Barclay and then Sir R. Lindsay, as chargés d'affaires, filled the interim period while likely and unlikely candidates for the post of ambassador were feverishly sounded out.[100] The search was revealing and sometimes bizarre because the government could not select an opponent of Home Rule, Balfour feared the charge that they were conveniently

96 Spring-Rice still awaits his historian, both contemporary and historical judgments of him vary, but the weight of opinion is condemnatory and some of it quite vicious (Hankey to Lloyd George, 20 Oct. 1917, citing Colonel E.D. Swinton and J.M. Keynes, ibid., F/23/1/25; Hyde, *Reading*, 234-6).

97 Cecil to Balfour, 17 and 21 May 1917, and Balfour to Cecil, 20 and 22 May 1917, Balfour Papers, 49738. Cecil and Balfour preferred Grey; Lloyd George, Curzon, and Milner, however, regarded Grey as too pacifist; Lloyd George wanted a businessman or Northcliffe, everyone else condemned Northcliffe, and the cabinet and King George v then turned to Chamberlain. Grey's principal merit was his intimate relationship with House.

98 Willert, *The Road to Safety*; Hyde, *Reading*, 234-6. Dixon, a British subject, appears frequently in the Balfour and Cecil papers and in relevant FO/800 files. As an unorthodox channel of communication he deserves further study.

99 Hyde, *Reading*, 234-312

100 Curzon to Lloyd George, 1, 14, 23, 30 July and 3 Aug. 1919, and Lloyd George to Curzon, 10 July 1919, Lloyd George Papers, F/12/1/20, 25, 26, 28, 30 and 34; Borden to Lloyd George, 13 Feb. 1919, and Kerr to Borden, 16

rusticating either the Tory or the radical leader in the House of Lords, J.W. Lowther confessed that he did not like Americans and that his wife actively disliked them, and some hinted that Austen Chamberlain might grasp at the post to escape the trials of the Exchequer for which he was not suited.

Finally, Grey left on his special and ill-fated mission which lasted from September to December 1919. Within weeks Grey, recognising the futility of his position, reported that any hopes that a new phase of Anglo-American cordiality and co-operation would ensue from his personal contacts were an illusion, for Wilson was unapproachable, House was in eclipse, and Wilson's European and anglophil policies were suspect.[101] Grey himself then started the search for his own successor, suggesting Reading, Walter Runciman, and Babington Smith, but, ideally, H.A.L. Fisher, historian, genuine liberal, and a scholar who could create the vital dialogue with American universities and intellectuals from which rapport over Ireland might result.[102] Clearly the search was still for a special kind of representative rather than for a career diplomat and Harmar Greenwood suggested that Aukland Geddes was qualified, as a Scotch Presbyterian, a person loyal to Lloyd George, a university man with business contacts, and someone acceptable to the Canadian government.[103] This nomination obviously received support and in April 1920 Geddes went to Washington for a prolonged tenure, only to be smuggled ashore in New York for fear of hostile demonstrations and to live for a long period under the threat of violence to his family. Geddes grew in experience, he rapidly established a personal relationship with Secretary of State Colby,[104] ultimately he seemed to satisfy his employers, and he left Washington only after a tragic accident which left

Feb. 1919, Borden Papers, OC no 474; Wiseman to I. Malcolm (BED Paris),
3 July 1919, Balfour Papers, 49741; Curzon to Balfour, 23 May, 16 and 27
June, 3, 6 and 20 July 1919, and Balfour to Curzon, 9 June 1919, ibid., 49734.
Balfour, Borden, Sydney Buxton, Austen Chamberlain, Lords Crewe, Finlay,
Peel, Grey, Haldane, and Salisbury, the Duke of Devonshire, H. Foster,
J.W. Lowther (the Speaker), and the Provost of Trinity College Dublin were
all approached or suggested as possible candidates.

101 Grey to Lloyd George, 5 Oct. 1919, Lloyd George Papers, F/60/3/7
102 Grey to Lloyd George, 5 Oct. and 11 Nov. 1919, ibid., F/60/3/7 and 8
103 Hamar Greenwood to Lloyd George, 3 Jan. 1920, ibid., F/19/2/3; Geddes,
     Forging of a Family, 323
104 Geddes to Curzon, 28 May 1920, FO/414/246

him virtually blind, and to resounding applause. In his early years as ambassador, however, he was less than satisfactory, many of his reports were inconsistent and unorthodox, his phraseology suffered from his medical training, his despatch of 15 April 1921, causing Curzon to question his mental balance, must rank as one of the most extraordinary diplomatic reports ever, and Curzon was quick to seize on his indiscretions.[105] In sum, and despite Geddes's improved touch, British representation in Washington was uneven and inconsistent and the necessary diplomatic lubricants were often applied inadequately to the machinery of Anglo-American relations. Equally, neither of Walter Hines Page's successors, John W. Davis and George Harvey, and especially the latter, satisfactorily represented the United States in London, neither established deep rapport with Lloyd George's government, and the circle of inadequate representation was complete.[106] The casualty in chief was Anglo-American accord.

Faced with such disheartening and embarrassing developments in 1919 and 1920 the Atlanticists were in retreat. The debate had continued about the principles which should underlie British foreign policy but, as 1920 drew to a close, the creation of an Atlantic entente seemed an unlikely prospect. Yet a final opportunity seemed to present itself in 1921, offering prospects for Anglo-American co-operation and emerging from Pacific and Far Eastern problems which were themselves part of the unfinished business of the peacemaking. The idea of using the settlement of Pacific and Far Eastern issues as a vehicle to create the Atlantic entente was not a wild dream and indeed was in some ways the most logical course of action. Both Britain and the United States had territorial possessions or dominions in the Pacific and their navies sought to preserve the security of that region. They were deeply involved in the economic, financial, and

105 Geddes to Curzon, 15 April 1921, Curzon to Geddes, 18 and 23 May 1921, and Geddes to Curzon, 20 and 25 May 1921, Lloyd George Papers, F/13/2/19 and 25. Curzon reprimanded Geddes for references made to European politics, Geddes protested, blaming deliberate press misrepresentation, and Curzon actually apologised.

106 This view of Davis is at best an interim one and Reading gave Davis unqualified praise to House (Hyde, *Reading*, 314). My assessment of Harvey stems from his conduct in 1921.

commercial life of the orient and their missionaries were active. Finally, immigration and broader racial issues concerned both London and Washington, and Japan had already challenged the status quo in Asia.

The world war had disrupted the balance of power in the Far East, eliminated Germany, reduced Russia's presence, and given Japan virtually a free hand. Japanese occupation of Shantung and islands in the North Pacific accompanied increased political and commercial pressure on China, Manchuria, and Inner Mongolia, and both Britain and the United States could not but recognise the threat to Pacific security, to their dominions and possessions, and to the integrity of China. Japanese-American relations had reached a low point at the Peace Conference, a naval race and racial antagonisms threatened to erupt, and rumours of war were heard on both sides of the Pacific. In fact the United States navy had already designated Japan as the most likely enemy of the future and Hawaii seemed vulnerable.[107] Britain herself, despite their alliance dating from January 1902, had ample cause for concern about Japan's lack of frankness and dubious policies. Indeed, without an excess of imagination Whitehall could envisage complications involving the stability of the whole area from Hong Kong to India. Australian alarm about the growth of Japanese naval power matched evidence of her penetration of South East Asia. Moreover, Japan's unco-operative attitude toward the financial consortium and her designs on the Chinese Eastern and South Manchurian railways accompanied her discriminatory administration at Tsingtao and acts of apparent barbarism in Korea.[108] Some of these problems had provided opportunities for Anglo-American co-operation, but although Curzon lectured Ambassador Chinda and Secretary of State Lansing pressed Minister Debuchi on occasions, co-ordinated Anglo-American representations were rare. Indeed, over the question of Japanese occupation of Eastern Siberia, while Curzon accepted the *fait accompli*, Wilson and then Charles Evans

107 Wheeler, 'The United States Navy and War in the Pacific'; 'The United States Navy and the Japanese Enemy'; *Prelude to Pearl Harbour*

108 Memorandum by the General Staff, 5 Aug. 1920, 'On the present political and military situation in China,' BD, 1st ser., XIV, no 86, 90–1; cabinet debate, 22 Oct. 1919, Cab. 23/12; W.M. Hughes to Lloyd George, 7 Oct. 1919, Lloyd George Papers, F/28/3/42; Fry, 'Anglo-American-Canadian Relations, 209–11 and 314

Hughes declared the territorial integrity of Russia as an aim of United States policy.[109]

This failure to secure Anglo-American co-operation in Asia stemmed basically from divergent attitudes toward Japan, for Britain's partial naval and military abdication from the Pacific seemed to dictate continued friendship with her ally, and financial stringency made the recreation of Britain's naval power in the Pacific impossible. In Britain's view, the rehabilitation of China could not be achieved at Japan's expense, Japan's need for outlets must be met, and an Asian barrier to Bolshevism must not be lightly discarded. Until 1921, therefore, Anglo-American co-operation in the Far East and Pacific had been hesitating and rare and this fact itself could be cited as evidence against the Atlanticist case. But the areas of initial concern and commitment remained, American eyes could be turned more easily to Asia than to Europe, and the very seriousness and urgency of the Pacific problems demanded an immediate attempt at a settlement. Moreover, the question of naval disarmament focussed attention on the Pacific powers rather than on Europe, and at the very worst there stood the remote possibility of a war between Japan and the United States in which Britain's position would at best be tragically difficult.

Clearly Britain hoped to avoid making a choice between Japan and the United States, wanting neither to sever links nor risk a breach with either power, and all these considerations became focussed ultimately on the question of the renewal of that last remnant of the old diplomacy, the Anglo-Japanese alliance. The question of renewal was a matter for decision apparently by 13 July 1921, and the whole range of Far Eastern, naval, and imperial security problems were affected. Viewed from London, Atlanticists could see the renewal question as the opportunity to secure a sufficient measure of Anglo-American co-operation to provide the basis of more sustained and far-reaching co-ordination. To more sceptical observers this could be the final test and the last occasion for a gesture from Washington. To those who were antagonistic toward Atlanticism, the renewal of the Anglo-Japanese alliance would be the occasion for another wearisome but vital debate in which they must ensure the retention of traditional realism as the foundation of British foreign policy.

The debate over the renewal of the Anglo-Japanese alliance would

109 Fry, 'Anglo-American-Canadian Relations,' 149–50, 207–8; Geddes to Curzon, 11 July 1920, BD, 1st ser., XIV, no 67, 70–1

provide the vehicle in 1921 which the Atlanticists could use, but why did 1921 seem to offer fresh encouragement and the possibility of improved relations between London and Washington? The answer lay in the recently elected Republican administration of President Harding which, although providing the prospect of mixed blessings at best, nevertheless seemed to offer sufficient hope. In the first place the mystery of who held power in Washington would dissolve, the vacuum would be filled, hopefully vigorous government would return, and at least meaningful talks could begin. Secondly, despite the use of anglophobe and isolationist sentiments and the courting of the Irish vote in the election, Harding's victory heralded the return of sections of the old Republican elite who were ideologically closer to the Conservative base of the Lloyd George coalition. Some of them were anglophil and all of them would reject ties with the radical-left in Britain.[110] The death of Theodore Roosevelt was a blow to Atlanticists like Lee, but at least they could hope for less doctrinal idealism, a reduction in public disputes, and more practical co-operation from the United States both on vital issues and broader questions.

As the Committee of Imperial Defence had speculated, a new administration taking office in March 1921 might make the grand gesture although the evidence at hand was at best indefinite.[111] The leaders of the Republican party were not oratorically 'big navy,' Congress had checked Daniels effectively, and the movement led by Senator Borah, however suspect his motives,[112] offered some hopeful signs. Furthermore, Geddes reported that demands for reductions in defence expenditure emerging from the mid-West, and for tax cuts as a preface to the elections of 1922, would clearly be popular. Consequently Lord Lee, after public statements in March, launched his informal but official approaches in April. He enjoyed Lloyd George's support, but by June Lee's initiatives ran aground on Edwin Derby's obstructionism and deliberate procrastination, for the United States refused to embark on bilateral and premature negotiations.

110 Long to Lloyd George, 16 Feb. 1919, and Geddes to Curzon, 29 June 1920, Lloyd George Papers, F/33/2/13 and F/60/4/4. Geddes, on balance, felt that a Democratic victory would be unfortunate for Britain.
111 Geddes to Curzon, 17 June 1921, FO/414/247
112 Historians have made much of Borah's crusade but Geddes dismissed his activities as pure politics, designed to show that he opposed navalism and militarism and aimed at securing places in the cabinet for his nominees (Geddes to Curzon, 5 Jan. 1921, FO/414/247).

At least, however, Lloyd George had thought the attempt worthwhile, his leftwing political opponents expected nothing less, and the signal from President Harding on naval disarmament was not too far distant.

The question of war debts was even more complex and the British cabinet merely procrastinated. They were unsure as to what the Republican victory meant, the election statements were ambiguous, and few could disagree with Curzon and Geddes that the evidence suggested that Harding must demand that the allies pay their debts. Yet Britain could hope for greater understanding despite certain discouraging reports, serious economic problems related to declining American exports might encourage new approaches, and the government expected Harding's administration to regard the economic revival of Germany and of Europe generally as a matter of urgent concern. Arthur Willert, *The Times'* Washington correspondent and reputedly an Atlanticist, noted, despite Harding's pledge to isolationism, a desire to water the wine of French policies on reparations and, consequently, suggested that the United States might increase her financial and economic involvement to secure, through Germany, European recovery.[113] Against this evidence, however, both Atlanticism and especially the 'Lafayette tradition' were tarnished in the United States and hopes for an accommodation on the debts question were tenuous at best.

Much of course would depend on the personnel in and the balance of Harding's cabinet and on the relationship of the executive to Congress, and on these critical points Lloyd George and his colleagues wrestled mainly with Geddes's remarkable reports. Early in June 1920 Geddes had stated that, despite the Irish question, if the right man were elected in November there was some prospect of a general agreement with the United States on international problems, covering naval, mercantile, and commercial matters. Negotiations were, however, pointless until a new administration took office.[114] Geddes's first report on the amiable Harding, however, described him as a party hack and a machine politician, lacking intellectual gifts, administrative experience, and knowledge of foreign affairs, and likely to be dominated by Lodge and the Senate on foreign

113 Craigie to Curzon, 2 Feb. 1921, and Willert to Tyrrell, memorandum, 26 April 1921, FO/371/5667. Mellon, appointed secretary of the Treasury, favoured a policy of granting extensive credits to Europe according to Craigie.

114 Geddes to Lloyd George, 4 and 8 June 1920, Lloyd George Papers, F/60/ 4/1 and 2

policy matters.[115] Lodge, Geddes described as cynical, cold, and disillusioned, but friendly to Britain and determined that the powers of the president be diluted.

In July both Geddes and Willert reported more fully.[116] Geddes, in addition to the usual political divisions, saw the United States as a bewildering kaleidoscope, divided in terms of nationalities between Irish-, German-, Italian-, Anglo-Saxon-, and American-Americans, separated racially between white, negro, and red peoples, split between 'Wilsonolatry' and 'Wilsonophobia,' torn between religious faiths, and, finally, divided over prohibition. In the Republican party Geddes distinguished between three groups: the extreme Conservatives who were anglophil; the mild progressives who were not hostile to Britain; and the radical-nationalists, such as Senators Borah and Johnson, who were extreme anglophobes. In the Democratic party Geddes saw idealist Wilsonians, Tammany Hall's men, and a group comprising northern and western Liberals and progressive southerners, containing many educated Americans, who were anglophil. Cox, the Democratic nominee, Geddes described as self-made, not a gentleman, ignorant of foreign affairs, and under the influence of a mysterious octogenarian lawyer called MacMahon. Moreover, the Democrats, clutching simultaneously at the British and Irish links, described themselves as anglophil and internationalist, and hoped for British aid to help defeat the Republicans. Harding, Geddes confirmed, was Lodge's creature and, professing to see little difference between the parties in their attitude toward Britain, Geddes advised neutrality in an election, the outcome of which no one could forecast.

Willert regarded neither Harding nor Cox as first class, both parties as isolationist, and Americans as disillusioned with foreign ventures, preparedness, dreams of world hegemony, and with Britain and France. Clearly they were more concerned with domestic reconstruction, the forced allied intimacies of the war had lost their attraction, and the sentimental utopianism of the peace had given way to practical politics. The Senate, in Willert's view, was determined to harness the executive and he expected Harding to bow before its pressure. Lodge was a gentleman but was wedded to politics of a baser kind and was unscrupulous, without convictions, deceptively

115 Geddes to Lloyd George, 30 June 1920, ibid., F/60/4/4
116 Geddes to Curzon, 13 July 1920; Willert, memorandum, 'An Appreciation of the Republican and Democratic National Conventions held at Chicago and San Francisco respectively in June and July 1920,' FO/414/246

parochial, and slippery. Willert expected him to court the Irish, seek to destroy the League, and show himself to be hostile to and envious of Britain. Johnson, Willert described as honest, but an ignorant demagogue, a provincial 'blatherskate,' and as hostile to the peace treaty. Borah seemed honest, but incurably provincial and isolationist, and Medill McCormick was brilliant, but a none too scrupulous anglophobe. The Senate as a body, Willert felt, was neither pro-League nor in favour of close Anglo-American relations. Willert forecast a Republican victory, resulting in isolationism and worship of the dollar, for America had neither national conscience nor unity, and unless she were blessed with higher class immigrants he doubted whether the United States could improve morally, physically, or in terms of efficiency. Indeed, the United States could regress and become 'flabbier' for her climate was not inducive to the perpetuation of the white race in its natural vigour. Willert concluded by recommending that Britain remain on good terms with 'this large and succulent jelly fish,' utilising the presence of the three-fifths of her population who were Anglo-Saxon, in power, and mainly anglophil. In crises and in general, Willert warned, Britain could expect little but economic aid from the United States, and she must rely on her own military and naval resources.

In October 1920, however, Geddes confirmed his belief in the possibility of achieving an Anglo-American settlement, assuring Curzon that for the first time since 1776 there was some chance of arriving at a working agreement with the United States, despite the hysteria of hatred aimed at Britain.[117] Geddes emphasised particularly that the United States had an embarrassingly bad conscience about her shoddy role in the world since 1914 in comparison with that of Britain, feeling on the debts question like a philanthropist caught picking the widow's pocket to steal her mite. Harding's election was now assured, but both presidential candidates were 'real mediocrities' and Harding's election pledges would result in certain unpleasant acts in foreign affairs. His secretary of state, however, not bound by those pledges, would bring a bigger mind to the task[118] and once the impact of electoral indiscretions had abated Britain would have an opportunity to reach an agreement with the United States, which she would honour for at least two presidential terms. To secure this

117 Geddes to Curzon, 18 Oct. 1920, Lloyd George Papers, F/60/4/8
118 Geddes's list of prospective secretaries of state did not include Charles Evans Hughes.

agreement Britain must show real firmness, refuse to yield to Washington's scowls, handle issues carefully, and avoid 'sentimental gush.' Once the American people had recovered their self-respect and influenced their government accordingly, Anglo-American co-operation was possible.[119]

By early January, however, the scene in Washington seemed to offer different prospects.[120] Geddes reported that the current battle within the Republican party would result in a victory for its extremist wing and Britain should prepare to face 'the least straight-laced' and 'the most anti-British' government ever. These extremist 'realists' intended to dominate the world, lead the English-speaking nations, build the strongest fleet and merchant marine, and treat Britain as a vassal state so long as her war debts remained unpaid, or force Britain to cede her Caribbean islands in return for the cancellation of her debts. They would raise the bogy of a Japanese menace to forge a bond between the English-speaking states bordering on the Pacific, wean the dominions from the empire,[121] and extend the boundaries of the United States south of the canal and north to the pole. This last aim was 'still whispered except in the small hours of an alcoholic morning.' Geddes insisted that his picture of extremist aspirations and ambitions was the sober truth rather than the product of his overheated imagination and would mean the transfer of the centre of English-speaking power to North America. Their target was the British government not the English people, but the policy was real enough. The colossal resources of the United States would provide the basis for overwhelming sea power and Geddes argued that Britain could not meet this challenge save through the development of Canada, joined to Britain in some organic union and providing a new basis for British power. Geddes did not expect an Anglo-American war but rather a deadly struggle disguised as peace. Britain's salva-

119 Geddes to Curzon, 2 Dec. 1920, FO/371/4548

120 Geddes to Kerr, 3 Jan. 1921, Lloyd George Papers, F/60/4/11. Geddes identified the 'irreconcilables' as Johnson and Borah, a less vigorous 'anti-everything-not-American group' including McCormick, their opponents, the Root Republicans, and the cynical and singular Lodge as participants in the power struggle. The 'irreconcilables,' including Hearst, Brandegee, and E.B. McLean, editor-president of the *Washington Post*, were the 'extremists.'

121 Similar sentiments, aims and phrases occur in the Gardiner-Lodge exchanges in early 1921, although Geddes did not include Lodge in the 'extremist' group.

tion lay in the development of submarine and air power, globally based, in the creation of a super-dominion government of the British empire, and in 'rubbing along' with the United States for the interim period, only to emerge successful in fifteen or twenty years. Success was possible for

they lack fixity of political purpose and the machinery to carry through to a long range objective that which requires continued self-sacrifice to attain, provided that they are not challenged to show their metal. The danger is that they can attain their first objective, naval supremacy, without conscious effort and without continued self-sacrifice. If they once have that they will hold fast to it, with what we are often pleased to call 'British' tenacity.

The British government, Geddes felt, was misled both by recurring waves of anglophobia and by the great volume of anglophilia which still existed in parts of America. United States governmental and defence circles were simply pro-American, wanting power and world leadership to fulfil the national destiny and regarding Britain's crippled position as their great opportunity. Geddes concluded this report by stating that a paper naval agreement on the basis of equality was possible if Britain did not appear overenthusiastic and if the British press kept quiet. Moreover the appointment of the next governor general of Canada was a vital factor along with others to prevent the sapping of Canadian loyalties, and Lloyd George should visit Canada and perhaps Washington to help improve the situation.

Craigie, in Geddes's absence, had more encouraging news once Hughes's appointment as secretary of state was confirmed, for he, Root, and Harding seemed to favour both an internationalist policy and closer Anglo-American co-operation.[122] Harding was even rumoured to be something of a Pan Anglo-Saxon, believing in the divinely inspired civilising role of the English-speaking peoples, but the evidence was less than definite.

Geddes returned to Washington in mid-February and resumed his gloomy but ambiguous and mixed prophecies.[123] Charles Evans Hughes, he reported, was a man of unimpeachable character and good judgment, but he was determined to assert America's position and continue Wilson's policies on specific matters such as oil rights

122 Craigie to Curzon, 17 Jan. and 2 Feb. 1921, FO/371/5667; Craigie to
  Curzon, 2 Feb. 1921, FO/414/247
123 Geddes to Curzon, 25 Feb. 1921, FO/414/247; Geddes to Curzon, 4 March
  1921, FO/371/5667

and cable facilities. Senator Knox, moreover, able to dictate the appointment of A.W. Mellon as secretary of the Treasury, A.B. Fall as secretary of the Interior, and H.P. Fletcher as Hughes's assistant at the State Department, wished not only to use war debts as a lever on European governments, but also favoured France over Britain. Geddes's suggested riposte was typically exaggerated; Britain should offer secretly to support France over reparations if France would agree not to hold independent negotiations with the United States on the reduction or cancellation of her debts.

In mid March Geddes commented on Harding's dubious private life and the unorthodox behaviour of some of his cabinet; in Geddes's words, 'chickens' came home to roost from an 'extensive poultry farm.'[124] Both the nomination of Harvey, a heavy drinker, as ambassador to London and certain embarrassing events at the inaugural ceremonies were attributed to the claims of the 'little chickens.' Turning to the question of policies and with appropriate comments on Secretary Hughes's Welsh ancestry, however, Geddes noted that both the Secretary of State and Harding were very cordial toward him personally and would welcome close relations with Britain rather than with any other country. Hughes personally seemed to feel that Anglo-American co-operation was essential for world peace and hinted that the United States might join a new association of nations outside the League, but Geddes noted that Harding's government was committed generally to oppose Wilsonian policies and had not really discovered any alternatives. In sum, Hughes was able, but ignorant of foreign affairs and Geddes did not see how Hughes could 'make the League look like no League' and pass co-operation off as isolationism. Harding's subsequent disenchantment with France's Viviani brought more gestures of goodwill toward Britain and even disclaimers of support for Sinn Fein, but prospects of American entry into the League remained dim and the President confirmed that he would encourage the development of America's merchant marine and would not actively pursue disarmament at that early stage.

In April Geddes felt Secretary Hughes was not only ignorant of foreign affairs but 'abnormal mentally and subject to attacks of mild mania. I do not think he can fairly be regarded as individually fully responsible for what he says during these attacks but he is Secretary of State and when the Secretary has spoken, America has spoken.

124 Geddes to Lloyd George, 17 March 1921, Lloyd George Papers, F/60/4/16; Geddes to Curzon, 5 April 1921, FO/371/5667

This situation is not without difficulty.'[125] His report then devoted several remarkable pages to Hughes's mental distress, revealed during the course of an astonishing interview in which Hughes, completely out of control and mentally irresponsible, became Dr Geddes's 'patient' and, aroused over the question of Yap, raved against Britain and Japan. To Geddes, Hughes symbolised in a sincere and compulsive way the national megalomania of the United States with its accompanying suspicion of Britain, and Geddes, to combat this situation, warned against either criticism of or fawning over the United States. Instead Britain should maintain a 'stoney silence.'

Whatever Curzon felt about this final particular piece of advice, he told Lloyd George that the despatch cast doubts on the mental balance of Geddes rather than of Hughes, that Geddes was afflicted with a mild form of mania, and that the appointment of an ambassador who was both professor and doctor opened up a style of diplomatic terminology that was new and frightening.[126.]

Finally, in the period preceding the Imperial Conference, Geddes came to the conclusion that the excitable, indiscreet, and finely balanced Hughes, faced with great senatorial opposition, would not even survive as secretary of state, especially as he was so ill-suited temperamentally to cope with the problems of his office.[127]

Hughes, however, did survive. In these fluctuating and even incredible despatches Geddes had given with the left hand only to take back with the right and Willert in turn offered little conclusive evidence. Geddes had analysed American politicians, frequently in derogatory terms, showed scant respect for United States political parties and institutions, and his comments on American national characteristics were hardly free from contempt. His prognostications about United States policies were at best speculative, and any anglophilia seemed invariably balanced by isolationism. In June and October 1920, Geddes suggested that a general Anglo-American

125 Geddes to Curzon, 15 April 1921, Lloyd George Papers, F/13/1/19
   Geddes's medical training was amply demonstrated in this report and he wrote
   later that Hughes, a great man and an anglophile, had a source of personal inspiration, his spirit, called the 'Black Dwarf.' At the Washington conference it
   forced him to accept a policy of naval equality (Geddes, *Forging of a Family*,
   328-9).
126 Curzon to Lloyd George, 20 April 1921, Lloyd George Papers, F/13/2/9
127 Geddes to Curzon, 5 May 1921, FO/371/5667. Tyrrell in a minute of 6 May
   disagreed with Geddes.

agreement was possible, by January 1921 it was less likely although a naval agreement was not an impossible proposition, and his subsequent reports offered scant encouragement. Clearly the British embassy in Washington had not clarified the situation beyond all doubt, and Geddes's evidence was not sufficiently conclusive either to discredit entirely or confirm to any significant extent the Atlanticist case.

The debate on policy would reopen and, as the renewal of the Anglo-Japanese alliance and the problem of imperial defence were high on the agenda for the Imperial Conference of June 1921, the Atlanticists could take heart and await their reinforcements from the dominions. Their bitterest critics, also buttressed from the dominions, were ready to oppose, while Lloyd George and the sceptics were willing once more to debate and test probable solutions to strategic political, and racial problems. Nothing was settled finally and the ebb and flow of discussion would continue. Consequently, in the proceedings of the Imperial Conference, which became the preface to the Washington Disarmament and Pacific Conference, British and dominion statesmen in their various ways hoped to arrive at solutions which would improve the prospects for peace and security.

TWO

1921
New Opportunities

To the Atlanticists 1921 seemed to offer encouraging prospects for co-operation between the United States and the British empire. Britain apparently could not delay a decision on the future of her alliance with Japan beyond 13 July and the question of renewal would reactivate consideration of global policy. A Republican administration would take office in the United States in March and the Imperial Conference of June would be the forum in which Britain and her dominions would debate the future of their joint policies. In consequence, the Atlanticists had a further opportunity to convince the sceptics and to convert the more hostile to the view that they could reduce or solve the vital political, racial, strategic, and economic problems troubling the world since the Peace Conference. To some extent the future of British foreign policy rested on the ability of the Atlanticists to win this debate. In their view, solutions might come by way of the Orient and the casualty-in-chief would be the twenty-year-old link between London and Tokyo.

This agreement, signed on 30 January 1902, widened in scope on 12 August 1905, and again modified on 13 July 1911 as a ten-year alliance,[1] came under scrutiny in London, Washington, and Ottawa from the early months of 1919.

The partnership of Britain and Japan, especially from 1906, had never been consistently harmonious and complex problems were not erased by enforced wartime co-operation. To many western observers Japan had frequently acted in fine disregard of the spirit and letter

[1] British and Foreign State Papers, CIV, 173–4; Dennis, *The Anglo-Japanese Alliance*; Chang, *The Anglo-Japanese Alliance*; Spinks, 'A History of the Anglo-Japanese Alliance, 1902–1922'; Nish, *The Anglo-Japanese Alliance*

of the alliance and during the Shantung negotiations at the Peace Conference Lloyd George, describing Japan as the Prussia of the Far East, stated that her terrorisation of China was one of the most indefensible and unscrupulous acts in history.[2] To find a convincing alternative, however, was another matter. Britain could not rebuff Japan and abruptly terminate their alliance and, as Lloyd George recognised, they could not say to Japan 'Nous avons été heureux de vous trouver en temps de guerre, mais maintenant bonsoir.'[3] In positive terms the alliance offered Britain some insurance against future dangers such as that resulting from a Russo-German combination, which a rebuffed Japan might join. Britain would tolerate, therefore, certain discomforts and irritations, and her global strategic predicaments seemed to dictate co-operation with Japan in the post-1919 period as it had in the years before 1914. British expert opinion differed both on the value of Japan's aid during the war and on her need for outlets and economic opportunities in East Asia, but on balance the British government tended to give Japan the benefit of the doubt. Consequently, although she was allied to a power she could not fully trust, Britain could neither contain nor coerce Japan and she seemed reluctant to attempt to coerce this barrier to Bolshevism in Asia.

The existence of the alliance, however, bred suspicion in the United States, placing a useful weapon in the hands of the anglophobes there and those who demanded 'a navy second to none.' Despite several categorical assertions by Britain that the alliance was not operative against the United States, the alliance became a matter of public concern in North America, a disturbing factor in Anglo-American relations, and consequently a problem of great significance to Canada. The Atlanticists argued, of course, that co-operation with the United States was the only avenue of escape from this predicament, but others had less confidence in such a solution.

Lloyd George's government investigated four courses of action as it studied the problem of the renewal of the link with Japan. Britain could retain her alignment with Japan in the form of a modified alliance. This approach would perpetuate a tried policy, enable London to exercise some restraint on Tokyo, and help provide for the security of imperial interests and possessions. It would, however, ag-

2 Council of Four, 22 and 28 April 1919, Mantoux, *Les Délibérations du Conseil des Quatres*, I, 335, 376–8
3 Fry, 'Anglo-American-Canadian Relations,' 145

gravate the problem of co-operation with the United States and antagonise the Atlanticists. Alternatively, Britain could attempt to move toward the United States principally by way of negotiations for a naval agreement, as in the Grey mission of 1919 and in the conversations between Lord Lee of Fareham and Adolph Ochs, publisher of the *New York World*, in April 1921. This course, involving the dual risk that the United States would prove unreliable and incurably isolationist and that Japan would become detached and embittered, would involve the termination of the alliance and the establishment of Anglo-American co-operation in the Far East. As a third but very distant possibility Britain could recreate her Pacific fleet and construct the Singapore naval base, as recommended by Admiral Jellicoe in his reports on imperial naval requirements written from September to December 1919.[4] This solution would enhance imperial security and British prestige, and offer greater independence from both Japan and the United States. But such a step would be provocative and would injure relations with both those powers, feed the flames of a naval race, challenge the disarmament credo, create problems with the dominions, and undermine the demand for financial retrenchment. Not surprisingly, therefore, Britain rejected it as unwise and unacceptable.

The fourth approach, generally regarded as the most desirable, rested on the creation of a tripartite or even wider Pacific agreement comprising at least Britain, Japan, and the United States. Such a policy had much to commend it and many regarded it as the ideal solution, for Britain would avoid the appearance of a choice between Washington and Tokyo. She would steer a middle course between friend and ally, retain her links with Japan and create new ties with the United States, and avoid both the appearance of under-writing Japanese policies in China and of desiring to co-operate with the United States in a way hostile to Japan. Moreover, a tripartite agreement seemed to offer the greatest opportunity to prevent both Japan's disengagement and American detachment and to enable Britain to retain the friendship of both, to influence both, and mediate between them. Obviously, however, this policy demanded drastic modification of the Anglo-Japanese alliance and a move by Britain away from her exclusive arrangement with Japan toward closer co-operation with the United States. While Atlanticists would applaud, their critics

4 Ibid., 289–315

doubted the practicability of the policy and could even dismiss it as wildly improbable.

Deliberation on these alternative policies prior to the Imperial Conference of June 1921 revealed certain significant divergences of opinion in two distinct phases of study. A report by the 'Anglo-Japanese Alliance Committee' of the Foreign Office on 21 January 1921 marked the end of the first period of investigation, involving principally the major government departments and diplomatic representatives in the field. The second and more urgent phase, providing the preface to the imperial meeting, involved exchanges with the dominions, the United States, Japan, and China, and resulted in precise cabinet recommendations by the end of May 1921.

The Foreign Office dominated the first phase, gathering and evaluating evidence and, surprisingly, the Atlanticists received sustenance as a result. Curzon, seeking the rehabilitation of China and stability in the Far East but admiring the skilfully bargaining Japanese much more than the hapless but demanding Chinese, favoured continued friendship with Japan.[5] He advocated a form of agreement or alignment which would facilitate scrutiny of Japan's activities in China, permit London to demand from Tokyo a larger measure of frankness in their dealings with each other, and allow Britain to moderate and influence Japan's policies. Curzon was convinced that Japan would be less troublesome in China if she were bound to Britain 'even by a loose alliance' and much less so than if Japan became an ally of Germany or Russia, or joined a hostile Russo-German entente. Japan herself, Curzon felt, generally favoured renewal of the alliance, and although he wished to avoid difficulties with the United States he did not believe in the feasibility of a triple agreement. Political considerations pointed, therefore, in Curzon's view, to the perpetuation of the alliance with Japan, and the strategic factors governing imperial defence reinforced his opinions.

The Admiralty in October 1919 demonstrated the fundamental relationship between imperial security in the Pacific and the renewal of the alliance with Japan.[6] Failure to renew the alliance would alter completely the naval situation in Asian waters, and Britain's position

5 Foreign Office to other departments, 21 Jan. 1920, BD, 1st ser., VI, no 789, 1053–4

6 Admiralty memorandum, 'The Naval Situation in the Far East,' 31 Oct. 1919, CP 54, Lloyd George Papers, F/143

in the event of war with Japan or of war between Japan and the United States would be extremely difficult. The Admiralty recalled that in June 1909 the Committee of Imperial Defence had concluded that British possessions in the Far East were secure while the alliance with Japan remained in force, that Britain must recreate her Pacific fleet before terminating the alliance to neutralise the danger from Japan's naval preponderance in the China seas, and that the Admiralty and the War Office must ensure that Hong Kong could hold out for one month in the event of war with Japan. At the present time, however, the Admiralty memorandum stated, Japan's naval building programme to complete eight dreadnoughts and nine battlecruisers by 1926 and Britain's financial problems made it unlikely that she could equal Japanese naval power in the Pacific in peacetime. In the event of war, Britain could not easily or rapidly convert this peacetime inferiority into a position of superiority, Hong Kong would likely fall, and Britain's influence in Asia would be irretrievably damaged. The Admiralty concluded, therefore, that if Britain did not renew her alliance with Japan, she must create a Pacific fleet capable of meeting a Japanese challenge, and strengthen the defences of Hong Kong to enable it to resist a prolonged seige.[7]

The Admiralty had offered a distressingly expensive alternative to preventive diplomacy and their recommendations of February 1920 continued in a similar vein. In a reply to the Foreign Office, the lords of the Admiralty stated that they considered 'a continuation of the alliance in its present form neither necessary nor desirable.'[8] While accepting the political desiderata of British policy, they saw little possibility of providing a force sufficiently powerful to support a strong policy which might involve coercing Japan. Therefore, in the Admiralty's opinion, naval weakness in the Pacific dictated the establishment of some satisfactory understanding with Japan, a conclusion with which Curzon entirely agreed.

Similarly the War Office advocated some form of alliance or understanding with Japan for, apart from the question of China, 'our military position in the Far East might be most embarrassing, to say

---

7 By 1921 the Admiralty had begun to emphasise Singapore rather than Hong Kong as their major concern.

8 Admiralty to Foreign Office, 12 Feb. 1920, BD, 1st ser., VI, no 789, 1054. Roskill, citing the letter from the Beatty Papers, omits the phrase 'in its present form,' misses the point of the Admiralty's recommendation and comments on illogical Admiralty reasoning (Roskill, Naval Policy Between the Wars, I, 293).

the least of it, in the event of hostilities with Japan.'9 The military were also impressed with the need to guard against a possible Russo-German combination and to deter Japan from joining it, but were even more impressed with the need to eliminate the possibility of a war with the United States, the preparations for which were simply beyond Britain's financial resources. Indeed, the problems raised by a war with Japan paled before those raised by a war with the United States, friendship with America was essential, and, therefore, if Britain renewed the alliance with Japan she must do so in such a manner as to avoid antagonising the United States. This considera-tion must be the dominant one in the debate over renewal, and the Army Council felt in fact that Britain could negotiate an agreement which would improve relations with both Japan and the United States, just as she had before 1914 in the case of France and Russia.10 In conclusion, however, the War Office returned to the idea of a renewed alliance with Japan which conformed with the principles of the League Covenant.

These expert views of the strategic factors involved were laid out for the Committee of Imperial Defence before the end of March 1920.11 This memorandum recalled the decision of 3 May 1911 which reiterated the judgments of June 1909 on the interdependence of imperial security in the Pacific and the maintenance of Britain's alli-ance with Japan, while emphasising the threat to Australia and New Zealand as well as to Hong Kong in case of war. With regard to the situation in the postwar period, the memorandum suggested that despite the defeat of Germany, which would permit an early concen-tration of naval forces in the Pacific in the event of hostilities with Japan, the position was still sadly difficult.12 With the United States neutral and unless Australia and New Zealand increased their naval

9 War Office to Foreign Office, 14 Feb. 1920, BD, 1st ser., VI, no 789, 1054–5

10 Using this precedent, the War Office also warned against obligations of honour, vague and secret understandings, and compromising and indeterminate commitments which involved Britain in 1914 in hostilities for which she was not prepared.

11 CID memorandum, 124-C, 'Strategic situation in the event of the Anglo-Japanese Alliance being determined,' 25 March 1920, Cab. 5/3. The CID was not func-tioning as a body at this time and in 1921 a standing defence sub-committee under Balfour supervised preparations for the Imperial Conference.

12 On the question of complications in home waters the paper stated that, while France and the United States maintained their current naval forces, Britain

forces, Japan would control the Pacific in the early stages of war, and would use her superiority initially to attack Hong Kong and Singapore and to gain control of the Straits of Malacca rather than invade Australia and New Zealand.[13] With strong echoes from Jellicoe's recommendations and from the Admiralty studies of October 1919,[14] the paper argued that the probability of such raids would vary inversely with the quality of dominion naval and military forces, and, if Britain failed to retain the alliance with Japan, imperial security would depend on whether the combined dominion and British forces could match those of Japan. This solution, the re-establishment of imperial naval power in the Pacific, however, foundered on the rocks of financial stringency and, despite the decision to recommend the construction of the Singapore naval base in June 1921, Britain was forced back on the intuitive and intellectual qualities of her diplomacy.[15]

The strategic implications resulting from an abrogation of the Anglo-Japanese alliance clearly suggested that Britain could not risk severing her links with Japan, and the Committee of Imperial Defence debate of December 1920 further refined the problem.[16] Churchill introduced the alliance as a political factor that they must weigh along with naval considerations when they assessed Britain's

could not station the main or a large part of the fleet far from home bases in peacetime. In the event of war with Japan, however, France and the United States would probably be benevolently neutral or even join Britain.

13 The memorandum stated, however, that Japan might reverse this strategy if Britain faced complications in Europe and the western Atlantic.

14 Fry, 'Anglo-American-Canadian Relations,' 291–3, 303–5

15 Hankey to Chamberlain, 'Notes on the imperial meeting,' 16 June 1921, and Admiralty paper, 'Empire naval policy and co-operation,' Austen Chamberlain Papers, AC 26; Oversea Defence Sub-Committee, 'Report on the Singapore naval base,' 7 June 1921, Sir George Foster Papers, vol. 66, file 160 and Lloyd George Papers, F/143. The Treasury representative, dissenting from the recommendation on Singapore, argued that defence decisions were premature until they settled the Anglo-Japanese alliance question, that forecasts of Japanese hostile actions were remote and hypothetical enough to be incredible, and that financial considerations demanded that Britain rely on diplomacy to obviate the risks produced by inadequate defence systems.

16 Minutes of the 134th meeting of the CID, 14 Dec. 1920, Lloyd George Papers, F/192/1/5

global strategic position. He favoured perpetuation of the alliance but argued that Britain could also amend it to allay United States fears and accommodate certain racial objections and pro-American sentiments prevalent in the dominions. To prevent a naval race, Churchill demanded, Britain must re-assess the situation and avoid renewing the alliance until they had held discussions on naval policy with President Harding's administration. Lloyd George's response seemed incredibly irresponsible; Anglo-Japanese naval co-operation would severely reduce the manoeuvrability of the United States fleet and compel the American government to station a significant part of its naval forces in the Pacific. The Premier had, therefore, without relinquishing the scheme for an Anglo-American naval agreement, speculated on the idea of using Japan as a counterweight to and a lever on the United States. Indeed, he even ruminated on Japan's value to Britain in the event of war with the United States. When Churchill denounced any suggestion of basing naval policy on co-operation with Japan against the United States, Lloyd George indicated that he preferred that policy to one which left Britain vulnerable to United States naval power. These exchanges were not particularly elevated and the Canadian government in 1921 felt it detected in its exchanges with London the idea of forcing the United States to accept a naval construction agreement or risk the renewal of the Anglo-Japanese alliance. Perhaps the Atlanticists faced both irresponsibility and opposition as the British government pursued its policy review.

Looking abroad, the Foreign Office assessed evaluations from four ambassadors in Tokyo, Peking, and Washington; Sir John Jordan, Sir Beilby Alston, Sir Charles Eliot, and Sir Aukland Geddes.[17] The most senior, Jordan, participating in the investigation of the alliance question up to and during the Washington Conference, was a rare enough person, a sinophil.[18] He did not regard Japan as a loyal ally, he had

17 Eliot, former high commissioner in Siberia, replaced Alston in Tokyo from 1 April 1920; Jordan left Peking at the end of February 1920, and Miles Lampson supervised the interim period until Alston arrived in mid-April; Geddes's tenure at Washington was uninterrupted. Jordan, Alston, and Geddes returned to London at some point to assist in the review of policy.

18 Jordan to Balfour, 23 Dec. 1918, Jordan to Curzon, 28 Aug. 1919, 17 and 19 Jan. and 27 Feb. 1920, BD, 1st ser., VI, 566–83, no 479, 691–5; nos 678, 679, 682, 683, 940–4, and no 759, 1015

opposed the Peace Conference decision on Shantung, he showed little faith in Japanese policies in northeast Asia, and he tended to dismiss the idea of Japan being a barrier to Bolshevism as a figment of Japanese propaganda. Not surprisingly, Jordan advocated co-operation with the United States, for she alone shared Britain's aims and interests in China and they were the only two powers in which China had any faith. Moreover, according to Jordan, only the United States had sufficient financial resources to guide China towards her great destiny. The two Atlantic powers should enforce a policy of co-operative internationalism and destroy the policy of spheres of influence, which tended to benefit Japan and harm both British interests and China herself. Jordan, however, did not expect Anglo-American co-operation to ensue so long as Britain retained her connection with Japan and while the United States retained her reluctant attitude. Although he advocated the abrogation of the Anglo-Japanese alliance, he could not really offer firm hopes of United States co-operation and was, therefore, an Atlanticist hovering reluctantly close to the ranks of the sceptics.

Sir Beilby Alston was less consistent than Jordan and his views on the alliance question underwent certain changes of emphasis which tended to bring him closer to the Atlanticists' position.[19] While in Tokyo, Alston expressed the view that the alliance had lost its raison d'être with the collapse of Russia and Germany, and that Britain could not renew it in its original form because of the alliance's incompatibility with the League Covenant. Alston also demanded the fullest co-operation with the United States in China, but he did not harbour hostility toward Japan. Indeed, he seemed to develop a growing faith in prospects for co-operative action with a 'liberal' and manageable Japan in China. Alston warned against isolating Japan from the Anglo-Saxon powers and against attempting to exclude her from the Asian mainland, suggesting that she feared isolation and that Britain could act in harmony with her to preserve China's integrity.

Consequently, Alston tended to recommend that Britain retain some form of agreement, entente, or friendly understanding with Japan, modified to meet League requirements, and negotiated only after having made a full explanation to the United States to remove

19 Alston to Tilley, 7 Oct. 1919, Alston to Curzon, 25 Nov. 1919, Alston to Tilley, 30 Dec. 1919, Alston to Curzon, 17 Jan. 1920, BD, 1st ser., VI, no 522, 761–5; no 598, 856–8; no 649, 912–14; and no 680, 943

her suspicions. Japan herself wished to retain the link and Alston felt that an entente would help dissolve Japan's doubts about the League, permit greater frankness between London and Tokyo, allow Britain to assert pressure on Japan, and permit her to mediate between Japan and the United States. Objectively, Alston regarded relations with the United States as of far greater significance than any arrangement with Japan, but he, like so many, could not offer with any conviction an affirmative reply to the principal questions; was the United States reliable, would she co-operate in China, and would she stand resolutely with Britain in a crisis? Ideally, Alston looked for a triple agreement pledged to the rehabilitation of China, but he regarded this policy as impracticable and returned, therefore, to the idea of an entente with Japan. In this phase Alston had swayed between the ideal and the practicable, a sceptic debating hypothetical alternatives.[20]

In mid-April 1920 Alston took over at Peking, but went on leave late in June, leaving R.H. Clive, counsellor and chargé d'affaires, in control. Alston obviously gained first-hand knowledge and confirmatory evidence on two important themes; the attitude of British commercial interests in China and the attitude of the Chinese government itself.[21] The Associated British Chambers of Commerce in China and Hong Kong and the Tsinan and Tsingtao British Chambers of Commerce denounced the alliance with Japan as a failure, as unnecessary because of the League of Nations, as injurious to British commercial interests, and as an instrument that encouraged Japanese ambitions while it undermined British hopes for a strong and independent China. The powers should return Shantung to China in full sovereignty and Britain, in negotiating any new agreement with Japan, should curb her ally's activities and secure a new deal for the Peking government. These views received support from the Board of Trade in London, which suggested that Britain rid herself of any obligation to endorse Japan's claims to 'special interests' in China. The Board of

20 Alston speculated on what policy Britain should pursue should the League collapse. Again he concluded that the likely absence of co-operation from the United States, coupled with the need to retain Japan's goodwill in China and avoid isolating her, pointed to the retention of an agreement with Tokyo.

21 Alston to Curzon, 4 and 21 May 1920, Clive to Curzon, 30 June 1920, BD, 1st ser., XIV, no 26, 21–2; no 35, 28; and no 59, 53–6; Clive to Curzon, 14 July 1920, Cab. 32/6; Board of Trade to secretary of CID, 28 June 1920, BD, 1st ser., XIV, no 61, 65, note 24

Trade regarded Japan as a dangerous competitor, suspecting that Japan had secured a substantial degree of control over China's economic development. The Peking government itself denounced the alliance as superfluous, as dangerous to China's survival, as an insult to her sovereignty, and as an obvious source of encouragement to Japanese imperialism. The Chinese authorities also demanded that Britain consult them before arriving at any decisions on renewal, and warned that they would not recognize the legality of those sections of a new treaty which referred to China, unless prior consultations were held.

En route for England, Alston, receiving a telegram in Toronto, hurried to Washington, arriving there on 26 July.[22] He found that he and Geddes were in complete agreement on questions affecting China, on Anglo-American relations in the Far East, and on the alliance with Japan, and that Secretary of State Bainbridge Colby, Assistant Secretary of State Norman Davis, and R. Morris, American ambassador in Tokyo, also shared many of his views.[23] Alston, lamenting the absence of an Anglo-Saxon policy in Asia, advocated that Britain and the United States, sharing a common language, mutual interests, and beliefs, and in view of their co-operation in the fields of religion, education, and medicine, should act in unison in China. The Atlanticist in Alston emerged even more strongly as he went on to suggest that they establish Anglo-Saxon naval control of the Pacific and convince China that Britain and the United States would ensure her independence and integrity. Alston later told J.V.A. MacMurray, head of the State Department's Far Eastern section, that both the United States and Britain were discredited in China, the former because of raising excessive hopes which were never fulfilled and the latter because of failing to speak and act in her defence. MacMurray agreed and, according to Alston, promised to support the idea of Anglo-American co-operative action.

Alston summarised his new expectations in a memorandum for the

22 Alston, 'Memorandum respecting talks at Washington in regard to future policies in the Far East,' 1 Aug. 1920, FO/414/246, and BD, 1st ser., XIV, no 79, 77–80

23 Alston and the United States officials agreed that the Chinese Eastern Railway should be under international control and that the Consortium would be a difficult means of organising financial support, but they disagreed over the issue of attempting to force Japan to permit Chinese control of the railway to Vladivostok.

Foreign Office.[24] The Japanese government, in which he had earlier shown increasing faith, he now denounced for a reckless violation of its pledges, its aggressive tendencies, and its failure to curb a powerful militarist clique. He suggested that Britain rid herself of her alliance with Japan, regain her diplomatic independence, and join with the United States to enforce the principles and interests which they held jointly. An Anglo-Saxon fleet based at Singapore and Hawaii would police the Pacific, remove any menace from Japan by checking the tendency of Japanese militarists to gamble, and help induce 'an Anglo-American-Japanese understanding regarding Chinese, Siberian and Pacific questions which would really make for permanent peace in East Asia and the maintenance of those principles which Great Britain, America and Japan have repeatedly declared to form the basis of their policy in the Far East.'[25] In Alston's opinion, Britain must seize the opportunity offered by the Anglo-Japanese alliance renewal question. If she decided on renewal, Britain must secure an understanding with Japan on fundamental policies,[26] demonstrate that Britain sought closer understanding with the United States,[27] and show Japan that their alliance had been a serious obstacle to an Anglo-American rapprochement because of the discrepancies between Anglo-Saxon principles and Japan's interests. He concluded with Colby's assurance that any American administration would favour this Anglo-Saxon policy and, without suggesting the destruction of all Britain's ties with Japan, he had clearly turned toward Atlanticism.[28]

24 Alston, 'Memorandum respecting suggestions for an Anglo-Saxon policy in the Far East,' 1 Aug. 1920, Cab. 5/3, FO/414/246, and BD, 1st ser., XIV, no 80, 81–6
25 Alston's statement of these principles was orthodox enough; the preservation of the mutual interests of all powers in China, the maintenance of China's independence and integrity, and the elevation of equal opportunity for the trade and industry of all nations above the search for special interests in China.
26 His assessment of Japan suggested that she wanted peace and the perpetuation of the treaty with Britain, that she was experiencing economic troubles and loss of prestige, that public opinion was restless and critical of the government, and that his Anglo-Saxon policy would bring Japan's extremists to heel.
27 He felt that an actual treaty between Britain and the United States was not necessary to secure his Anglo-Saxon policy.
28 Crowe's minute of 9 August was sceptical, bordering on hostility.

Sir Charles Eliot, Alston's successor in Tokyo, took quite a different view and, unmoved by opinions to the contrary, consistently favoured renewal of the alliance with Japan, modified in the light of the League Covenant.[29] At times Eliot ran ahead of the Foreign Office in assuring Japan of Britain's devotion to their treaty and in comforting Japanese officials on her intentions. He also emphasised to London Japan's dedication to the alliance and her desire for harmonious relations with Britain and the United States.[30] But more than that, Eliot's despatches, often circulated to the cabinet, met with a favourable response from Crowe and Curzon, or simply reinforced views at which Curzon and his senior officials had already arrived.[31] Eliot emphasised the strategic benefits of the alliance, with a loyal Japan providing for the security of Hong Kong, Singapore, Australia, and Canada's Pacific coast, and also the diplomatic advantages gained from Britain's ability to restrain and moderate her ally. He deplored the 'myth' of a beleaguered and democratic China terrorised by a rapacious Japan and described majority Japanese opinion, her commercial groups, civil administration, and higher officials as favouring reasonable, moderate, and honourable policies. In addition, Eliot advocated renewal of the alliance in order to avoid any rebuff to Japan, to guard against Japan orientating toward Germany or a Russo-German combination, and to remove possible threats to India.

He did not feel that Britain could count on the United States in Asia, her objections to the alliance were ill-conceived and emanated only from an inferior class of American, and the United States seemed blind to the advantages which Britain and she herself gained. Moreover, in Eliot's view, as Japan was willing to renegotiate the alliance and remove the grounds for Washington's objections, the United

29 Eliot to Curzon, 23 May, 8 and 17 June 1920, BD, 1st ser., XIV, no 36, 28–9; no 45, 38; and no 52, 42–8; Eliot to Curzon, telegram, 12 Dec. 1920, Cab 32/6

30 Curzon found it necessary to restrain Eliot, both on the question of discussing the terms of renewal of the treaty and on the need to preserve the executive position of the forthcoming imperial meeting (Eliot to Curzon, 16 July and 3 Aug. 1920, and Curzon to Eliot, 25 July 1920, BD, 1st ser., XIV, no 70, 72; no 81, 86–7; and no 74, 74–5).

31 Crowe minuted on Eliot's despatch of 17 June, 'good reading and carries conviction,' while Curzon added, 'It is a good general statement of the case, but says little or nothing about China or India.'

States had no right either to denounce the alliance's past record or to warn against it in the future. Similarly, skilful negotiations could remove any conflict between the alliance and the League Covenant and Eliot dismissed as folly the view that the League rendered the alliance superfluous. Dominion objections[32] he brushed aside as the product of confusion, linking immigration matters with the operation of the alliance, and of ignorance, which blinded the dominions to the strategic benefits they gained. Moreover, Peking was mistaken in its belief that the alliance threatened China's interests rather than the reverse. Finally, Eliot suggested, the exaggerated complaints from British commercial interests about Japanese discriminatory policies could be met in the renewal negotiations. In return, British commercial and governmental officials should treat the Japanese with greater frankness and cordiality and with less suspicion and contempt. Honourable negotiations between equals would produce neither a derogatory treaty nor a mere exchange of notes but what all the best elements in Japanese life desired, a renewed alliance in harmony with the League Covenant.

With Jordan and Alston ranged to some degree against Eliot, what of Dr Geddes, attempting to assess Washington's reactions and American opinion in an election year? In April 1920 Geddes warned London of the possible injurious effects not only of a decision to renew but also of a failure to seize the opportunity to abrogate the alliance.[33] Anglophobe influences could exploit either decision, stimulate a wave of opinion hostile to Britain, and injure the prospects for American entry into the League. As a remedy, Geddes suggested a joint Anglo-Japanese declaration, deferring the decision on renewal until the League of Nations was so firmly established that the alliance would be superfluous or at most a form of insurance against the League's collapse.[34] Again in June 1920 Geddes suggested a public explanation

32 Eliot described Canada and Australia as sharing the same views on the alliance.

33 Geddes to Curzon, 30 April 1920, FO/371/5359

34 Geddes's report struck a responsive chord at the Foreign Office and helped to initiate the Anglo-Japanese moves in June to reconcile their alliance with the League. Bentinck, Wellesley, Hardinge, Curzon, and Balfour all agreed that they must avoid violations of the Covenant and that such a step would improve Britain's image in the eyes of the world and in the United States. Hardinge noted, however, that whatever Britain did she would certainly be hotly criticised in the United States.

of British policy to offset damaging press rumours,[35] but by November, despite his concern over United States reactions, Geddes advised retention of the alliance with Japan.[36] He reiterated that American opinion would denounce renewal in any form unless the alliance were diluted and made virtually meaningless, but he doubted that this issue could greatly exacerbate feelings already aroused over the oil and Irish questions. Finally, Geddes seemed to feel that at least the alliance could serve as a restraint on and a sober warning to extreme anglophobes.

Ideally, Geddes, echoing Alston, saw considerable merit in an exchange of notes between Britain, Japan, and the United States, laying down a common policy with respect to China, coupled with an Anglo-American naval agreement to outclass Japan in the Pacific. He felt, however, that Senate objections to an alliance, constitutional difficulties, and the lack of constancy in United States policy would render such schemes ineffective. Even more than that the United States was in a competitive mood, jealous of Britain, blaming Britain for her errors and problems, trailing a bad conscience, demonstrating ignorance of international affairs, confirming her isolationism, and bowing to the will of an unscrupulous and dynamic anglophobe minority, which sought to force 'John Bull' to disgorge 'Ireland of course but also sea power and anything else America may fancy, principally the British West Indies, the resources of Canada and more recently Australia.'

Geddes, therefore, suggested that Britain should attempt to help avoid the election of a hostile president and then tie each president down at the start of his term of office to a policy of co-operation in the Far East and the Pacific. This would result in a series of four-year agreements, which Geddes described as introducing a 'periodicity' into United States foreign policy. Geddes forecast, however, considerable difficulty with Harding's administration and warned that the price of an agreement would be that London give way on every major issue. In Geddes's opinion a decision against renewal of the alliance with Japan would be premature unless Britain had already accepted the view that close Anglo-American relations was the principal aim of her foreign policy, and he concluded:

35 Geddes to Curzon, 5 June 1920, BD, 1st ser., XIV, no 43, 38
36 Geddes to Curzon, 15 Nov. and 3 Dec. 1920, ibid., no 162, 177–8; no 175, 187–9, and Cab. 32/6

I believe that for a period of years it will remain an important British interest to secure co-operation with America even at the price of introducing some periodicity into our own policy, but it would be a high and I believe unnecessary price to pay to purchase it at the cost of Japanese enmity.

He recommended then that Britain renew the alliance with Japan, modified to accommodate the League Covenant, omitting either a military or an adhesion clause,[37] and remaining in force for four years to coincide with one American presidential term. Britain should also attempt to reach a four-year agreement with the United States which did not require Senate ratification and then renegotiate it with each new president for as long as seemed desirable, or until the Senate changed its attitude.

The Foreign Office, in drawing up its recommendations, had, therefore, Alston moving closer to Jordan, with Geddes somewhere between them and Eliot, and all four finding common ground in the ideal if apparently impracticable solution of achieving co-operation between Britain, Japan, and the United States. However, Jordan and Alston, returning to London, had greater opportunities to influence the review of policy. This review by the Foreign Office in 1920 passed through three phases. A preliminary investigation resulted in Lord Hardinge's summary in April. During the second period the Foreign Office accepted the obligations of the League Covenant and the Atlanticists increased their impact. Finally the study which resulted in the report of the Anglo-Japanese Alliance Committee, presented in January 1921, reflected a further movement of opinion away from that of Hardinge and Curzon toward the Atlanticists. Again all participants found a point of agreement in the concept of achieving tripartite co-operation in the Far East. However, by May 1921 Curzon clearly had reasserted himself and was bent on undermining Atlanticist influence.

Initially, H.W. Malkin, assistant legal adviser at the Foreign Office, ruled, and his view was never challenged, that the Anglo-Japanese alliance was incompatible with the League Covenant.[38] Consequently, although the alliance could be operative in cases where a

37 The idea of an adhesion clause, permitting the United States to join a renewed Anglo-Japanese treaty, had already emerged from Foreign Office studies, although Eliot opposed the idea.
38 Malkin, memorandum, 'Anglo-Japanese alliance as affected by the Covenant

war occurred and did not receive League disapproval, Britain must bring the alliance into complete accord with the Covenant. Curzon accepted Malkin's ruling and the Foreign Secretary's general position on the alliance received support from C.H. Bentinck, a member of the Far Eastern department and later head of the Russian department.[39] Curzon and Bentinck admitted that fundamental differences existed between British and Japanese policies in China, and realised that Japan regarded the alliance in part as an instrument to remove the threat of British or Anglo-American opposition to her policies. However, while recognising the problems raised by commercial rivalry and racial-immigration questions, while conceding that Japan might bid for the hegemony of East Asia, and despite acknowledging the possibility of Anglo-American co-operation in pursuit of common goals, both Curzon and Bentinck insisted that Britain must retain her alliance with an honourable and loyal Japan. In their view, political factors reinforced strategic considerations and promised that the alliance would benefit both parties in the future as it had in the past.

At the same time, Curzon and Bentinck hoped to accommodate the United States as far as possible. Bentinck, describing relations with the United States as the dominant consideration from the point of view of both material interests and racial affinity, insisted that Britain must divest Japan of any expectations of support in a war against the United States. Indeed, Bentinck argued that if Britain could rely on the United States the alliance with Japan would be unnecessary, but London had received no assurances of co-operation from Washington. Furthermore, the abject state of relations between Washington and Tokyo made it impossible to conduct policy in harmony with two powers who seemed set on a collision course. A tripartite agreement was therefore impracticable. Bentinck concluded that Britain must renew the treaty with Japan and attempt to achieve friendly co-operation with the United States and France.

Our future course lies between our ally with whom our interests conflict and our friend who is united to us by race, tradition and community of interests and ideals. It will be difficult for us to steer a straight course, both

of the League of Nations,' 18 Feb. 1920, BD, 1st ser., VI, no 744, 1001–3, and Cab. 5/3

39 Foreign Office to Admiralty, 21 Jan. 1920, BD, 1st ser., VI, no 789, 1053–4, and Bentinck memorandum, 'Effect of the Anglo-Japanese alliance upon Foreign Relationships,' 28 Feb. 1920, ibid., no 761, 1016–23 and Cab. 5/3

parties will no doubt reproach us, as they have done in the past, for not giving them more whole-hearted support against the other, but this course as outlined must be steered; our interests demand it.[40]

F.T.A. Ashton-Gwatkin's memorandum of March 1920, counselling delay and opposing a decision on renewal until the unsettled Japanese domestic scene had become clarified, was more significant for the dissenting minutes it produced than for its own content.[41] Bentinck, H.G. Parlett, former counsellor at the Tokyo embassy, and E.M. Hobart Hampden, former secretary at that embassy, denied Ashton-Gwatkin's assumptions, evidence, and conclusions. Britain could neither denounce the alliance nor delay and leave it untouched, and Hardinge drew the following conclusion: 'It seems to me that they all tend to a renewal or continuation of the Alliance in a new and modified form. What that form should be will require much discussion.' Curzon did not disagree and Hardinge informed the United States ambassador that Britain would retain the alliance for a further year and then attempt a reappraisal, inferring that this would be done with the dominions at the next imperial meeting.[42]

40 Bentinck noted, in support, that France and Holland would welcome renewal of the Anglo-Japanese alliance and Portugal would not object. He also suggested that France might be included in a triple agreement, thus foreshadowing the arrangement reached at the Washington conference.

41 Ashton-Gwatkin was second secretary at the Foreign Office and a member of the Far Eastern department. Ashton-Gwatkin, memorandum, 'The Anglo-Japanese alliance and constitutional changes in Japan,' 23 March 1920, BD, 1st ser., VI, no 789, 1049–53. He feared that renewal would bolster the oligarchic bureaucracy and the military faction in Japan, and hoped that prosperity, liberalism, intellectual dissent, and responsible government would result in democratic control of foreign policy, an end to military influences, a reduction in defence expenditures, and a nausea with sabre politics. These developments should, in Ashton-Gwatkin's view, reduce the threat to China and to British interests, help alleviate tension between Japan and the United States, and avoid the possibility of Japan joining Russia or Germany. Subsequently, Ashton-Gwatkin suggested using the alliance renewal question to force Japanese co-operation in the Consortium, coupled with offers to recognise her special interests in South Manchuria, and to save her face by a British offer to restore Wei-hai-wei to China (Ashton-Gwatkin, memorandum, 'Japan and the Open Door,' ibid., XIV, no 61, 57–66).

42 Davis to Secretary of State, 28 April 1920, Papers Relating to the Foreign Relations of the United States, 1920, II, 680 (hereafter cited as FR).

The second phase, in the summer of 1920, saw the Foreign Office accommodate the obligations of the League Covenant and witnessed a new emphasis from Atlanticist opinion. In a series of harmonious exchanges with Japan, Curzon was able to solve or shelve the problems created by inconsistencies between the alliance and the League Covenant, also ensuring that the alliance would not continue unamended after 13 July 1921. As Curzon told Eliot and Geddes, he was not denouncing the alliance but merely suggesting a joint statement to the League to improve Britain's moral and diplomatic position, without prejudicing the freedom of action of the dominions.[43] Consequently, on 8 July Curzon and Ambassador Chinda despatched their note to the League from the Spa Conference, affirming the adherence of Britain and Japan to their obligations under the Covenant.[44]

V. Wellesley, assistant secretary at the Foreign Office and superintending the Far Eastern department, fired the first round for the Atlanticists, after listening to guarded approaches from Butler Wright, counsellor at the American embassy, on the question of co-operation in China.[45] Wellesley denounced the alliance as a notorious failure and attacked Japanese policies as antagonistic to Anglo-American aims in China, as more ruthless, brutal, and insidious than German policy and as an attempt to establish control over China to the exclusion of the western powers. At best, Wellesley argued, the alliance was an unnatural and artificial compact, which would become a shallow and negative marriage of convenience if retained, placing Britain in an ignominious and preposterous position in relation to China. Wellesley advocated, therefore, that they respond to

43 Curzon to Eliot, 3 and 16 June 1920, Curzon to Geddes, 13 June 1920, and Eliot to Curzon, 8 and 22 June 1920, BD, 1st ser., XIV, no 41, 36–7; no 51, 42; no 42, 37; no 45, 38; no 46, 39; and no 55, 50

44 British foreign and state papers, 1920, 113, 370 and Lloyd George, statement, House of Commons, 24 June 1920, 130, *Debates*, 5 ser., cols. 2365–6

45 Wellesley, memorandum, 'Anglo-American co-operation in the Far East,' 1 June 1920, BD, 1st ser., XIV, no 40, 32–6. Wellesley and Bentinck met Butler Wright on 21 May and the latter claimed to speak on behalf of his ambassador. They met again on 14 June, but Wellesley received little encouragement from Hardinge, who advised against further meetings for the present. Wellesley recognised of course that Washington could disavow these approaches and probably would not pursue them in the face of strong anglophobe and anti-Japanese sentiments in the United States.

any overtures from the United States offering the slightest prospect of success, that they build on any hopeful foundations such as the Consortium, and that Britain seek a tripartite agreement involving the United States. This was a practicable course in his view as Washington might follow up the Consortium with 'a political understanding, in order to give definite expression to the similarity of British and American aims in the Far East.' Wellesley also felt these steps would raise both British prestige and Chinese hopes and would earn the applause of the British communities in China. He sought, however, to avoid a rebuff to Japan which would make her feel isolated and insecure, and he envisaged either an agreement with the United States accompanied by renewal of a modified alliance with Japan, or even a triple agreement which at the very least would secure a clear statement of American policy.[46] If Britain modified the alliance to meet her obligations under the League and remove the military clauses, she would encourage United States adherence, and Wellesley concluded that the time was ripe to reach for what had been regarded as utopian, a tripartite agreement. His superiors were clearly less impressed and Hardinge merely assured Ambassador Davis that the alliance, when renewed, would not be aimed at the United States.[47]

In combination with Jordan, and reinforced by Alston, however, Wellesley continued to attempt to influence the Foreign Office's review of policy.[48] He stated that Britain should seek 'a carefully planned constructive policy for China and the creation of a proper equilibrium of economic interests in that country after a full and frank discussion with the Americans,' and he explored four alternative courses of action. His alternatives were abrogation, renewal of the alliance modified only to satisfy the League Covenant, renewal in a form different from an alliance and with an adhesion clause to attract the United States and other powers, and renewal as in the third alternative but without an adhesion clause and with a parallel agreement with the United States. Eventually Britain might consolidate these parallel arrangements.[49] Without being entirely consis-

46 Wellesley expected the Japanese military to resent this check on their China policy, but he felt they would recognise the value of a detente with the United States and in any case would not dare undermine this course of action.

47 Davis to Colby, 7 June 1920, FR, 1920, II, 682.

48 Wellesley, memorandum, 'Respecting the Anglo-Japanese alliance,' 1 Sept. 1920, BD, 1st ser., XIV, no 97, 106–13

49 In expanded form the fourth alternative meant a five-year treaty with Japan,

tent in his reasoning and despite being attracted to the third alternative, Wellesley opted for the fourth policy as offering the best chance of success with the least possible risk.[50] An assurance of United States moral support would strengthen Britain's hand in her negotiations with Japan, who could not risk isolation from Britain and the possibility of an exclusive Anglo-American combination. Consequently, Wellesley expected Japan would meet Britain's terms and, should a multilateral arrangement ultimately result, then Japanese policies would be subject to adequate restraints.[51]

Wellesley's proposals received the support of Sir Conyngham Greene, former ambassador to Japan, and of Jordan, despite the latter's criticism of the cumbersome procedures involved in implementing the fourth alternative and his preference for an exchange of identical notes with Japan and the United States. Wellesley suggested that a committee study the renewal problem and the broader questions of Far Eastern policy, and clearly there existed within the Foreign Office a challenge to Curzon. Moreover, when Ambassador Hayashi reached London on 4 September to replace Chinda he found evidence of public concern over the possibility of war between Japan and the United States, fear of British connivance or involvement, and coolness toward Japan.[52] Yet Lloyd George personally had just given Chinda a very different impression in their farewell talk on 17 August,

in harmony with the League Covenant and without a military or adhesion clause, and a parallel agreement with the United States for the same period of time. Then Britain would attempt to consolidate the two agreements into a multilateral treaty including China and possibly other powers, but recognised as an agreement, rather than a treaty requiring ratification by the United States Senate. This agreement would be a consultative and self-denying arrangement rather than a defensive or offensive treaty and would involve prior consultation with China and the omission of all reference to India.

50 Wellesley lamented the fact that economic restraints checked the development of Britain's naval and military forces and he urged that a strong British or Anglo-American fleet police the Pacific.

51 Wellesley suggested that Britain could use Japan's dependence on Indian cotton as a lever in their negotiations and regarded as essential minimum terms a pledge of Japanese frankness, an assurance that Japan would not repeat her 'twenty-one demands,' and an agreement to pursue the economic stability and independence of China. In return Britain would promise to restore Wei-hai-wei to China.

52 Nish, 'Japan and the Ending of the Anglo-Japanese Alliance,' 374. Hayashi

assuring him that Britain would retain the alliance as a matter of course. The Foreign Office intercepted Chinda's despatch to Tokyo of 20 August and Curzon, lamenting the Premier's sortie, pointed out to Lloyd George that he seemed to have gone further than anyone else in favour of retaining the alliance.[53] Chinda was impressed with Lloyd George's assertion that Anglo-Japanese co-operation was one of the prime factors contributing to world stability, and that while Britain would consider dominion and American views and while he personally favoured the inclusion of the United States in their treaty, Britain would maintain the alliance.[54] The British public favoured this policy, according to Lloyd George, and the current chaos in American politics made it impossible to open negotiations on a triple agreement.

Lloyd George was, therefore, the source of some confusion although his remarks to Chinda were probably more general and trite, as Curzon conceded, than the departing ambassador claimed. In mid-December the Premier told Senator Medill McCormick, an envoy of President-elect Harding, that he would welcome an American representative to work out the problems associated with the League, the peace treaty, naval matters, and the alliance with Japan.[55] He assured parliament later that month that his government would act on the alliance only after full consultation with the dominions.[56] Both these statements were too general to be really significant, clearly neither the Foreign Office nor the government had made final recommendations or decisions, and other influences were still at large. Perhaps the Foreign Office's expert committee, suggested by Wellesley, and meet-

inserted a rejoinder in *The Times* on 4 January 1921 to a particularly damaging article of 30 December.

53 Curzon to Lloyd George, 25 Sept. 1920, Lloyd George Papers, F/13/1/20, including Chinda to Foreign Minister (Tokyo), 20 Aug. 1920; Nish, 'Japan and the Ending of the Anglo-Japanese Alliance,' 373–4.

54 Chinda was impressed neither with the prospects for a triple agreement nor with the chances of the dominions altering British policy, and Tokyo drew comfort from the fact that as Anglo-American and Japanese-American relations were so wretched the triple alliance would not materialise, and the Anglo-Japanese alliance would remain in force.

55 McCormick to H.C. Lodge, 22 Dec. 1920, Henry Cabot Lodge Papers, file 1921, Sept.-Dec. (misfiled)

56 Lloyd George, statement, House of Commons, 23 Dec. 1920, 136, *Debates*, 5 ser., cols. 2113–14

ing between 19 October and 30 November 1920, would narrow the alternatives?[57]

Wellesley, Jordan, and Conyngham Greene, along with Sir William Tyrrell, assistant under-secretary of state, comprised the expert committee and produced a predictable report.[58] The committee stated that Far Eastern problems hinged on Japan's policy toward China and that Britain must decide whether her policies and those of Japan were close enough to make renewal of their alliance either practicable or desirable. On this point the committee was emphatic: Japan's actions were dangerously and persistently expansionist, discriminatory, and at variance with Britain's interests. The report specifically rejected the assertion that the alliance had acted as an effective restraint on Japan and accepted the view that postwar circumstances suggested non-renewal. However, financial and strategic considerations, in the committee's opinion, demanded a policy that would terminate any naval competition, allow reductions in defence expenditure, and still provide for the security of the Pacific.

The reverse side of the question was that of relations with the United States, and the committee had no hesitation in citing the alliance as a formidable obstacle to the realisation of close Anglo-American relations and their full and indispensable co-operation in China. The treaty with Japan, therefore, threatened a cardinal principle of Britain's global and Far Eastern policies and the committee decided unanimously that Britain must relinquish the alliance and replace it with a tripartite entente with Japan and the United States 'consisting in a declaration of general principles which can be subscribed to by all parties without the risk of embarrassing commitments.' Furthermore, to achieve this declaration of principles, Britain should co-operate closely with Washington rather than with Tokyo. Only as a regrettable second choice, necessitated by United States unwillingness to join in a triple arrangement, would the committee advocate an agreement with Japan. Even this agreement, reconciled with the League Covenant, must contain provision for the eventual participation of the United States.

While supporting the idea of a triple entente, the committee had un-

---

57 Curzon to Eliot, 21 Oct. 1920, and Curzon to Clive, 23 Oct. 1920, BD, 1st ser., XIV, no 139, 158–9, and no 144, 102. The Colonial and India Offices were consulted before the committee submitted its final report to Curzon.

58 Report of the Anglo-Japanese Alliance Committee, 21 Jan. 1921, ibid., no 212, 221–7. Tyrrell, of course, had been an intimate of Grey.

mistakably restated the case for reorientating British policy away from Japan and toward the United States. They had virtually avoided the question of the practicability of their suggested policy, but Curzon's position had received an additional challenge and developments prior to the imperial meeting brought further Atlanticist pressures.[59] Whether the Foreign Office committee could influence policy, however, remained undecided, and in fact Curzon, when making recommendations to the cabinet in May 1921, rejected its principal suggestion and turned to the second alternative.

The period prior to the imperial meeting of June 1921 brought three significant developments. First, an Anglo-Canadian debate in which Ottawa demanded that Britain seek a tripartite or even wider agreement by way of a conference of Pacific powers. Second, a series of Canadian-United States contacts which reinforced Ottawa's Atlanticism but did not initiate it. Finally, the cabinet's vital decisions of 30 May after a further review of political, strategic, and other factors. Significantly, Curzon carried the cabinet to a great degree and yet Lloyd George's government adopted a plural approach toward the question of the alliance and the impending discussions at the Imperial Conference. The Atlanticist thesis received support from Ottawa as it had from within the Foreign Office itself and expectations were perhaps justifiably raised. In any event the Atlanticist arguments could not simply be dismissed, but those who were antagonistic wielded formidable powers. This then was still the nature of the debate.

The Canadian government, now led by Arthur Meighen but in Borden's shadow, was at the core of these developments, demonstrating its faith in the Atlantic entente.[60] Ottawa acted with dual intent.

59 A cabinet committee, chaired by Leo Amery, supervised and prepared the agenda, Cab. 27/112; Milner to Governor-General, 28 Jan. 1921; Churchill to Governor-General, 26 Feb. 1921, King Papers, file 1922 (Chandler-Churchill).

60 The first important account focussing on the Imperial Conference itself was Brebner, 'Canada, the Anglo-Japanese Alliance and the Washington Conference.' Brebner based his article largely on information acquired from J.W. Dafoe of the *Manitoba Free Press*, through Professor J.T. Shotwell, and both Borden and Meighen accepted it as an accurate account of the imperial meeting (Dafoe to MacGregor Dawson, 23 May 1935, J.W. Dafoe Papers, reel 5, M 77). More recent accounts of some interest are Galbraith, 'The Imperial Conference of 1921 and the Washington Conference,' and Fry, 'The North

As a function of North Atlantic triangular diplomacy Meighen sought to interpret the North American viewpoint and demanded the maintenance of that order of priorities which placed Anglo-American accord at the summit of expectations. In terms of interimperial relations he attempted to use Canada's voice of persuasion to deflect if not reverse policies and alter the order of preferences that the emerging commonwealth should pursue. Canada had growing commercial interests across the Pacific, her missionaries were active in Korea, her immigration laws discriminated against orientals, and yet she was indebted to Japan for naval protection received during the recent war. Canada's principal concern, however, accentuated by participation in the allied intervention in Siberia, was the antagonism growing between Japan and the United States. Renewal of the Anglo-Japanese alliance would undermine Anglo-American accord, be injurious to the creation of an Atlantic entente, and set the empire's foreign policy irrevocably on the wrong path. Meighen's government was prepared to gamble, therefore, in opposing renewal of Britain's exclusive alliance with Japan, on the willingness of the United States to participate in world affairs. Meighen, guided by Christie and like the Atlanticists in London, viewed the Republican administration of President Harding with greater expectations.

In pursuance of this Atlanticist policy, the Canadian government welcomed and sought out sources of information and contact with receptive Republicans. Prominent on the American side were Senator Henry Cabot Lodge and William Howard Gardiner, a member of the executive committee of the American Navy League and a former president of the American branch of the English-Speaking Union.[61]

Atlantic Triangle and the Abrogation of the Anglo-Japanese Alliance.' Of less value are Tate and Foy, 'More Light on the Abrogation of the Anglo-Japanese Alliance,' Vinson, 'The Imperial Conference of 1921 and the Anglo-Japanese Alliance,' and Lower, 'Loring Christie and the Genesis of the Washington Conference of 1921–1922.'

61 In the course of their correspondence Brebner thanked Dafoe for his lead on Gardiner, described as an element in 'the 1921 affair' and mentioned the possible existence of more dramatic information. Brebner also suggested the possibility of links between Gardiner's activities and those of 'Putnam Weale.' Gardiner told Dafoe that the views of the American government had been imparted unofficially to Meighen and that he himself was involved. Dafoe urged Brebner to see Gardiner and to 'get him to tell you what he knows about the means that were taken in 1920–1921 to impress upon Mr. Meighen's mind

Gardiner was the more active but Lodge's sympathy and support, when other Republicans were lukewarm or dubious, was of considerable value to him.[62] Neither was an isolationist, and Gardiner sought a new phase of co-operation in the Pacific and East Asia to secure the interests and possessions of the English-speaking peoples. He regarded the existence of the Anglo-Japanese alliance and the probability of its renewal as the principal obstacle to this goal. In Gardiner's opinion, Britain's desire to retain her alliance with Japan reflected doubts about the security of India, threatened in fact by sedition inspired from Tokyo, and showed Britain's selfish desire to reinforce her position in Asia. Curzon, Gardiner felt, epitomised these views, supported by Balfour and Churchill, and their devious policy attempted to ensnare the United States in a triple alliance that would strangle American initiative and her Open Door policy, and ensure the perpetuation of Britain's links with Japan. Gardiner, supported by Lodge, attempted, therefore, to secure the orientation of the dominions toward the United States and to use them as a bridge, leading to an Anglo-American alignment against the common enemy, the leader of the yellow races, Japan.[63]

Gardiner laid down a specific plan with three clear goals. The United States should create and lead an entente of the English-speaking peoples bordering on the Pacific, dedicated to a common policy.

the advisability of offering resistance at the Imperial Conference of 1921 to the renewal of the Anglo-Japanese Alliance' (Dafoe to Brebner, 26 April 1935, and Brebner to Dafoe, 30 April 1935, Dafoe Papers, reel 5, м 77).

62 Gardiner to Lodge, 5 Jan. and 14 Feb. 1921, William Howard Gardiner Papers, box 3, file H.C. Lodge, and Lodge Papers, file 1921, A-G, Jan.–April. Gardiner claimed to have influenced Lodge's views on foreign and defence policy by expounding his thesis of 'insular America' (Gardiner to Lodge, 7 Jan. 1937, Gardiner Papers, box 3, file H.C. Lodge Jr, and Gardiner to H.L. Stimson, 28 June 1926, ibid., box 6, file Philippines, 1921). Gardiner's role is referred to by R.G. Albion in Gardiner, *Writings on Sea Power and American Naval Policy*, foreword, and Albion, *Makers of Naval Policy, 1798–1947*, 454, 675.

63 Gardiner to W.S. Sims, 25 Nov. 1920, 1 Oct. and 22 Dec. 1921, and 19 Feb. 1922, Gardiner Papers, box 2, file Rr Adm. Sims; Gardiner to Hornbeck, 11 Dec. 1921, ibid., box 4, file S. Hornbeck; Gardiner to Bywater, 31 March 1923, ibid., box 3, file H.C. Bywater; Gardiner to Fletcher, 30 July 1921, ibid., box 3, file H.P. Fletcher; Gardiner to Lodge, 5 Jan. and 14 Feb. 1921, see note 62

This entente should ensure the demise of the Anglo-Japanese alliance through the influence of the dominions. Finally, the United States should reassert the Open Door policy, rejuvenate China, check Japan, and provide for the security of the Philippines.[64]

Such was Gardiner's policy, and with the approval of Lodge he used his contacts with the Navy and State departments, once the Republicans had their mandate, to initiate the appropriate steps. He was dedicated to the task, convinced of its vital nature, and equally convinced of the ultimate success of his mission, for, as he told Senator R.O. Brewster from Maine, 'on my initiative Canada vetoed the renewal of the Alliance.'[65] Gardiner exaggerated his own role and erred in his analysis of Canada's impact, but the significance of his activities remain. From April 1920 he prepared the ground in expectation of a Republican victory in the presidential election and on the assumption that the question of the renewal of the Anglo-Japanese alliance would be taken up by Britain and the dominions at the next imperial conference. Harding's success in November fulfilled Gardiner's basic expectation and he launched into a flurry of activity, discussing the renewal question and the broader issues involved with Canadian and Australian 'representatives' in Washington and New York. He told Admiral W.S. Sims that they had assured him that if the United States evinced some understanding of their problems, Canada and Australia would oppose renewal of the alliance. Gardiner also pursued with Canadian officials the idea of joint naval defence in Pacific coastal waters, regarding this plan as an important basis for an entente and as a step toward the establishment of United States leadership.[66]

64 Gardiner to Sims, 21 April and 30 July 1921, ibid., box 2, file Rr Adm. Sims; Gardiner to Roosevelt, 29 July 1921, ibid., box 2, file Col. T. Roosevelt Jr; Gardiner to Fletcher, 6 Sept. 1921, ibid., box 3, file H.P. Fletcher; Gardiner to Lodge, 16 and 19 Feb. 1921, Lodge Papers, file 1921, A-G, Jan.–April

65 Gardiner to Brewster, 23 Feb. 1944, Gardiner Papers, box 3, file R.O. Brewster. Gardiner in the course of numerous accounts given to a variety of people from 1921 to 1944 did not embellish or expand his thesis. The story did not grow with each successive telling.

66 Gardiner to Sims, 10 June 1920, ibid., box 2, file Rr Adm. Sims; Gardiner to Fletcher, 6 Sept. 1921, see note 64; Gardiner to Edwards, 26 Jan. 1921, ibid., box 3, file Lt-Comm. W.A. Edwards, Naval War College. Gardiner named F. Hudd and Col. J.A. Cooper of the Canadian Bureau of Information in New York, but did not identify the Australian officials.

Gardiner's second task involved convincing eminent Republicans and prospective members of the new administration that the United States must pursue a vigorous policy in Asia and the Pacific based on his three-point programme. In this campaign he received apparently only the active and sustained support of Lodge, and actually wrote subsequently of Lodge that 'soon after that he pulled off his entente of the Pacific Britannic Dominions and ourselves.'[67] Later he wrote to Lodge, urging that the United States avoid antagonising Canada on tariff matters to help promote the entente between the English-speaking peoples under America's aegis, which would result from Lodge's initiatives in December 1920.[68] The entente would include Australia, New Zealand, South Africa, Canada, and the United States and, whatever its precise nature or form, Gardiner felt that it implied an understanding to oppose the renewal of the Anglo-Japanese alliance. Perhaps equally surprising, although Gardiner was not alone in mistakenly coupling Australia and Canada together in a supposed joint determination to oppose the alliance, he assumed that Australia would lead the offensive at the imperial meeting.

Unfortunately detailed documentation of this phase of the Gardiner-Lodge programme is lacking, but more than hints reached London, and Miles Lampson at the Foreign Office warned of the possibility of joint Canadian-United States action on Pacific questions, and noted specifically a report in the *Morning Post* of 1 December 1920. This article spoke of a possible agreement among the United States, Canada, Australia, and New Zealand on Asian immigration, which Senator Lodge favoured. The Canadian government had denied that such an agreement existed but Lampson was impressed neither with the denial nor with the idea that immigration matters were the sole reason for contacts, and he warned of the possibility that Canada, and even Australia and New Zealand, might gravitate toward the United States to create a union of 'Pacific Nations of the Anglo-Saxon stock.'[69] Tyrrell, commenting on the possibility of Cana-

67 Gardiner to Sims, 21 April and 30 July 1921, see note 64; Gardiner to Roosevelt, 29 July 1921, see note 64; Gardiner to Edwards, 26 Jan. 1921, see note 64
68 Gardiner to Lodge, 30 July 1921, Lodge Papers, file 1921, A-G, Jan.–April; Gardiner to Johnson, 21 April 1921, Gardiner Papers, box 2, file H.W. Johnson
69 Lampson, memorandum, 8 April 1921, 'On correspondence with the Canadian Government relating to the Anglo-Japanese Alliance,' BD, 1st ser., XIV, no 261, 271–6. As late as mid-September Geddes reported on Lodge's desire to isolate

dian initiatives in Washington, warned that independent action by Ottawa prior to an agreement with Britain would play into Lodge's hands, for Lodge wished to detach Canada and possibly Australia and move the centre of the English-speaking community from London to Washington. Tyrrell seemed impressed with the anglophobic nature of Lodge's policy but perhaps Lodge's priorities were different. He warned President-elect Harding against unilateral reductions in America's naval building programme, suggesting that the threat of a naval race was the most potent lever to use on Japan to force a settlement of Far Eastern problems in favour of the United States. Furthermore, he hoped that Canada, Australia, and New Zealand would join with them to secure the co-operation of Britain and to show Japan that she could not control the Pacific.[70]

Whatever the details, Gardiner seemed optimistic in December 1920 and Australia appeared to be the most promising of the dominions to carry out his policy. Indeed, as late as May 1921 Geddes reported comments by Mark Sheldon, the Australian commissioner in Washington, on the advisability of an alliance between the United States and the Pacific dominions, and cited press articles to the effect that Premier Hughes of Australia and Lodge agreed on the need for such an understanding.[71] Despite such rumours and reports, however, Gardiner soon became aware of the real attitude of Australia and New Zealand on the alliance question, and consequently Canada remained as the only avenue of approach through which to influence the Imperial Conference. Gardiner surmised that Foreign Office representations to Premier Hughes insisting that the alliance was vital to Pacific security and that United States policy was unreliable accounted for Australia's apparent volte-face. In fact, despite Australia's well pub-

Japan and have the United States assume control in the Pacific and embrace the dominions (Geddes to Curzon, 16 Sept. 1921, Grigg Papers, reel 11).

70 Lodge to Harding, 25 Feb. 1921, Lodge Papers, file 1921

71 Geddes to Curzon, 23 May 1921, received 1 June, FO/414/247. Geddes referred to a recent article in the *Christian Science Monitor* which stated that Hughes and Lodge favoured an understanding on immigration and defence policies and that Premier Massey of New Zealand agreed. Canada would also be included in such an agreement, which Lodge and Hughes felt would be a more effective instrument than the Anglo-Japanese alliance and would be signed by states who shared the same ideals and faced a common danger. Hughes of Australia, of course, passed through the United States en route to the Imperial Conference.

licised opposition to many of Japan's policies, Premier Hughes does not seem to have changed his attitude on the alliance renewal question, but in any event the road to London seemed to pass through Ottawa.[72]

In February 1921 Gardiner approached the State Department and principally Henry P. Fletcher, Norman Davis's successor-designate as under-secretary of state. Gardiner called for action to secure the abrogation of the Anglo-Japanese alliance and, as Fletcher did not feel that the State Department could approach Britain directly, Gardiner urged that they act through Ottawa. He personally had maintained his contacts with Canadian officials and he could arrange to make a speech in Canada within two weeks, to meet members of the Canadian cabinet and privy council and inaugurate discussions to help subvert Curzon's policy. Gardiner assured Fletcher that the Canadians accepted his voice as an authoritative if unofficial one. Other Republicans consulted, except Lodge, remained sceptical, for they expected the dominions to toe the Curzon line and to be unable, even if they were willing, to block the Foreign Office. The State Department, however, accepted Gardiner's suggestions, since they required neither official sanction nor action, and Gardiner proceeded to implement his programme.[73]

Three days after Harding's inauguration Gardiner spoke to the Canadian Club of Toronto.[74] The contents of his speech then became the subject of consultations with Ottawa and Gardiner subsequently

72 Gardiner to Sims, 21 April 1921, see note 64; Gardiner to Fletcher, 13 April 1921, Gardiner Papers, box 3, file H.P. Fletcher; Gardiner to Lodge, 13 April 1921, ibid., box 3, file H.C. Lodge. B.L. Simpson told Gardiner that Massey would not oppose the Foreign Office lest he prejudice New Zealand's chance of raising a five-million pound loan in London.

73 Gardiner to Lodge, 14 Feb. 1921, see note 62; Gardiner to Brewster, 4 July 1944, Gardiner Papers, box 3, file R.O. Brewster; Gardiner to P. Kennedy, 24 Oct. 1921, ibid., box 4, file Foreign Press Service; Gardiner to Knapp, 18 May 1922, ibid., box 5, file Rr Adm. H.S. Knapp; Gardiner to Fletcher, 13 April 1921, see note 72 and 6 Sept. 1921, see note 64. On another occasion Gardiner said that he warned against direct approaches to Britain, suggesting his procedures to ensure that Britain opted for the English-speaking peoples (Gardiner to E. Sedgewick, 29 Dec. 1921, Gardiner Papers, box 4, file *Atlantic Monthly*).

74 W.H. Gardiner, 'Political and Naval Problems of the Pacific,' speech of 7 March 1921, Pamphlet no 2–5061 (Public Archives of Canada, Ottawa)

described his speech as the prologue to Meighen's efforts in London.[75] In late March Gardiner prepared for further speaking engagements in eastern Canada and for a conference with the Canadian government in which he expected Meighen to participate.[76] On 23 April he left for Ottawa, the details of his visit having been arranged with a Colonel McCullough (probably C.R. McCullough, former chairman of the Belgian Relief and Reconstruction Fund), and with C.A. Magrath, Canadian chairman of the International Joint Commission.[77] The conversations in Ottawa, according to Gardiner, ranged over the whole area of Far Eastern affairs and the problems associated with a joint defence policy in the Pacific. As a result Meighen accepted the task of attempting to veto the renewal of the Anglo-Japanese alliance.[78]

Clearly Gardiner was well satisfied with his venture into diplomacy and tended to luxuriate in his efforts. He looked forward confidently to the Imperial Conference, continued to attempt to assert influence, and claimed later that Canadian officials kept him and the authorities in Washington informed of the proceedings in London.[79] What ap-

75 Gardiner to Jones, 1 Feb. 1923, Gardiner Papers, box 3, file Adm. H.P. Jones; Gardiner to Cooper, 14 March 1921, ibid., box 5, file Col. J.A. Cooper; Gardiner to Fletcher, 13 April 1921, see note 72; Gardiner to Sims, 21 April 1921, see note 64; Gardiner to Roosevelt, 29 July 1921, see note 64

76 Gardiner to Sims, 21 April 1921, see note 64 and 1 May 1921, Gardiner Papers, box 2, file Rr Adm. Sims; Gardiner to Fletcher, 13 April 1921, see note 72. Gardiner was no doubt gratified by the applause his views received from C.A.C. Jennings, editor of the Toronto Mail and Empire and a close friend of Meighen (Cooper to Gardiner, 27 April 1921, ibid., box 5, file Col. J.A. Cooper).

77 Gardiner to Cooper, 14 April 1921, ibid., box 5, file Col. J.A. Cooper. Magrath became Meighen's nominee for the post of Canadian ambassador to Washington.

78 Gardiner to Sims, 1 May 1921, see note 76 and 30 July 1921, see note 64; Gardiner to Fiske, 16 April 1921, Gardiner Papers, box 3, file Rr Adm. B.A. Fiske. Gardiner suggested to Fiske that the United States should orientate Canada toward the 'Orange Plan,' ie the Navy Department's plan in case of war with Japan.

79 Gardiner to Sims, 30 July 1921, see note 64; Gardiner to Brewster, 4 July 1944, see note 73; Gardiner to Fletcher, 30 June 1921, Gardiner Papers, box 3, file H.P. Fletcher; Gardiner to Phillips, 'An estimate of the war situation,' 12 March 1943, ibid., box 4, file W. Phillips. Gardiner knew of the difference of

plause or credence he received, however, from the Harding administration is difficult to say, but Lodge wrote within days of Gardiner's
visit to Ottawa that he expected Britain to modify the alliance and
provide specific exemptions for the United States at the insistence of
Canada.[80] In June, Edwin Denby, rejecting Lord Lee's proposal for
a naval agreement under which Britain would patrol the Atlantic and
the United States would police the Pacific, observed elsewhere that
the United States counted on dominion opposition to offset the impact
of the Anglo-Japanese alliance unless Britain made the treaty inoper-
able against America.[81] Moreover, Geddes reported from an 'unimpeachable and authoritative source' that the United States had
decided to concentrate its diplomatic, naval, and commercial efforts
in South America and Asia rather than across the Atlantic.[82] The
security of the Pacific must be in American hands and, as a corollary
to this policy, the United States would attempt to organise a union of
the English-speaking peoples bordering on the Pacific. Secretary of
State Charles Evans Hughes had insisted, however, that they must
avoid the risk of hostilities with Japan and seemed determined personally to control policy in regard to the Anglo-Japanese alliance,
Anglo-American relations generally, and naval disarmament.

What precise impact Gardiner had in Ottawa is also difficult to
assess, for Meighen's government had other sources of information

opinion between Meighen and Curzon by 30 June 1921. He believed that the
Imperial Conference, convinced by Meighen, had rejected renewal of the
alliance in order to pursue the policies he advocated. Gardiner, therefore, misinterpreted the decisions reached in London and the reasons for them, and,
consequently, exaggerated his own role.

80 Lodge to Lord Charnwood, 16 May and 2 July 1921, Lodge Papers, file 1921,
A-G, Jan.–April. Lodge suggested that the renewed alliance must not threaten
the United States and that they must achieve co-operation between the British
empire and the United States. An interesting and perhaps significant point is
that Lodge here assumed that Britain would renew a modified alliance rather
than terminate it.

81 Young, *Powerful America*, 48–52. These exchanges were the result of the Lee-
Ochs conversations which had Lloyd George's blessing. The Denby Papers
contain no information on this subject, but Denby repeated the myth that
Canada and Australia held a common attitude toward the alliance.

82 Geddes to Curzon, 3 June 1921, FO/414/247, Cab. 32/6 and Lloyd George
Papers, F/210/2/11. The report came from the Consul-General in New York,
quoting Col. Theo. Roosevelt Jr.

and had already taken the initiative in exchanges with London before Gardiner's appearance. Elder statesman Newton Rowell had met pro-League Republicans, Elihu Root, Hughes, and William Howard Taft in February.[83] Root confirmed Colonel House's view that Harding would propose an alternative to the League but would consider entering an amended League should his proposals fail. Both Root and Hughes spoke of the need to develop co-operation between the Anglo-Saxon peoples and between Britain and the United States, and Taft expressed similar sentiments. Taft had also pointed out that Harding was not an isolationist, that he realised that the American people expected positive action to secure peace, and that he favoured United States involvement in world affairs, perhaps through a permanent court of international justice. These opinions, while from eminent enough sources, were expressed in general, even speculative terms and House's congenital optimism could be misleading. However, there was some encouragement for Meighen and his advisers.

No one was more convinced of this than Loring Christie, Meighen's principal source of inspiration on foreign policy. Christie, after a formative session in Geneva at the League Assembly and after meeting Kerr and Lloyd George in London and discussing the Anglo-Japanese alliance, laid out his assumptions and propositions in a memorandum of 1 February 1921, and thereby established his control of the question.[84] Indeed, Christie's paper provoked the ensuing Anglo-Canadian debate. Christie saw the alliance as a vital factor affecting the future of the British empire and of relations within the English-speaking world, and he suggested that Britain faced three alternatives; renewal, abrogation, and amendment by removal of the military clauses. He opposed renewal on the following grounds: the demise of Russia and Germany had removed the reasons for the alliance; current policy decisions could not be based on the future possibility of a Russo-German revival and only an immediate crisis

83 N. Rowell to Meighen, 9 Feb. and 3 March 1921, Meighen Papers, xxvi, no 97. Borden, Lloyd George, and Kerr also received copies of these letters.
84 Lower, 'Loring Christie,' 38–48. This article contains a number of errors. Lower recalls submitting an earlier account to Brebner and Christie to ensure accuracy, but the documents do not bear out either of his informants or Lower's own views in some respects. Lower ignores other contributions to the subject, and myths about Meighen's role seem difficult to disperse. Christie's historical facts were not always sound, but he seemed well informed on British attitudes toward the alliance.

could justify any alliance; dominion public opinion opposed the alliance with Japan; Britain's ability to restrain Tokyo was largely fictional; China had no faith in the alliance and felt it implicated Britain in her rape; and, above all, as a devotee of English-speaking concord, Christie believed that the United States opposed any special relationship between Britain and Japan and that renewal would injure prospects for Anglo-American co-operation. Christie also dismissed an amended alliance as 'mere window dressing and dishonest' and as involving Britain in incalculable liabilities and consequences with an ally comprising a 'people remote, little understood and radically different from our view.' In search of a method to secure the empire's interests in the Far East and to promote understanding with the United States, Christie proposed to involve Japan, China, and the United States with Britain, not in an alliance or an entente but by 'a pooling of the counsel and experience of all interested powers for the purpose of arriving at a common policy in the Far East.'

Christie proposed, therefore, a conference of Pacific powers where Britain could reconcile her position with that of the United States and China, where the powers could act in line with the methods and spirit of the 'new diplomacy,' and where they might create the basis of a working Pacific concert founded on common interests and necessities. A dedicated Atlanticist, Christie could not dismiss American co-operation as a chimera and he suggested that a Canadian envoy, despatched secretly on behalf of Canada, should sound out the United States. Even if Washington rejected the idea of a conference, Christie still demanded an end to the Anglo-Japanese alliance and the pursuit of informal Anglo-American discussions to arrive at a working agreement with each secretary of state during his tenure of office. Christie was not impressed with the dangers of Washington dictating policy to London nor with the prospect of the United States seizing the moral leadership. The empire must have the substance, not the shadow, it must 'take the cash and let the credit go,' and even draw strength from 'another bond of sympathy within our humour-loving Empire' should it face empty boasting from Americans. Curzon would have turned pale at such levity, or red, but Christie's final paragraph could not be dismissed:

These notes have been written on the assumption that the American is a political animal as we believe ourselves to be; that in his instincts and methods he is nearer to us than any other; that in our and the world's highest interest we should work together; and that it is our business to meet and cope with him on the political plane depending upon our skill there as against his. Consistently with our actual safety we should do all we can to prove our friendship and nothing to alienate his. It has not yet been demonstrated that he has definitely rejected our friendship. And if there is to be any rejection of friendship it must never come from our side; if the choice is to be rejection, the choice must be his; and we must see to it that it is quite plain to the world that the choice was his. Otherwise we shall have failed in the highest art of politics.

Christie's case won Meighen's immediate acceptance and on 15 February Meighen telegraphed Lloyd George to begin implementation of Christie's proposals.[85] Meighen dismissed the Anglo-Japanese alliance as obsolete and demanded that Britain seek an understanding with the United States:

In view of her tendency towards the abandonment of her attitude of isolation generally, her traditional special interests in China, which is [sic] as great as ours and of the increasing prominence of the Pacific as a scene of action, there is a danger that a special, confidential relationship concerning that region, between ourselves and Japan, to which she was not a party, would come to be regarded as an unfriendly exclusion and as a barrier to an English speaking accord.

Instead of renewing the alliance Britain should call a conference of Pacific powers which would terminate the alliance gracefully and seek a working Pacific concert, all to the betterment of Anglo-American relations. Finally, Meighen proposed that Borden meet with the Harding administration, thus rejecting in part Christie's idea of a secret and independent Canadian move. The British cabinet debated Meighen's propositions on 18 February and Curzon, not surprisingly, led the opposition.[86] In his view, such matters could not be placed in the hands of a dominion envoy, the Foreign Office and the Committee of Imperial Defence were studying the question, and, as there was much to be said for retaining the alliance and as Ambassador Geddes urged renewal, Curzon hoped that the cabinet would not rush to the conclusion that they should denounce the alliance because

85 Governor General to Colonial Secretary, 15 Feb. 1921, Borden Papers, post-1921 series, folder 253; Lampson, memorandum, 8 April 1921, 'On correspondence with the Canadian Government relating to the Anglo-Japanese Alliance,' BD, 1st ser., XIV, no 261, 271–6

86 Minutes of cabinet meeting, 18 Feb. 1921, Cab. 23/24

of dominion opposition. Churchill, now colonial secretary, countered to some extent, urging the cabinet to treat the Canadian proposals with some consideration. They must recognise dominion special interests with regard to the alliance, promise that Britain would take no decision without consultation, and ask that Borden come to London to consult on the advisability of a prior and independent approach to the United States. The cabinet then agreed that Lloyd George should draft a reply to Meighen on the lines suggested by Churchill, securing the latter's approval and that of Curzon, and that they should also inform Australia.

Although Lloyd George's reply of 26 February[87] accepted the proposition that they should consider the renewal question from the point of view of relations between the United States and the British empire, inevitably it exasperated Christie.[88] Lloyd George demanded that the imperial meeting retain complete freedom of action and suggested that a proposal for a Pacific conference, especially if Washington responded favourably, would impair that freedom. Britain must consult with all the dominions before taking any steps and although the Pacific conference idea had much to commend it as a possible ultimate solution, other political, economic, and strategic issues were involved and were under study by expert committees. Naval construction, the League, and disarmament were specifically mentioned and Lloyd George's reply inferred, or so it seemed to Ottawa, that the renewal issue was a potential lever on the United States to secure a naval agreement. Lloyd George invited Borden to London to discuss the broad issues involved and the question of sounding out the United States, but clearly he frowned on independent moves by Ottawa, and insisted on the preservation of the executive role of the Imperial Conference.

Christie prepared his rebuttal, indignant, cutting, and couched

87 Colonial Secretary to Governor General, 26 Feb. 1921, Borden Papers, post-1921 series, folder 253, and King Papers, file 1922 (Chandler-Churchill). Lampson's memorandum dated the reply as 22 February, and the draft in the Lloyd George Papers (F/9/3/30) has that date, but the telegram was not sent until 26 February.

88 Churchill authorised Meighen to give the substance of this reply of 26 February to the House of Commons but he warned against statements which might arouse misgivings either in Washington or Tokyo (Governor General to Colonial Secretary, 1 March 1921, and Colonial Secretary to Governor General, 9 March 1921, King Papers, file 1922 (Chandler-Churchill)).

in vigorous nationalist and Atlanticist terms, by 3 March.[89] In his view, the very failure to approach the United States would itself prejudice the liberty of action of the Imperial Conference, leaving the empire for at least two years with only the alternatives of renewal or denunciation of the alliance with Japan. Britain would not countenance denunciation, regarding it as an unfriendly act toward her ally, and Christie therefore argued that Canada must direct the Imperial Conference toward acceptance of a policy based on Anglo-American co-operation. She should investigate Washington's attitude and build on any encouraging response. Christie found it incredible that Lloyd George could suggest that a favourable American reply to the idea of a Pacific conference would be unfortunate, and he rejected any attempt to force a naval agreement on the United States prior to a settlement of the alliance question. In his view, to compel Washington to cease naval construction and to enter the League would be diplomatic blackmail, equivalent to saying 'In short we may need the Japanese to throw in the balance against the power of the United States.'[90] Canada must reject such propositions for they suggested a new justification for the Anglo-Japanese alliance, assumed that an American menace had replaced a Russo-German threat, and inferred a whole new approach toward Anglo-American relations. In Christie's view, Britain might transform the alliance from a limited Far Eastern arrangement into the very pivot of her world policy and call in Japan to redress the balance of the Western world.

In addition, Christie dismissed Curzon's expert committees as mere excuses for delay and their findings as irrelevant to the question as to whether Canada should support a policy that would alienate the United States and force increased defence expenditures. He sought to secure an Atlantic entente through the reassessment of Far Eastern and Pacific issues, the alliance renewal question was the most suitable vehicle, and he could not accept the views of those who dismissed his policy as impracticable and argued that Britain must retain the friendship of Japan until the United States disarmed. Christie denounced the British reply as insincere and as designed to

89 Christie to Meighen, 3 March 1921, Borden Papers, post-1921 series, folder 253
90 Christie had clearly seized on the crucial relationship between strategic and diplomatic factors and his indictment of British policy forces the historian to recall Lloyd George's irresponsible conjectures at the CID meetings of December 1920.

impose Britain's will on the Imperial Conference. Lloyd George's despatch did not recognise Canada's role in Anglo-American relations, it ignored her intermediary position, and it failed to recognise her voice as the most vital one in imperial discussions on North American problems.

Christie, therefore, rejected Britain's reply as unacceptable and recommended that Canada send Borden to Washington as soon as possible. Canada must defy Britain because her own interests as a neighbour of the United States and as a Pacific dominion were more vital than those of Britain in this matter. In his view, the welfare of the Canadian people outweighed the value of Britain's possessions, and Ottawa possessed superior knowledge of and qualifications for dealing with Washington. The Canadian government should, therefore, Christie argued, sound out Harding's administration on its own behalf and for its own information, so that Meighen could participate in the review of imperial policy and prevent decisions inimical to Canada's interests.

Although Christie's memorandum reached Meighen on 3 March, Ottawa delayed its note to London until 1 April, and then sent an abbreviated and somewhat muted version of Christie's blast.[91] Meighen did not send Borden to Washington, but doubtless Gardiner's mission in reverse made Borden's visit somewhat superfluous. Although Ottawa's despatch of 1 April was quite moderate in tone and phraseology, the threatened refusal to participate in a renewal of the alliance with Japan was unmistakable and London could not ignore the significance of such a stand. The Foreign Office had wind of Lodge's moves if not of Gardiner's, and Lampson, convinced that Ottawa was determined to sound out Washington, urged immediate action to avert the danger of Canada joining with the United States in an independent Pacific and Far Eastern policy.[92] Lampson pointed out that the Foreign Office's own expert committee was in substantial agreement with the Canadian government,[93] he himself believed

91 Governor General to Colonial Secretary, 1 April 1921, King Papers, file 1922 (Chandler-Churchill)

92 Lampson, memorandum, 8 April 1921, 'On correspondence with the Canadian Government relating to the Anglo-Japanese Alliance,' BD, 1st ser., XIV, no 261, 276

93 The Foreign Office committee had suggested a tripartite entente whereas Canada advocated a conference of Pacific powers to achieve a working agreement.

their views to be correct, and he felt that the solution proposed by the expert committee was most likely to unite the empire. Lampson proposed, therefore, that they send the committee's report to Ottawa, to show Meighen's government that experts in London were aware of the issues involved and to comfort those in Ottawa who worried lest wide differences of opinion still existed between Canada and Britain.[94] Tyrrell feared the machinations of Lodge and the dangers inherent in any initiative taken by Borden while London and Ottawa remained divided. He avoided, however, Lampson's erroneous inference that the Foreign Office's expert committee's views were shared by Curzon and the cabinet, and that Meighen had reason to feel comforted.

While both Lampson and Tyrrell viewed the matter as urgent, the cabinet, distracted by domestic problems, had other priorities. They did not turn to the question until 21 April and even then, pleading the pressure of other work, instructed Churchill to inform Ottawa that labour unrest and Curzon's illness prevented them from replying to Meighen's telegram.[95] Churchill offered some hope at least of rapid action and on 26 April Lloyd George responded to Meighen.[96]

94 Britain had sent a copy of the Foreign Office memorandum of February 1920, recognising a triple agreement as the ideal solution but advocating renewal of the alliance with Japan as the practical policy, to the dominions, and Lampson felt that the more recent committee report would do much to show Ottawa that different attitudes now existed in London. Bentinck wrote the February 1920 paper under Curzon's supervision (Foreign Office, memorandum, 28 Feb. 1920, 'Effect of Anglo-Japanese Alliance upon Foreign Relationships,' BD, 1st ser., VI, no 761, 1016–23).

95 Minutes of cabinet meeting, 21 April 1921, Cab. 23/25; Churchill to Governor General, 22 April 1921, King Papers, file 1922 (Chandler-Churchill)

96 Churchill to Governor General, 26 April 1921, King Papers, file 1922 (Chandler-Churchill) and BD, 1st ser., XIV, no 261, 276, note 15. Curzon drafted the telegram after consulting Tyrrell, according to the official British documents, but Curzon was ill and Churchill's hand is also evident. He wrote to Lloyd George pointing out that they had not answered Meighen's telegram of 1 April; that Curzon was ill; and that Kerr's draft reply, referring to shipbuilding, the League, and to disarmament, was unacceptable. Churchill's suggested reply was somewhat on the lines laid down by Tyrrell although he went further, suggesting that the Pacific conference, held either in Canada or the United States, might well be the final solution and that it could convene almost immediately after the imperial conference, should the

He assured the Canadian Premier that decisions on the alliance would wait on the imperial 'cabinet,' that they would so inform Japan, and that the empire would lose nothing by this procedure. Meanwhile to gain time Britain would negotiate a three-months' renewal of the alliance. As to the proposed Pacific conference, Lloyd George expected the imperial meeting to discuss it, but he raised the question of Australia's attitude which made it impossible for Britain to prejudge Canada's suggestion.[97] In conclusion, Lloyd George asked Meighen to refrain from consulting the United States independently, but suggested that Britain might use Canadian resources should the Imperial Conference decide on such approaches.

This somewhat belated British reply ended the Anglo-Canadian debate prior to the Imperial Conference,[98] although Christie's pre-

dominions and the United States accept it. Furthermore, Churchill seemed willing to permit Borden to go to Washington to sound out the United States on the Pacific conference scheme, providing that Borden could not commit the empire in any way by his consultations. Churchill also warned that although Canada would oppose the Foreign Office's idea of a one-year extension, she would accept a three-months extension of the alliance, and Lloyd George should urge the Foreign Office to ask Japan for the shorter extension. In Churchill's view Britain should enter a Pacific conference with the alliance intact and should permit its abrogation only after satisfactory negotiations at the meeting of Pacific powers (Churchill to Lloyd George, 25 April 1921, Lloyd George Papers, F/9/3/30). Clearly the Foreign Office, the Colonial Office, and the Prime Minister's secretariat were all involved in the 26 April reply and some confusion existed about the views of each participant.

97 The specific reference to Australia suggests that a definite expression of opinion had reached London, and Prime Minister Hughes had spoken in the House of Representatives on 8 April. Hughes had stated the familiar dilemma. Naval defence was the essence of Australia's security, the Anglo-Japanese alliance affected the question of imperial defence, the hope of the world lay in co-operation between the English-speaking peoples, but security lay in the renewal of the alliance with Japan modified to be acceptable to both allies and to the United States. In full circle, then, the Anglo-Japanese alliance was essential for imperial security and for peace. Churchill circulated this speech to the cabinet on 28 April 1921.

98 Lampson had suggested that they send the committee's report to Canada, but there is no evidence that the Foreign Office acted on his proposal. One might speculate on the reasons why a report which reinforced Ottawa's views was withheld from the Canadian government.

paratory work continued. His memorandum of 23 April, to guide Meighen's comments in parliament, added little except to call for friendly relations with Japan as well as with China and the United States, and to describe Japan as a great and ambitious nation, a faithful ally, and a valuable member of the world community.[99] Christie's final paper before the Imperial Conference, however, had more to offer and provided Meighen with additional ammunition for the forthcoming debate in London.[100] Its tone, spirit, and message were predictable. Christie issued another manifesto, calling for co-operation between the two commonwealths, the empire, and the United States, and denying that Britain could renew the alliance in any form acceptable to Washington. Furthermore, anglophils in the United States were adamant that renewal would injure Anglo-American relations, whereas their counterparts in Japan looked for British benevolent neutrality in the event of war with the United States and then for British support at the peace table. Christie, however, made other points, some quite novel and even curious. Britain, by renewing the alliance, could drive China into Russia's arms but she should seek rather to rejuvenate China than alienate her. Canadian opinion, Christie continued, had rallied to the League of Nations and opposed all alliances as incompatible with the Covenant. Moreover, suggestions emanating from the State Department, the White House, and Republican party headquarters that a decision to denounce the alliance would greatly enhance the prospects for disarmament were acceptable wisdom, but blackmail from London to secure a naval agreement with the United States as the price for Britain severing her exclusive arrangement with Japan was unacceptable folly. In conclusion, Christie felt that the Pacific conference scheme was now even more valid than in March and should the Atlanticists lose the debate at the Imperial Conference Meighen must not accept its decisions as binding on Canada without parlia-

99 Christie memorandum, 23 April 1921. 'The Question of the Renewal of the Anglo-Japanese Alliance,' King Papers, file 288. Christie urged that Canadian public opinion be heard on the alliance question and clearly Meighen's opposition to renewal had the support of the majority of the Canadian people, of the Canadian press, and the Liberal opposition. The crucial debate took place on 27 April 1921. Canada, House of Commons, *Debates*, 1921, III, 2626–80

100 Christie memorandum, 1 June 1921, 'The Anglo-Japanese Alliance,' Department of External Affairs (Ottawa), Monthly Bulletin, September 1966, XVIII, no 9, 402–13

mentary approval. No one had stated the Atlanticist case more forcibly than Christie and though the British cabinet expected to dominate the Imperial Conference, a confrontation with Canada seemed unavoidable.

In addition to these exchanges with Ottawa, the British government reappraised other political and strategic factors prior to the crucial cabinet meeting of 30 May, and then again in the final days before the opening of the Imperial Conference. Through sources, orthodox and otherwise, Peking continued to emphasise its opposition to renewal of the Anglo-Japanese alliance. Alston, back in Peking, reported renewed pressure, rumours of boycotts, and even of American-inspired attacks on the alliance. He also confirmed the opposition of British commercial opinion in China to renewal and their support of the idea of a Pacific conference.[101] Curzon, however, refused to commit himself to prior consultations with Peking, merely assuring China that her views would receive due consideration, and no doubt China helped undermine her own position by irritating Curzon with such demands.[102] The Foreign Secretary's anger eventually spilled over to B. Lennox Simpson (Putnam Weale), the roving envoy from Peking who pleaded China's case in Ottawa, Washington, and London, and probably did more harm than good to his cause.[103] Simpson met Meighen on 3 May, handed him a draft of a revised Anglo-Japanese alliance which Britain supposedly would present to the Imperial Conference, and hinted at a possible Sino-American defence agreement or Sino-Russian co-operation should Britain retain the alliance.[104] Simpson then visited Washington, met Secretary of State Hughes and certain senators, reported back to Meighen on their hostility to the Anglo-Japanese alliance, and departed for Eng-

101 Alston to Curzon, 17 May, 3 June, and 2 July 1921, BD, 1st ser., XIV, no 280, 290; no 292, 299–300; and no 318, 321, and Cab. 32/6

102 Curzon to Alston, 16 June 1921, BD, 1st ser., XIV, no 303, 306–7

103 Curzon to Alston, 28 June 1921, ibid., no 311, 314–15. Simpson's own account is *An Indiscreet Chronicle from the Pacific*, 92–124. Curzon took particular exception to Simpson's use of that 'Communist organ,' the *Daily Herald*.

104 B.L. Simpson, 'Report of a Confidential Mission to Canada, the United States and England in 1921. A Campaign against the Anglo-Japanese Alliance,' King Papers, file 288. The draft treaty was not an accurate document, but his hints of possible Sino-Russian contacts may not have gone unheeded, for Christie, for the first time, referred to this future danger in his memorandum of 1 June.

land, arriving on 1 June. There he met with Lord Riddell, Grigg, Hankey, and Tyrrell and attempted to influence opinion through the press. The Foreign Office, however, dismissed him as a clever and at times unscrupulous propagandist, prepared to sacrifice accuracy in the interests of his employers, and this verdict remained unchallenged.[105]

Japan had also launched a propaganda campaign to influence British public opinion and to gain support for renewal of the alliance. From March Japan used the columns of *The Times* and the *Daily Telegraph*, and in May the Crown Prince made a successful state visit to London, helping to improve the public atmosphere between the two countries.[106] Curzon no doubt welcomed such attempts and his negotiations with Tokyo to extend the alliance for three months beyond 8 July 1921, to permit the Imperial Conference to debate the renewal question, were far more cordial than his dealings with Peking.[107] Curzon, approaching Ambassador Hayashi on 9 May, initiated a curious set of exchanges[108] in which initially Curzon and the Japanese government were ranged against Cecil Hurst, the Foreign Office's chief legal adviser, and Ambassador Eliot. Curzon then petulantly accepted Hurst's ruling but failed to win the Japanese over to this view before the Imperial Conference convened, only to have Birkenhead rule against Hurst and in favour of Japan on 1 July. On 2 July, therefore, Curzon returned to his original position after this long exercise in frustration.

105 Wellesley to Geddes, 1 June 1921, King Papers, file 1921 (Carey-Churchill). Riddell seemed more impressed with Simpson, but was the exception in this case. Riddell diary, entry of 14 May 1921, *Diary of the Peace Conference and After*, 301

106 Lampson and Leeper, minutes on Foreign Office documents, March 1921, FO/800/329; Eliot to Curzon, 3 June 1921, King Papers, file 288; Nish 'Japan and the Ending of the Anglo-Japanese Alliance,' 374–5. The Japanese government entertained hopes that Lloyd George would make a return visit.

107 The question of urgency sprang from the joint Anglo-Japanese note to the League of 8 July 1920. If this was a notice of intention to abrogate their alliance, then the Imperial Conference had little time for comprehensive debate.

108 Curzon to Eliot, 11, 13, and 26 May and 7 June 1921, Curzon to Hayashi, 8 and 27 June and 2 July 1921, and Eliot to Curzon, 20, 27, and 31 May and 11 June 1921, BD, 1st ser., XIV, no 277, 287–9; no 279, 289–90; no 287, 295–6; no 295, 301–2; no 297, 302–3; no 310, 313–14; no 320, 322; no 283, 292–3; no 288, 296–7; no 291, 298–9; no 300, 305; and no 301, 305, and FO/414/247

The principles of the debate were clear. Hurst ruled that the joint note to the League of Nations on 8 July 1920 constituted a notice of intent to abrogate the Anglo-Japanese alliance and that the alliance was 'self-extinguishing' on 8 July 1921 unless prolonged. Britain and Japan must, therefore, negotiate a three-months' extension, make a new declaration to the League, and give notice that the procedures of the League Covenant would prevail over those of the alliance during the three-month period. The Japanese government, however, denying Hurst's interpretation of the joint note of 8 July 1920 and rejecting the view that the alliance was 'self-extinguishing' unless renewed, insisted that the alliance remained in force automatically unless a signatory specifically denounced it. Tokyo suggested that the Imperial Conference might terminate the alliance but that renewal was not required, and concluded that although both partners had admitted to the League that their alliance was imperfect and to some degree inconsistent with the Covenant, they must also assume it to be self-perpetuating. Birkenhead, of course, ruled precisely that for the Imperial Conference, they must decide on abrogation of a self-perpetuating treaty, not renewal of a self-extinguishing alliance, and consequently on 2 July Curzon could propose to Japan that they merely genuflect again before the League Covenant.

Lloyd George personally and the cabinet collectively were subject to two other sources of influence prior to the 30 May debate. Edward Grigg, Kerr's recent successor and of the same political vintage, urged the Prime Minister to consider his interpretation of the problem and his proposed solutions.[109] Grigg saw the alliance renewal question essentially as a question affecting the relations between the white and the Asian sections of the empire, with India, presenting a psychological problem, as the most sensitive area. He described the empire as a bridge between the West and Asia, showing that Britain believed in equal opportunity for and mutual self-respect between white and coloured peoples. Grigg saw the alliance with Japan both as a valuable instrument giving proof of Britain's desire to treat Asians fairly, and also as a complicating factor because of ambivalent attitudes toward the renewal question. Ordinarily, Grigg pointed out, India would applaud Britain's support of China against Japan, but should they renounce the alliance because of Canadian

109 Grigg to Lloyd George, 25 May, and memorandum, 'The Anglo-Japanese Alliance,' 25 May 1921, Lloyd George Papers, F/86/1/3 and Grigg Papers, reel 11; Kerr, 'Anglo-Japanese Alliance'

and United States pressure, Delhi would charge London with racial discrimination and Britain's position in India would be endangered.

Grigg, however, in the interests of cordial Anglo-American relations, sought the ideal solution of continued links with Japan and close co-operation with the United States. He recommended that they fuse Christie's views with those of the Foreign Office committee and that Britain seek a tripartite agreement, which would form the basis of a standing Pacific conference to meet periodically and deal with relevant problems. Such a policy, Grigg suggested, would 'bridge the colour line in the Pacific,' preserve Japan's prestige, and persuade her to co-operate with the West.[110] Tactically, Grigg urged that they put Britain's case to Ambassador Harvey, discuss the problems involved with India, and ask for Anglo-American co-operation in the economic rather than the political sphere. If Harvey responded sympathetically, Lloyd George would enter the Imperial Conference with a clear policy. He could warn the dominions of the dangers resulting from racial friction, soothe the Indian delegation, and forestall Canadian opposition, for Meighen would not dare oppose a policy already accepted by Harvey. Having carried the Imperial Conference, Britain could then approach Japan and the United States and summon a Pacific conference to London before the dominion premiers left.[111]

110 The tripartite agreement, between the empire, Japan, and the United States, might be based on a recognition of the Open Door and equal opportunity in China, and on arrangements dealing with immigration, cable communications, Yap, shipping facilities, and defence expenditure. The Pacific conference would have the same composition and would handle all outstanding and new issues.

111 Grigg returned to this tactical move of using prior talks with Harvey to forestall Meighen, although, as Grigg looked to a Pacific conference and co-operation with the United States, it is difficult to see why he should have expected Meighen to oppose such a policy if Britain suggested it to the Imperial Conference. At the same time Grigg saw the triple agreement as modifying rather than destroying the alliance with Japan and as ensuring against any charges of adopting an anti-Asia policy. Grigg recommended the quiet approach to Harvey rather than a public appeal to Washington also as a way to avoid rekindling American suspicions of Lloyd George. Whatever frailties were inherent in Grigg's scheme, clearly the most glaring was the assumption that Harvey's relationship with Secretary of State Hughes made him a suitable

Grigg had drawn Lloyd George's attention to political and racial considerations and Lord Lee raised again the connection between strategic and political factors.[112] Lee, expressing fears of a schism within the empire over the alliance question, called for an immediate cabinet decision in which Admiralty and Treasury opinion should carry equal weight with that of the Foreign Office. The Admiralty, Lee noted, could neither frame an imperial naval policy nor give but academic and inconclusive advice to the dominions, and could not even determine the cost, strength, and distribution of the British fleet until they settled the broader political questions relating to the Pacific. He personally, however, called for the termination of the alliance with Japan and for the fullest co-operation with the United States. In Lee's view, this policy would avert a war between Japan and the United States, eliminate a source of anglophobe, jingoist agitation in America seeking to secure a large navy, avoid the crippling burden of a three-power naval race, reassure Washington of London's good faith, and undermine the influence of Japan's extremists and Prussian-minded military caste who advocated dangerous policies. He conceded that the link with Japan helped guarantee the security of Britain's possessions and trade in the Pacific, but the risks involved, such as friction with the United States and the destruction of any hope of a disarmament agreement, demanded that Britain adopt an alternative policy. Lee regarded an Anglo-American alliance as an ideal solution but he saw a tripartite Pacific agreement as the most practicable, and he expected the United States to accommodate Britain on many issues, including a naval agreement, if Britain ended her alliance with Japan. Tactically, Lee, like Grigg, urged immediate negotiations with Harvey and with Japanese officials accompanying the Crown Prince to find an alternative to a policy of drift and avoid both a schism within the empire and war between Japan and the United States.

The review of defence policy, underway since early May, was not complete, but Lee had gone further than anyone in his demand for Anglo-American co-operation. Curzon, however, unmoved by views from the 'lower deck,' spoke for the Foreign Office in authoritative

avenue of approach (Grigg to Lloyd George, 4 June 1921, Lloyd George Papers, F/86/1/4 and Grigg Papers, reel 11).

112 Lee, memorandum, CP 2957, 21 May 1921, 'Anglo-Japanese Alliance,' Cab. 24/123 and Lloyd George Papers, F/143

fashion when the cabinet met on 30 May 1921.[113] He outlined for the cabinet the arguments for and against renewal, dealing with the negative and 'weaker' case first. The case against renewal rested on the following grounds: because of the eclipse of Russia and Germany the alliance was superfluous, but Curzon regarded the future as less secure; the alliance was a source of irritation and suspicion in the United States, but Curzon tended to dismiss these sentiments as mere excuses for naval construction;[114] and Britain would forfeit the friendship of China, who would regard renewal of the alliance as a direct encouragement of Japanese imperialism.

Curzon's support of renewal rested on equally familiar arguments relating to the Pacific balance of power. The alliance had been a successful and valuable instrument since the Russo-Japanese war and now ensured against a resurgent Russo-German menace which an isolated Japan might support. The alliance helped London restrain Tokyo and fulfilled strategic desiderata by removing the need for Britain to maintain large military and naval resources in the Pacific and the Far East. Moreover, Britain's treaty with Japan was popular with her other allies, France and Holland, and Japan herself, on the whole a faithful ally, wanted their alliance to continue. A rebuff from Britain would certainly bring resentment and possibly retaliation.[115]

Curzon then analysed dominion attitudes. He stated that Australia and New Zealand preferred renewal, that South Africa's views remained obscure, but that Canada, because of her own interests, American influence, her attitude on immigration, and her missionary activities in Korea, opposed renewal. Indeed, Canada actually threatened independent action and had proposed a conference of Pacific powers to seek a new solution. A triple alliance was, however, in Curzon's view, impracticable because of hostile influences in control of the United States Senate and the absence of any guaranteed stability in American policy. Instead, Curzon proposed renewal of a modified four- or five-year alliance, after prior consultation with

113 Minutes of cabinet meeting, 30 May 1921, Cab. 23/25. Most cabinet members were present and Lloyd George instructed Hankey to make a full record of their discussion.

114 Curzon made a similar report to the imperial premiers but omitted this reference to naval construction.

115 Curzon gave the misleading impression that Japan would accept the three-months' extension and, in comparison with his statement at the imperial meeting, said nothing to the cabinet about racial considerations.

China and the United States. Britain should also secure if possible
an agreement with the United States of the same duration and this
suggestion marked the limit of Curzon's concessions to Atlanticism.

Churchill welcomed the news from Australia and New Zealand,
for this would ease the delicate task of securing the consent of the
Imperial Conference to Britain's policy. Their differences with Canada, he felt, were largely on the methods of securing peace and
stability, of preventing a clash between Japan and the United States,
and of forestalling a naval race, and he urged that they take up
Meighen's conference scheme. Unfortunately they did not have adequate information on American policy, but Churchill suggested that
they ask the dominions to accept renewal, perhaps as a temporary
measure, along with the conference proposal. Then if the conference failed, Britain would retain the modified alliance with full
assurances to the United States. Both Austen Chamberlain and
Arthur Balfour spoke in support, with the former urging that President Harding rather than the British government call the conference.

Lord Lee conceded that the United States had lapsed into isolationism, that she was suspicious both of the Anglo-Japanese alliance
and of British motives in general, as Admiral W.S. Sims had recently
confirmed, and that renewal would provoke fresh demands for a
naval building programme. However, in view of America's potential
resources and the extent of Japan's armaments burden, Lee rejected
Geddes's views and proposed that a conference, summoned by Harding, would provide a solution and apply some form of Monroe Doctrine to the Pacific. In Lee's view, of course, Britain must not risk a
confrontation at the Imperial Conference.

Edwin Montagu, secretary of state for India, wanted all reference
to India removed from the terms of the alliance in order to secure
the cessation of Japan's dubious activities there, but he supported
renewal since it would be a wedge to help weaken the idea of 'Asia
for the Asiatics.' Montagu also tended to support the Conference
proposal, but this support only provoked Curzon who pointed out
that a conference required time to arrange, its decisions would not
necessarily conflict with renewal, and that Britain must retain the
alliance before entering into any such meeting. Lloyd George agreed
with Curzon, for abrogation of the alliance would upset Japan, injure
Britain's prestige in Asia, and give the impression that the United
States dictated British policy. He also expressed apprehension about
Russia and Germany and described Japan as a faithful ally who, although inscrutable and lacking in conscience, had stood by him in

the postwar round of conferences. In any case Japan would be a greater nuisance in India without the restraints of treaty obligations and Lloyd George came down firmly on Curzon's side, urging renewal of the alliance before participation in a conference.

This debate produced a quintuple decision. Curzon would explore the possibility of President Harding calling a Pacific conference, but only after assuring the powers that Britain would retain her alliance with Japan. The British government expected to renew the alliance for a period of less than ten years and modify it to make it consistent with the League Covenant and not offensive to the United States. Britain would achieve these safeguards in prior negotiations with China and the United States. The Foreign Office would negotiate a provisional renewal of three months and the cabinet expected to secure the concurrence of the Imperial Conference without great difficulty. Finally, the appropriate officials would prepare a study of Japan's aid during the recent war and an appreciation of the Far Eastern strategic position should the alliance be terminated.

The scale of priorities and the degree of emphasis involved in these decisions favoured Curzon's views over those of the Atlanticists, for the cabinet had agreed to renew the alliance and only then to explore the conference proposal. An element of pluralism, however, had emerged because the merit of a Pacific conference and the value if not the practicability of a tripartite agreement were generally acknowledged. Moreover, Britain would attempt to reconcile improved relations with China and the United States with the retention of the alliance modified to meet the obligations of the League Covenant. Perhaps the most surprising feature was the assumption that Britain could carry the Imperial Conference without great difficulty, for Meighen's opposition was predictable and Smuts's views were not likely to support those of Hughes and Massey.[116]

Between this crucial cabinet debate and the opening of the Imperial Conference Lloyd George's government received additional information of a political nature and the results of the review of defence

116 As the dominion delegations converged on London Grigg sounded them out for Lloyd George. Christie was unmoved, he reported, Meighen would oppose Britain's policy on the alliance, and Canada would not even discuss defence matters. Even more alarming, according to Grigg, was the possibility of an embarrassing Canadian-South African front to propose isolationist principles for imperial foreign policy and to force consideration of delicate constitutional problems (Grigg to Lloyd George, 16 June 1921, Grigg Papers, reel 11).

policy. The politically orientated material was inconclusive and could be freely interpreted in London. Geddes reported increased anti-British propaganda, renewed criticism of the alliance, and a tendency to view an act of renewal as an unfriendly gesture toward the United States.[117] Official circles in Washington were not immune to exaggerated claims that Britain, by her decision on renewal, could make either an enemy of the United States and a friend of Japan or the reverse. Moreover, Secretary of State Hughes had inferred that renewal would be disastrous. Such attitudes, Geddes felt, reflected excessive American ambitions in the Pacific and an equally exaggerated feeling of virtue with regard to commercial competition. On the specific question of renewal, however, Geddes, modifying his advice of November 1920, suggested that instead of renewing the alliance Britain should try and reach a tripartite agreement with Japan and the United States. Geddes had thus changed the emphasis of his advice but he offered little to suggest that a triple agreement was any more practicable. Arthur Willert also reported that H.P. Fletcher had discouraged the idea of a tripartite arrangement, and Curzon was not converted.[118]

Moreover, Eliot saw no reason to modify his view that Britain should renew the alliance. He reported that Japanese opinion was both more anglophil and more anxious to retain the alliance than in the past, and that the Japanese government was more realistic and moderate.[119] Churchill's report of a conversation with Ambassador Hayashi tended to confirm Eliot's views,[120] and the adjournment debate in the House of Commons on 17 June showed Curzon that his policy had a substantial degree of support.[121] Members of parliament were concerned about the China trade and were critical of

117 Geddes to Curzon, 6 June 1921, BD, 1st ser., XIV, no 294, 300–1 and Cab. 32/6

118 Willert report, 31 May 1921, Vinson, *The Parchment Peace*, 106

119 Eliot to Curzon, 9 June 1921, BD, 1st ser., XIV, no 298, 303–4

120 Churchill memorandum, CP 3048, 17 June 1921, 'The Anglo-Japanese Alliance,' Lloyd George Papers, F/143. Churchill told Hayashi of the divisions over the renewal question, describing himself, the Foreign Office, Hughes, and Massey as ranged against Canada. He placed great emphasis, however, on the dangers of a Pacific naval race and said that he did not want an exclusive Anglo-Japanese arrangement to hinder the settlement of naval and other great problems.

121 143, *Debates*, 5s, col. 783–859

Japan's policies in Asia, but although they showed little love for Japan they revealed even less inclination to lose her friendship. Some members favoured a Far Eastern or a naval conference and looked to a quadruple agreement embracing Britain, China, Japan, and the United States, but few opposed the renewal of a revised alliance which would satisfy China, safeguard India, and preserve Anglo-American accord. Austen Chamberlain, replying for the government, assured the House that ill-informed sections of American opinion rather than the United States government itself opposed the alliance, and that Britain hoped to reconcile Anglo-American co-operation with a modified agreement with Japan.

The review of Pacific defence policy, because it of necessity pondered the question of future conflict in that area, contained many references to possible hostilities with Japan, but again strategic factors, even if they suggested steps to achieve preparedness, did not point to the termination of the alliance with Japan.[122] Moreover, financial considerations tended to reinforce these strategic factors. Balfour's committee was ready to report to the cabinet by 13 June on the Singapore naval base and favoured construction of the base in view of pressing strategic considerations which dictated that the British fleet should be able to operate in the Pacific.[123] The Treasury's demands that financial stringency should dictate against premature decisions on costly defence programmes and that Britain must rely on diplomatic instruments such as the Anglo-Japanese alliance to reduce the risks produced by her inadequate Pacific defensive system were also accepted, to the extent that the committee realised that major expenditures were impossible in the near future. The committee looked, however, to a gradual development of the Singapore base as funds became available, and to possible dominion contributions.

122 The Standing Defence Sub-Committee, chaired by Balfour and acting for the Committee of Imperial Defence, co-ordinated the study of dominion contributions to imperial naval defence, of the need to construct the Singapore naval base, and of what the strategic situation would be should Britain terminate her alliance with Japan. See note 15

123 Standing Defence Sub-Committee, 6th meeting, 13 June 1921, Cab. 2/3; Hankey to Lloyd George, 14 June 1921, Lloyd George Papers, F/25/1/39; and 'Singapore's development as a naval base,' Hankey note covering conclusions of the Standing Defence Sub-Committee, 13 June 1921, CP 3039, ibid., F/143

The cabinet met on 16 June without the recuperating Lloyd George, and Balfour, while admitting that renewal of the alliance with Japan would reduce the probability of danger in the Pacific, denied that renewal removed the need for the Singapore base.[124] Singapore, Balfour claimed, was vital to imperial security, serving the needs of the oil-burning fleet and enabling the navy to conduct operations in the Pacific. The cabinet in general agreed with Balfour, noting in addition the advantages to Canada's Pacific coast defences, the value of showing the dominions that Britain possessed a naval policy, and the merits of countering claims by the United States that her fleet would protect the white races and their civilisation. The cabinet decided, therefore, that, providing no major expenditures were envisaged in the next two years, it would approve the recommendations on Singapore and explore the problem with the dominions, while retaining all major decisions in its own hands.

Balfour's committee also recognised certain tactical problems involved in discussing these decisions with the dominions, for Britain must not allow the dominions either to feel complacent about the one power standard or assume that Britain herself could afford greater contributions to imperial naval defence.[125] Yet Britain must show the dominions that her defence preparations were adequate on a global scale, being based on the ability to move the main fleet to the Pacific from home waters in an emergency. This in turn depended on eliminating any idea that the development of the Singapore base was unnecessary if Britain retained her alliance with Japan. These problems were summarised finally in the Committee of Imperial Defence paper of 17 June which concluded that Britain must construct the Singapore naval base irrespective of the decision on the Anglo-Japanese alliance.[126] However, should Britain decide to end the alliance, then the need for the naval base was urgent, any hope of gradual construction disappeared, and Britain must develop Singapore rapidly and even at great cost in order to offset the attendant risks. Obviously, therefore, the empire would receive strategic

---

124 Minutes of cabinet meeting, 16 June 1921, Cab. 23/26, and Hankey to Lloyd George, 17 June 1921, Lloyd George Papers, F/25/1/44. Balfour did not expect Britain to complete the base before she would again face the alliance renewal question, ie in five years' time.

125 Standing Defence Sub-Committee, 7th meeting, 17 June 1921, Cab. 2/3

126 CID memorandum, 144-c, 17 June 1921, 'Strategic Situation in the event of the Anglo-Japanese Alliance being determined,' Cab. 5/4

benefits and avoid a large financial outlay in the near future by renewing the alliance. Curzon's position was reinforced on the very
eve of the Imperial Conference and the Atlanticists faced as impressive an array of opposition as they had in the previous two years.
Their opportunities were also Curzon's, Hughes of Australia might
counter Meighen, and would Grigg be an effective substitute for
Kerr? Would Balfour and Smuts assert themselves, in which direction
would Lloyd George turn, and to what extent would Washington
influence London? Perhaps in the final analysis the Atlanticists must
cling to the singular fact that the British government could not be
irresponsible enough to rebuff directly the United States. Nor, however, could she reject Japan. Realism at the very least should breed
compromise and an imperial consensus was hardly beyond the limits
of diplomatic ingenuity.

THREE

The Imperial Conference

The Imperial Conference, seemingly the pivotal meeting where the imperial elite would settle the future of British Far Eastern policy and rule on the Atlanticists' case, was, in terms of personalities, a volatile mixture of old and new. Lloyd George and Curzon, the former recently ill and still bedevilled by domestic problems and the latter heavily committed in European affairs; Hughes of Australia, reputably fiery, caustic, and truculent, known for his outbursts in private and his leakages to the press, but now reported as chastened, tired, and looking to Lloyd George for guidance; Massey of New Zealand, an effective prop for Hughes; Smuts, the urbane South African nationalist and pro-League internationalist, but regarded as uncommitted on many issues and most concerned with constitutional developments; and Meighen, youngest in age and experience, a fresh-man in imperial circles, but confident, intellectually sound, eloquent, and recognised in London as the most difficult of the dominion premiers and as being under Christie's influence.[1] Meighen would lead the Atlanticists in oratory and substance, with Smuts giving considerable and effective support and even at times assuming the leadership. Hughes, in fact unrepentant and unchastened, stood ready to direct the opposition with monumental powers of repetition. Inevitably the debates at the Imperial Conference would mock the usual published statements of cordial unanimity and tolerance.

1 Hankey to Lloyd George, 15 June 1921, Lloyd George Papers, F/25/1/41. Hankey noted Meighen's unyielding attitude on the question of the alliance and urged Lloyd George to meet Meighen personally to counteract Christie's influence. Most other observers seemed impressed with Meighen, but Smuts found him depressed and hesitant and expecting political defeat at home.

In his opening statement on 20 June, Lloyd George merely outlined the problems involved in securing peace, stability, and arms limitation in the Pacific and justice for China.[2] His government wished to preserve the well-tried friendship with Britain's faithful ally, Japan. The empire, a bridge between the races of east and west, must prevent the division of the world on racial lines, but friendship with the United States was a cardinal principle of policy, dictated by the 'proper nature of things,' by instinct, reason, and by common sense. Britain must, Lloyd George suggested, work closely with the United States in all parts of the world, but though they were prepared to discuss arms limitation with Washington, his government could not ignore the fundamental relationship between sea power and imperial security. Then with a now characteristic flourish of patrician flattery, Lloyd George praised the empire's role in war and peace and conceded that 'There was a time when Downing Street controlled the Empire; today the Empire is in charge of Downing Street.' Lloyd George had bowed to Tokyo, genuflected to Washington, courted the dominions, and had suggested the basic question was one of priorities and emphases which familial negotiations would solve.[3]

Hughes, acutely conscious of the problems of Pacific security and the financial and strategic obstacles to the recreation of imperial naval power in Asian waters, was far more precise.[4] He accepted the need to amend the alliance with Japan to satisfy the League Cove-

2 Notes of meeting, E1, 20 June 1921, Cab. 32/2 [imperial meetings 1921, notes of meetings nos E1–34, 20 June–5 Aug. 1921]. The published record is
Great Britain, *Parliamentary Papers 1921*, XIV (Reports, Commissioners, VII), Cmd. 1474.

3 Meighen spoke briefly but not without significance on the value of conference diplomacy, the League, and the commonwealth, and on the need to mitigate racial divisions.

4 Notes of meeting, E 2, 21 June 1921, Cab. 32/2. Hughes, during the war and at the Peace Conference, had opposed Japan's retention of former German islands in the north Pacific, had opposed the militarisation clause in the C class mandates to restrain Japan, and had helped defeat the racial equality amendment. In general, therefore, Hughes had adopted attitudes hostile toward Japan, but, in addition, he had little faith in the United States and feared that the 'new world' would dictate imperial policy. Hughes, *The Splendid Adventure*, 119–26; Galbraith, 'The Imperial Conference of 1921 and the Washington Conference,' 143–52; and Whyte *William Morris Hughes*, 424–46

nant, but stressed that 'the case for renewal is very strong if not indeed overwhelming.' In Hughes's view, the alliance enabled Britain to restrain Japan and renewal would prevent Japan's isolation from the western nations, avoid a blow to Japan's national pride, and would aid China, the empire, and the prospects for peace. At the same time he acknowledged the problem of relations with the United States. Australians admired America, regarding her as a model for their own future, and, in Hughes's opinion, the alliance must specifically or implicitly exclude the possibility of war with the United States and be renewed in such a manner as to remove all grounds for suspicion and criticism from Washington. He doubted whether they really understood American opinion and the reasons for their hostility toward the alliance, and he proposed, therefore, that they summon a conference with the United States and Japan to clear the air, search for mutually acceptable policies, and construct a reasonable basis on which to renew the alliance.[5]

Hughes received predictable support from Massey, but Smuts intervened with a curious combination of internationalist, Atlanticist, and isolationist phrases, which, however, clearly carried considerable weight.[6] To Smuts, sanity and reason demanded that the empire avoid an arms race with the United States and sentiment and history dictated Anglo-American co-operation. The United States was closest to the empire in 'all the human ties,' she was the 'oldest Dominion' who had left their circle because of a great historical error, but they must repair the loss and return her to the fold. Smuts regarded the United States as a staunch and true friend whose intervention, though late because of her failure to appreciate the issues at stake, had been decisive in the recent war. Since then, the empire and the United States had drifted apart, due, in Smuts's opinion, to differences of viewpoint and to statesmen's errors, but the fundamental special relationship remained intact and the only safe path was that of Anglo-American co-operation. Smuts the Atlanticist, however, did not advocate an alliance or an exclusive arrangement with the United States, for such instruments were undesirable, unnecessary, and be-

5 Hughes also suggested a disarmament conference, in which Britain, France, Japan, and the United States would participate, and pointed out that a successful conference would affect the alliance question and the broader issue of imperial security.

6 Notes of meeting, E 2, 21 June 1921, Cab. 32/2 and C. Sifton to Dafoe, 8 July 1921, C. Sifton Papers, file 1921

yond their grasp. Instead he advocated that the empire, the world's greatest power, shun alliances as such and turn to universal friendship, global co-operation, and a union of all free peoples in a consultative system of conferences; in fact to a true society of nations. Smuts the imperial isolationist then pronounced on the demise of Europe and on the need to avoid preoccupation with and involvement in that disturbed and tortured continent, urging that wisdom rather than selfishness suggested the avoidance of entangling commitments. To Smuts, the Far East and the Pacific were now the vital areas and the empire must choose between co-operation in a society of nations and competition in rival groups and exclusive alliances; the former policy would bring peace and the latter, war. Smuts suggested, as a solution to this dilemma, that the imperial meeting lead the world to a conference or a system of conferences where the empire would mediate between east and west.

Smuts had clearly provoked Massey. Deterrent naval power and alliances, not the League, were still the fountains of security, and Massey favoured alliances with France and with Japan, the latter treaty having made possible the recent Australasian war effort. Massey spoke of co-operation with the United States; he would give due consideration to her views, and join with her to prevent war, but Britain could not secure an alliance with the United States and must, therefore, renew the alliance with Japan with whatever modifications seemed necessary.[7] Already, then, by the end of this second session the Atlanticists and their opponents had skirmished and the afternoon meeting added substantive and personal differences.[8] Hughes and Meighen indulged in testy exchanges over Canadian diplomatic representation at Washington and, significantly, Lloyd George issued a gloomy prognosis on the future of the League and of Atlantic co-operation, which Smuts countered in a sanguine expression of faith.

At the fourth and fifth sessions, on 22 June, Curzon reviewed the

7 Sir John Findlay, an elder New Zealand statesman, who had accompanied Premier Sir Joseph Ward to the 1911 Imperial Conference, had also travelled to London to offset Massey's views. Findlay agreed with Meighen and threatened that renewal of the alliance would force New Zealand to leave the empire and seek the protection of the United States. He did not of course participate in the conference and his influence seems minimal (Tate and Fay, 'More Light on the Abrogation of the Anglo-Japanese Alliance,' 541–2).

8 Notes of meeting, E 3, 21 June 1921, Cab. 32/2

spectrum of imperial foreign policy and wasted little time in rejecting Smuts's propositions and in praising the Anglo-Japanese alliance as a factor which enabled Britain to exercise a controlling influence on the 'sometimes dangerous ambitions of Japan.'[9] Curzon then launched into a sustained attack on recent United States policies, denouncing Wilson's administration both for its withdrawal from and its ill-judged sorties into world affairs, and laying the blame for the breakdown in Anglo-American relations squarely at Washington's door. The Middle East, Curzon cited as a typically disastrous American defection, and he pointed to the problems of Yap and cable communications as examples of her lamentable interference. Wilson's foolish policies, Curzon suggested, were responsible for making the United States 'nervous, useless and impotent at the critical period after the war,' but he regarded Harding's administration in a somewhat different light. The Republicans, Curzon felt, would ignore the League but explore the idea of some international association for peace, and would avoid entanglements in Europe but at least participate in certain bodies such as the Supreme Council, the Reparations Commission, and the Conference of Ambassadors. Curzon, therefore, professed to see hopeful signs of future Anglo-American co-operation and looked to limited American help in the task of world reconstruction.

On naval policy, Curzon saw the United States as balancing between completion of the 1916 programme and Senate pressures for a disarmament agreement, but he reported that no approaches had been made or received. On other specific issues he pointed to America's dislike of the Anglo-Japanese alliance, her 'stiff and rather ungenerous' policy on war debts, and to the continued irritation over the Irish question, but in general he returned to the theme of a Republican tendency to rebuild Anglo-American rapport and of the need to reciprocate when Harding made his advances. Curzon concluded with a typical flourish: 'My own belief is that in the troubles and turmoils of the east, if we look to the west and re-establish excellent relations with America, we shall see a dawning of light in a sky which is so overcast in almost every other quarter of the globe.' He had followed his slashing attack on Wilson with some Atlanticist oratory which surely deceived no one about the priorities he preferred. In any case, Churchill dispelled any momentary illusions with a strong denunciation of Wilson's vacillations on the Middle East

9 Notes of meetings, E 4 and E 5, 22 June 1921, Cab. 32/2

and of the 'absolute hiatus' in Washington, and with a derisive and angry attack on the United States' attitude on mandates which he felt reflected a fatuous delusion that the mandate areas were a source of large profit to Britain.

The Imperial Conference did not hold a formal session on Thursday, 23 June, and the significant development of that day took place in Washington where the internationalist secretary of state, Charles Evans Hughes, and Ambassador Geddes met for a prolonged discussion.[10] Geddes announced that Britain would probably retain the alliance for another year to allow further study, and Hughes, in reply, left no doubt that he opposed the retention of the alliance, regarding it as a stimulus to Japan and not as a restraint imposed on her. The Secretary of State described Britain's attitude as vital in the current strained situation with Japan and he looked for British support and co-operation in the execution of American policies in the Far East. Geddes then posed the basic question: would the United States join in tripartite co-operation? Hughes, in reply, rejected any involvement in an alliance, suggesting that co-operation meant the pursuance of common policies, and he looked rather for agreement on ends than on means. Geddes replied that Britain could not discard Japan abruptly, but she need not renew the alliance and he suggested that an exchange of notes as a triple declaration of common policy would be an adequate substitute. Hughes, giving a personal view and being non-committal until he had consulted Harding, stated that if the declared policies complied with those of the United States they would participate. Meanwhile, Geddes could inform London that the United States opposed renewal of the Anglo-Japanese alliance, and Hughes reminded the ambassador that those in Congress who supported Ireland's cause would gain strength from any such renewal.

Hughes then discussed this conversation with assistant secretaries R.W. Bliss and J.V.A. MacMurray and on the following day he informed Geddes that he could report to London that Hughes personally accepted the idea of a triple declaration of policy. The nature of the declaration and its practical application would, however, deter-

10 Memorandum of conversation between Hughes and Geddes, 23 July 1921, Charles Evans Hughes Papers, box 175, folder 76a. This is a more detailed account than the record in FR, 1921, II, 314–16. Hughes wanted greater American participation in world affairs and a multilateral disarmament agreement, and he sought improved Anglo-American and Japanese-American relations. Pusey, *Charles Evans Hughes*, 2 vols; Glad, *Charles Evans Hughes*

A.J. Balfour and C.E. Hughes drive through Washington

mine the attitude of the United States government. Hughes had, therefore, offered the prospect of Anglo-American co-operation as a substitute for the Anglo-Japanese alliance, but he had given no official and definite commitment, he had eliminated the idea of the United States entering an alliance, and he had not resisted the temptation to apply pressure on Britain.

Clearly, the reaction in London to these exchanges would be a vital consideration and Geddes's reports were received on 25 June before the substantive discussions on the renewal question took place in the Imperial Conference. Geddes first reported growing public interest in the whole problem and, as a result of the State Department publicly denying the receipt of any information or assurances from Britain, mounting hostility to the alliance, to Britain, and toward Japan, the inevitable enemy of the future.[11] Geddes then reported specifically on his discussion with Hughes and emphasised that the Secretary of State opposed renewal of the alliance in any form and had denied that the United States would be appeased even by her specific exclusion from the operation of a revised treaty.[12] Geddes gave the impression that Hughes was 'very hopeful' about the idea of a tripartite declaration of policy and concluded with further phrases to emphasise United States hostility to the alliance.

The Imperial Conference resumed its meetings on 24 June with Meighen prominent for the first time.[13] He devoted himself, however,

11 Geddes to Curzon, 24 June 1921 (received 25 June), BD, 1st ser., XIV, no 307, 310–11. For Hughes's public statement, see Hughes to Harvey, 22 June 1921, FR, 1921, II, 313.

12 Geddes to Curzon, 24 June 1921 (received 25 June), BD, 1st ser., XIV, no 308, 311–12. Geddes's report differed from Hughes's own account on two particular points; Geddes said that he explored the idea of the United States signing an identical or similar agreement or treaty with Japan, which Hughes rejected because of Senate opposition to any treaty; and Geddes did not report that he himself raised the idea of a triple declaration of policy embodied in identical notes, leaving the question of initiative somewhat vague. Geddes also omitted any reference to Ireland.

13 Notes of meeting, E 6, 24 June 1921, Cab. 32/2. Here Meighen laid down his three principles, calling for regular or even continuous consultation, the weighing in London of dominion advice, and the recognition of the principle that where a dominion was specifically and heavily involved, its views should receive commensurate attention when the empire debated its policy toward that area.

to the principles which should form the basis of the conduct of imperial foreign policy and of the role that the dominions should play, and he pointed to Canada's special concern and paramount interest in matters relating to the United States as a test case. When the empire debated the question of its relations with America, he expected Canada's views to receive special consideration and he demanded that improved relations with Washington should be 'the pivot of Britain's world policy.' Meighen also demanded that the empire give the fullest support to the League, that they turn away from alliances and groupings and that a dominion could reject obligations entered into by Britain. Such views, clearly the result of Christie's prompting, made an obvious appeal to Smuts, forging a Canadian-South African front against the assault from the Antipodes.

Smuts denied either that he advocated a policy of 'splendid isolation' from Europe or that he condoned recent United States policy, but he confirmed his dislike of an alliance with France and his belief in Atlanticism as the proper basis for imperial foreign policy, whether or not the United States joined the League. Lloyd George and Massey were sceptical about the League's future unless the United States became a member, and Hughes professed to fear both an American attempt to dictate policy and that Britain could secure an agreement with Washington only if she let the United States seize the leadership. Furthermore, Hughes accused Smuts of inconsistency by opposing an alliance with France but proposing ties with the United States. Smuts, in reply, argued that the United States and the empire shared similar positions in world affairs, that their co-operation did not mean American control, but that alignment with France meant entanglement in Europe's internal affairs. Smuts wanted Britain to remove the causes of friction with the United States, to seek a general settlement, create a new atmosphere, and to dedicate herself to Atlanticism as the basic principle of her foreign policy. The world was bankrupt and half mad, Smuts asserted, the empire must make a fundamental strategic decision about policy, but his critics were unmoved.

At the next session, following the weekend recess, Lloyd George, primed by Grigg and Hankey, rejected Meighen's principles, singling out as dangerous the idea that a dominion or Britain herself should have a decisive voice on any issue in which she had special interests, and then he attacked Smuts's views on Europe.[14] Churchill and

14 Notes of meeting, E 7, 27 June 1921, Cab. 32/2; Hankey to Lloyd George,

Chamberlain supported Lloyd George with gestures of Anglo-French solidarity, Meighen rallied to Smuts, and the meeting decided to discuss the Anglo-Japanese alliance on the following morning.[15] Curzon, with Geddes's reports of 24 June received and digested, presented his arguments for and against the renewal of the alliance and the proposals adopted by the cabinet on 30 May.[16] He confirmed the urgency of the matter, although expressing optimism about the negotiations for a three-month extension with Japan,[17] and turned to the vital question of Washington's attitude. Curzon insisted that Secretary of State Hughes was aware of Britain's interpretation of article four of the 1911 treaty, excluding the United States from its operation, but that the American press and public opinion were more extreme than just in their reactions. Geddes, in November 1920, had advised retention of the alliance, but just prior to the conference he had reported that Hughes would regard renewal as disastrous and his most recent despatches were even less encouraging. Hughes had discussed with Geddes the idea of a tripartite declaration of policy in identical notes, but there the matter rested and Curzon saw neither a concrete offer nor any commitment from Washington.[18]

25 June 1921, Lloyd George Papers, F/25/1/48, and Grigg to Lloyd George, 26 June 1921, Grigg Papers, reel 11

15 Notes of meeting, E 8, 28 June 1921, Cab. 32/2. Lloyd George arrived late, having dealt with the coal crisis.

16 Curzon, however, made no mention, as he had on 30 May, of the United States using popular opposition to the alliance as an excuse for naval construction and he made much more of racial considerations in his speech to the imperial meeting.

17 The extension would remove the 13 July deadline and give Britain until 13 October to settle the alliance question. Interestingly enough, Meighen, foreshadowing Birkenhead's ruling, expressed the view that the alliance was self-perpetuating and did not need renewal, but Curzon insisted on the reverse interpretation.

18 Curzon was absolutely frank in his comments on Geddes's telegrams of 24 June and obviously he did not feel that Hughes had offered a tripartite pact or a clear commitment. J.C. Vinson's view thus exaggerates the categorical nature of Hughes's reply to Geddes and misinterprets the reception given Geddes's reports in London. The debates at the imperial meeting were still sharp and urgent, wide differences of view and of orders of priority still existed, and the Atlanticists' task was still formidable (Vinson, 'The Imperial conference of 1921,' 257–66).

On the question of Asian opinion, Curzon ridiculed B.L. Simpson, gave guarded praise to Japan, and mixed contempt with sympathy for China, while admitting that they must consider Peking's views and co-operate with the United States in China's economic development.[19] He also suggested consultations with the United States and the need to meet their obligations under the League Covenant, but, predictably, he favoured the case for renewal. He emphasised the past value of the alliance, dwelt on the possibility of a future Russo-German menace, and applauded Japan's reasonableness in their negotiations, a fact which contrasted sharply with the humiliation, anger, and resentment which Japan would feel should Britain rebuff her. He personally disliked the prospect of severing links with a faithful and valuable ally and he did not regard the need to improve Anglo-American relations as a justifiable reason for doing so. Moreover, the alliance soothed racial antagonisms, offered prestige to the Asians, increased the self-respect of non-white peoples, and helped to remove prejudice. In Curzon's opinion, the alliance was an asset of considerable value, the War Office, the Admiralty, Hughes and Massey agreed, but Meighen opposed renewal and suggested a Pacific conference. Curzon acknowledged that Meighen's proposal had considerable support but he felt the scheme might be consistent with renewal.

The Foreign Secretary then considered the alternative courses of action. He opposed both abrogation of the alliance and its perpetuation amended merely to accommodate the League, India, and the United States. Curzon did not regard a triple agreement as practicable and he also dismissed it as vulnerable to United States senatorial and public opinion and as dependent on continued favourable results in American presidential elections. Consequently, the Foreign Office favoured renewal in a different form, after consultation with the League, China, and the United States, and proposed that Britain simultaneously express a willingness to join the United States in a Pacific conference. This conference, according to Curzon, would obviously be far-reaching and protracted. Before it convened, therefore, Britain must sign a new four- or five-year treaty with Japan, fully acceptable to the United States, China, and the League, and

19 Simpson was a man 'of doubtful character and antecedents'; the Japanese had great intellectual gifts, resolution, order, discipline, and a fierce patriotism, but were rather unscrupulous, expansive, aggressive, and Germanic; China was a hopeless, inert, and impotent mass.

with provision for the adherence of the United States.[20] Curzon added that the cabinet favoured this policy and did not feel that Geddes's recent telegrams altered the situation.

Churchill did not agree with Curzon's last point but Balfour reinforced the Foreign Secretary's analysis with the familiar and simple proposition that naval unpreparedness dictated that Britain retain the alliance with Japan just as it demanded the construction of the Singapore naval base. Moreover, Balfour, impressed with Beneš's recent scheme for a Central European entente in harmony with a revised League Covenant, argued that Britain could negotiate an effective defensive and benign alliance, offending neither the League nor anyone but 'an embittered controversialist.' On that apparently hopeful note the meeting adjourned, with Lloyd George to return to the coal crisis and Curzon to see Ambassador Harvey that afternoon before the next session of the Imperial Conference.

Curzon, in his conversation with Harvey, intended to clarify the position of the United States but in fact their discussion became a source of confusion.[21] Curzon, attempting to distinguish between governmental views and those of the press, asked Harvey whether the mere fact of renewal, apart from the form, would likely meet with a necessarily unfavourable response from Washington. Harvey, according to Curzon, assured him that he need entertain no such fears, that the views of the press were not those of the administration, and that the United States would respectfully examine any decision reached by Britain. Curzon then speculated on the possibility of broadening a naval disarmament conference into one covering all issues related to the Pacific and especially to China, and Harvey again gave an encouraging reply. Curzon concluded from

20 Curzon, memorandum on the alliance, 28 June 1921, E 21, Cab. 32/6. This
   course of action was alternative A, which Curzon preferred, and he pointed
   out that renewal would be independent of the Pacific conference but not inconsistent with it. Scheme B, which Curzon did not recommend, suggested a
   temporary renewal of the existing alliance, brought into line with the League
   Covenant and omitting any reference to India. The renewal period would be
   one year from October 1921, and the Pacific conference would meet in the
   intervening period.
21 Curzon to Geddes, 29 June 1921, BD, 1st ser., XIV, no 313, 316–18, and Cab.
   32/6. Harvey, appointed ambassador as a reward for his political services to
   Harding, did not enjoy Hughes's confidence and was hardly a model of
   reliability.

this conversation that Washington's reaction to his policy would be a favourable one and he professed to see few obstacles, but clearly he had paid insufficient attention to Harvey's cautionary words that he had received no instructions from Hughes and that the United States did not intend to take the initiative. Consequently, Meighen could differ in his interpretation of this conversation, Geddes's next reports seemed to conflict with Harvey's views, and the American ambassador's reliability, status, and even his veracity were questioned amid much irritation and confusion.[22]

On the following morning the Imperial Conference reassembled for a session which Meighen dominated to a large extent.[23] He confirmed Canada's opposition to renewal of the alliance in any form, and gave a detailed rebuttal of Curzon's analysis. The alliance had not preserved peace, and he cited as evidence the Russo-Japanese war; no menace actually existed from Russia and Germany, and Britain could not renew the alliance on the speculative possibility of their resurgence, whether singly or in combination, and, indeed, renewal would invite such a development; Japan was not a loyal ally and Meighen sarcastically indicted Japan for exceeding her rights, violating her covenants, committing acts of aggrandizement, and being prepared to repeat the performance in the next twenty years with the alliance providing similar restraints. Clearly, in Meighen's opinion, the alliance had not deterred Japan, and renewal would make Britain a willing accomplice and lower her prestige. Moreover, China opposed renewal and yet the avowed aim of the alliance was the preservation of her integrity. In addition, Meighen claimed, an alliance modified to accommodate the League, China, and the United States would be superfluous, and exclusive treaties merely subverted the League, stimulated counter-arrangements, and encouraged a revival of the dangerous situation existing before 1914. Meighen could not accept the dangers incurred by the loss of Japan's friendship and her possible orientation toward Russia and Germany as valid reasons for renewal. He emphasised rather the loss of China's friendship and the danger that renewal would ensure that the United

22 Johnson, *George Harvey*, 325; Pusey, *Hughes*, II, 493; Butler, *Across The Busy Years*, II, 124–34. Johnson concluded that Harvey had expressed ignorance of Washington's attitude, but that he felt the United States opposed renewal.

23 Notes of meeting, E 9, 29 June 1921, Cab. 32/2

States achieved a monopoly of China's commercial and financial development.

Moreover, Meighen asserted, the alliance would prevent an improvement in Anglo-American relations, and Canada wished neither to suffer because of a deterioration in those relations nor to become another 'Belgium' in the event of war. If British policy really pivoted on the maintenance of 'Atlantic harmony,' then Britain must judge all major issues in the light of her relations with the United States. In Meighen's view, any exclusive arrangement with Japan would jeopardise Anglo-American accord, anger American public opinion, encourage every anglophobe, and would be regarded as a provocative rebuff to the United States. He dismissed the proposal for special provisions or exemptions for the United States as inadequate and regarded Japan's desire to retain the alliance despite the probability of such exemptions as curious and sinister. Japan required, Meighen felt, to secure Britain's support in Asia, her benevolent neutrality in the event of war with the United States, and then Britain's aid at the peace table.

The United States, Meighen assured the meeting, looked for fresh approaches, a new atmosphere prevailed in Washington, and Harding's administration expected the Imperial Conference to provide a lead. Britain should not demand a naval disarmament agreement as the prerequisite for abrogating the alliance with Japan, for renewal would provoke a naval race whereas termination would produce an agreement on armaments. Meighen challenged Britain's priorities and rejected the idea that Japan would be estranged by non-renewal, for Canada wished to replace the alliance with a tripartite agreement affording equal treatment to all signatories. Furthermore, Canada would not participate in a renewal of the Anglo-Japanese alliance aimed at 'a menace' from the United States. Meighen regretted that Britain had opposed Canada's idea of sounding out the United States prior to the imperial meeting to see whether Washington would welcome a Pacific conference, and he charged that Britain had bungled the whole affair. In consequence, the imperial meeting did not know whether the United States would accept a Pacific conference and join in the search for a tripartite agreement, and Britain faced the stark alternatives of renewal or termination of the alliance by 13 July.

This accusation produced quibbling exchanges on the validity of the 13 July deadline and the proposed three-months' extension to the alliance, and Meighen then demanded immediate negotiations with the United States and any other interested power to secure an agreement or an exchange of notes by 13 July.[24] He rejected any plan for renewal followed by an approach to Washington and urged acceptance of the fact that renewal was untenable and that a conference must be convened. He then called on Geddes's recent reports to support his own position and focussed the discussion on the double duets, involving Geddes and Hughes in Washington and Harvey and Curzon in London, as competing sources of reliability. Meighen clearly preferred the former as the more accurate source of information on American policies and he would admit no possibility of reconciliation between the conflicting reports. Curzon, while accepting that Harvey and Geddes disagreed, rejected Meighen's assessment; Harvey, sent to London specifically to secure closer Anglo-American co-operation, had had ample opportunity to state that his government would not tolerate renewal, and yet, on the contrary, Harvey seemed to think that renewal was the most natural course of action. Curzon and Meighen could not even agree on the significance of various signs of American friendship. To Curzon they indicated that Washington would accept renewal, but to Meighen they demonstrated that Britain must not rebuff the United States by renewal and must encourage her participation in a triple understanding.

Balfour then came to the point; had Meighen any evidence that the United States would enter a tripartite agreement? Meighen hedged; he could have been more definite had they allowed Borden to sound out opinion in Washington, but, on balance, he felt that the United States would join in a broad inclusive arrangement that was neither a formal nor a rigid treaty. There Meighen rested his case, having presented it with great force and some skill and having emerged beyond Smuts as the most formidable Atlanticist voice, but his efforts provoked a violent attack from Billy Hughes, challenging and at times distorting Meighen's proposals.

In Hughes's opinion, the facts were clear until Meighen spoke, and yet the Canadian Premier, without justification and in defiance of Curzon's reports, had merely stated that they must not renew the alliance because the United States was opposed. Meighen claimed a special understanding of American opinion, seemed willing to ignore

24 Although the negotiations with Japan for an extension were incomplete, Curzon claimed that they had until 13 October to decide on a policy. Meighen opposed even the three-months' extension and claimed, wrongly so, that Britain had not consulted Canada on that question.

Ambassador Harvey, was excessively attuned to his North American environment, and he appeared ready to permit the United States to dictate the empire's policies. Hughes, in contrast, would not toe Washington's line, Meighen's voice must not outweigh his, especially as Australia's security rather than that of Canada was directly involved. The United States, Hughes emphasised, had contemptuously rejected her own creation, the League, and was constructing immense naval forces, and he could see no evidence either that she would discuss disarmament or discontinue her naval programme. To Hughes, the United States, refusing to respond to British initiatives on disarmament, was an irresponsible and militarist power, and he rejected Meighen's view that renewal of the alliance with Japan would destroy the prospects for a disarmament agreement. Furthermore, he denied that Meighen really had an alternative to renewal. Australia, naturally, would prefer the United States to Japan as an ally, but the choice did not exist. Washington offered only the shadow and not the substance and in particular offered no aid to Australia's security. Meighen, Hughes charged, ignored the two fundamental facts: America's real objection to the alliance lay in her fear of Japan and, secondly, deep hatred of Britain existed among certain sections of American opinion. Hughes warned against delay, Britain could not achieve a disarmament agreement, imperial security was the acid test, and they must renew the Anglo-Japanese alliance.[25]

When the conference resumed that afternoon Hughes returned to the attack.[26] Japan had rendered indispensable service during the war and, had she joined Germany, the Central Powers would have emerged victorious. Meighen had failed to make a case against the alliance, Balfour had shown that they could renew it in a way compatible with the League, and he personally regarded the alliance as consistent with the League, with Anglo-American friendship, and with disarmament. They must reject the suspicions and hostilities of the voice of the people of America as invoked by Meighen and, instead, heed the words of Harvey. In any case, Hughes asserted, Britain's rejection of Japan would not convert the American hymn of hate, swelled by the bitter and irreconcilable Irish question, into a song of eternal friendship. Rather, Britain's capitulation to American

25 At this point, Lloyd George interrupted Hughes and suggested that it would be as well for Meighen, who had gone to lunch with the Prince of Wales, to hear the indictment.
26 Notes of meeting, E 10, 29 June 1921, Cab. 32/2

pressure would merely earn the empire contempt and cost them prestige and respect. The empire, Hughes demanded, must formulate its policies without weakness or vacillation, with faith in its cause and in the justice of its motives, but with due regard for and in consultation with the United States. They could neither risk isolation nor court the enmity of Japan at a time of strategic vulnerability. In conclusion, Hughes denied that the United States would ally with Britain, join the League, disarm, or defend China and Meighen's conference offered little comfort, whereas the Japanese alliance offered concrete and proven advantages.

Hughes had been repetitious but forceful, opting for the potentially menacing Japan rather than the unreliable United States, and Smuts then re-entered the debate. In his view, they must avoid a rebuff to Japan and secure the correct basic alignment in policy which, for himself and Meighen, meant a new bout of co-operation with the United States. Smuts attempted to merge the alliance question with all the other issues in Anglo-American relations, calling for a general settlement rather than a piecemeal approach to each separate issue. This course of action suggested a triple declaration of policy in identical notes drawn up at a three-power conference. Smuts agreed with Meighen that Geddes's reports indicated that Secretary of State Hughes would join in negotiations and that Harvey's conversation with Curzon showed that Hughes would go beyond disarmament talks. In conclusion, Smuts advocated non-renewal of the alliance and the pursuit of a triple entente by way of a Pacific conference. Lloyd George suggested that Curzon's 'Plan B'[27] would serve the same purpose and Smuts agreed, providing they inform both the United States and Japan that Britain desired a triple entente.

After further irresolute and even confused debate on the meaning and value of the Curzon-Harvey conversation, Massey spoke in support of Hughes and opposed renewal for a mere twelve-month period to permit a conference to meet.[28] They must renew the alliance forth-

27 See note 20

28 Curzon admitted that Harvey had not spoken officially on behalf of the United States government and Chamberlain felt that Harvey had been more favourable to renewal than had Hughes. Meighen and Smuts applauded Geddes's reports because they emphasized American hostility to renewal and the possibility of American participation in a triple agreement. Curzon and Hughes preferred Harvey's comments which suggested that the United States would

with as the foundation of the empire's policy despite the need to consult the United States. Massey feared the possibility of war between Japan and the United States and the outbreak of serious racial conflicts. Moreover, he expressed doubts about the future stability of a state so racially diffuse as America. He also referred to a secret source of information, indicating that the United States sought to control the Pacific and wean Canada, Australia, and New Zealand away from the empire, a prospect which attracted neither himself nor Hughes.[29]

Massey continued at the next session very much in the same vein and was followed by the Maharaja of Cutch.[30] While accepting a triple understanding as ideal, he supported renewal of an alliance with Japan, modified so as to omit any reference to India, for the empire must not discard Japan to court the United States. Lloyd George then made a major contribution for the first time since the opening session and his speech reflected a cabinet discussion that had taken place earlier that day.[31]

Curzon, summarising the views of the dominions for the cabinet, had expressed surprise at the vigour and extent of Meighen's attack and reported that Hughes had met Meighen head on, with Smuts, both helpful and embarrassing, balancing between them. Curzon conceded that Geddes's reports showed that renewal of the alliance would have a serious effect on United States opinion and that the Senate would not ratify a triple alliance, but that a declaration of policy in an exchange of identical notes was possible. Curzon, however, felt that Japan would not accept an exchange of notes as a substitute for the alliance. They must clarify further the views of Japan and the United States and they should suspend debate at the Imperial Conference until he had interviewed Harvey and Hayashi.

The cabinet, after speculating on the possibilities of war between Japan and the United States and between Japan and the empire, examined the merits of a diplomatic approach to secure both a defensive alliance with Japan relating to China and the Far East, and a tri-

not object to renewal. Harvey had also, however, supported the idea of a conference, encouraging Meighen and Smuts to some degree, and hence the discussion on the relative value of Anglo-American exchanges in London and Washington could become confused and cyclical.

29 Although Massey made no specific revelations at the meeting, the Lodge-Gardiner policy seemed to have surfaced again.

30 Notes of meeting, E 11, 30 June 1921, Cab. 32/2

31 Minutes of cabinet meeting, 30 June 1921, Cab. 23/26

partite agreement to cover the Pacific and provide for the security of Australia. Lloyd George, in summary, insisted on certain points as fundamental: Britain could neither quarrel with the United States nor insult Japan and a settlement of the Yap controversy might moderate Washington's opposition to the alliance; the empire must secure China's support for any new arrangement, particularly as they could not permit the United States to gain control of the lucrative China market; and the ruling that the joint Anglo-Japanese note to the League was an act of denunciation presented the immediate problem to which the cabinet must find a solution by reversing or withdrawing the legal opinion. Meighen, as Lloyd George pointed out, would then be forced to demand denunciation and not merely non-renewal of the alliance, abrogation would become the immediate issue, and a conference would provide the solution. The Premier's ingenuity clearly appealed to his colleagues and, after consulting Lord Birkenhead, the cabinet agreed to propose to the imperial meeting that Curzon sound out Harvey and Hayashi. Meanwhile, Birkenhead would prepare himself to reverse the ruling on the joint note to the League in order to remove pressing deadlines and avoid the need for a three-months' extension of the alliance.

Lloyd George then went to the Imperial Conference to show how they could reconcile the views of Meighen and Hughes and avoid a choice between Japan and the United States. Despite attempting mediation and indulging in some Atlanticist oratory, however, he still denied that renewal of the alliance would create a quarrel with the United States, and insisted that a refusal to renew would provoke a breach with Japan, indicating that he regarded Hughes's case as the stronger. In Lloyd George's view, the empire must not rebuff her gallant if opportunistic ally, they must behave like gentlemen, divest themselves of the view that war between Japan and the United States was inevitable, preserve Britain's position in China, and consult Washington and Peking. He favoured a Pacific conference to establish common ground between Japan and the United States, and this conference would have ample time to meet as Britain now accepted the Japanese view that they had not shown intent to denounce their alliance. Birkenhead dutifully gave his ruling, the alliance was self-perpetuating, Meighen was deflated, and Lloyd George contentedly suggested that they study the broad issues of policy in the light of the Pacific conference proposal while giving Meighen a chance to reconsider his position.

Lloyd George seemed satisfied that he had cooled Meighen's ardour and lowered the temperature of the meeting, and the renewed Canadian offensive on the following day must have been as unpleasant as it was unexpected.[32] Meighen attacked both Hughes's misrepresentation of Canada's position and Lloyd George's apparent acquiescence in the falsification. He had not suggested that they rebuff Japan so as to court the United States, he had not proposed ungentlemanly conduct, and he was not the 'voice of America.' Meighen, turning to the new situation created by Birkenhead's decision, suggested that before 13 July they must remodel the alliance to meet their obligations under the League Covenant and the wishes of India, limit its life-span to one year, and call a Pacific conference. This conference, completing its work in 1921, Meighen suggested, should create a four-power understanding, embracing the former allies, the United States, and China, which would then replace the alliance.

Lloyd George, in reply, continued to preach reconciliation, but he could not accept the idea of placing a one-year time limit on the alliance. They must leave the treaty untouched except for modifications to accommodate the League and seek a permanent solution at the Pacific conference. Meighen and Lloyd George were, therefore, still opposed and a debate ensued, becoming less coherent with constant repetition of positions which the advocate thought consistent and his audience clearly did not, and in which Hughes still proposed renewal when everyone else realised that renewal was no longer the issue and opposed the idea of a conference when everyone else agreed that a conference was desirable. Finally, Hughes demanded that the Imperial Conference itself decide without delay on renewal and then, but only then, would he accept a Pacific conference.

Curzon, to restore symmetry and coherence, proposed a five-point plan of procedure: inform Japan of Birkenhead's new ruling and assure her that the alliance remained in force; notify the League that they hoped to deal with Far Eastern and Pacific questions on a larger plane and in harmony with the Covenant, and that meanwhile they recognised the pre-eminence of the Covenant over the alliance;[33] sound out Japan, China, and the United States on the question of a Pacific conference and, as the fourth step, report back to the imperial

32 Notes of meeting, E 12, 1 July 1921, Cab. 32/2
33 Curzon to Hayashi, 2 July 1921, BD, 1st ser., XIV, no 320, 322

meeting; and finally, reaffirm that Britain would not renounce her alliance with Japan until the Pacific conference had reached a settlement or a new treaty had emerged to replace the alliance. The inference was clear; should the conference fail, the modified alliance would continue in force and naturally Hughes was quick to applaud. Meighen, however, could express only partial assent, for Curzon's compromise lost its impartiality by the wording of the fifth proposal. Equally, Smuts disliked the specific emphasis on the need to perpetuate the alliance should the conference fail, for this proposal would hand the initiative to Japan who could wreck the Pacific conference at will, secure in the knowledge that her alliance with Britain remained intact.

Continuing on the same theme at the afternoon meeting, Smuts proposed the omission of Curzon's fifth point, Hughes and Massey insisted that this proposal was the only basis on which they would agree to a Pacific conference, and Lloyd George continued to conciliate while favouring the Australian attitude.[34] Meighen joined Smuts in demanding that they leave all options open in case the conference failed and avoid any commitment to Japan which would make her the arbiter, for he did not agree that Tokyo really preferred a triple arrangement as Lloyd George suggested. Moreover, Meighen did not see how Curzon could approach the respective ambassadors with a supposedly agreed imperial policy; Curzon's further assurance to Hughes that Britain would retain the alliance if the Pacific conference failed, whether the meeting accepted his fifth proposal or not, seemed to confirm Meighen's view. However, the premiers agreed that Curzon should see the ambassadors and Meighen was left to draw comfort from assurances of an opportunity for further debate.

At this point, on Friday, 1 July, the Imperial Conference turned the alliance question over to Curzon and did not formally debate the matter again until 8 July. Curzon, still plagued by the confusing disparities between the views of Harvey and Geddes,[35] met Hayashi on 4 July and assured him that Britain would not denounce the alliance

34 Notes of meeting, E 13, 1 July 1921, Cab. 32/2

35 Geddes to Curzon, 2 July 1921, BD, 1st ser., XIV, no 317, 320 and FO/414/248.
Geddes, to correct Harvey, insisted that Hughes disliked the prospect of any exclusive Anglo-Japanese agreement, that the Washington press was privy to Hughes's attitude, and that Harvey did not enjoy Hughes's confidence. Crowe, noting that Geddes's views changed with 'bewildering intensity,' was sceptical of the value of his reports and Curzon did not disagree with Crowe.

without good cause and without an acceptable substitute.[36] However, despite their determination to permit no deterioration in Anglo-Japanese relations, the government, Curzon explained, must seek a more satisfactory and broader solution to allay the fears of the dominions, China, and the United States. The imperial meeting favoured a course of action whereby the United States, prompted by Britain, would call a Pacific conference to be held in America and Curzon asked for Japan's approval.[37] Hayashi, while expressing doubts on the participation of China, agreed to recommend Curzon's proposal to Tokyo and the Foreign Secretary responded by assuring Hayashi that while he hoped they could replace the alliance with a broader agreement, he still wanted the old allies to walk side by side in Asia.

Curzon then met with Wellington Koo and, though they succeeded in irritating each other, both seemed sure that China would accept the Pacific conference proposal.[38] On the following day Curzon discussed the whole question with Harvey, reporting the favourable response of Hayashi and Wellington Koo, and proposing that Harvey immediately consult with and ask his government to call a Pacific conference in the fall or winter.[39] Harvey, in response, seemed sanguine enough and even anxious to avoid any delay. Curzon concluded their interview by emphasising that the Anglo-Japanese alliance's value and relevance was not confined to the Pacific and that, whatever the outcome of the proposed conference, Britain wished to maintain close relations with Japan and avoid racial divisions.

Curzon, in the course of these meetings, had attempted faithfully to interpret the will of the Imperial Conference and to capture its nuances and emphases. A flurry of information followed from Washington which, if not uniformly encouraging, at least clarified the

36 Curzon to Eliot, 4 July 1921, King Papers, file 1176, and Curzon to Eliot, 8 July 1921, BD, 1st ser., XIV, no 328, 331–4

37 The conference would include the United States, Japan, China, Britain, and the dominions, and possibly France and the South American countries. Details of the participants, the venue, and the convener were not included in Curzon's five-point proposal of 1st July and were still somewhat vague.

38 Curzon to Alston, 4 July 1921, King Papers, file 1176, and Cab. 32/6, and Curzon to Alston, 8 July 1921, BD, 1st ser., XIV, no 327, 329–31

39 Curzon to Geddes, 5 July 1921, King Papers, file 1176, and Cab. 32/6, and Curzon to Geddes, 9 July, 1921, BD, 1st ser., XIV, no 330, 336–8

major outstanding problem.[40] Secretary of State Hughes, undermining the value of the Curzon-Harvey discussions, confirmed that he had not communicated in any way before 7 July with Harvey on the question of America's attitude to the alliance. Moveover, the United States government, as the press knew, irrevocably opposed the alliance or any special relationship between Britain and Japan. Hughes, insisting on secrecy and irritated by press revelations in London that Britain, Japan, and the United States had already agreed on a declaration of policy to replace the alliance, applauded, however, the idea of a Pacific conference. He had informed Harvey on 7 July that he would probably welcome British proposals to replace the alliance with a triple declaration of policy.[41] In addition, Geddes reported, Hughes felt that the problem of naval armaments might be investigated along with detailed questions such as cable communications, and, in Geddes's opinion, settlement of political and economic questions was the necessary prerequisite to a naval armaments agreement. The Irish question remained, however, according to Geddes, as a major obstacle either to a political detente or an armaments settlement with the United States.[42]

After an interval of one week the Imperial Conference returned to the alliance question to study the results of Curzon's endeavours.[43] Hughes, supported by Massey, appeared distinctly unhappy at Cur-

40 Geddes to Curzon, 6, 7, and 8 July 1921, BD, 1st ser., XIV, no 323, 326, no 325, 327, no 326, 328–9, and no 329, 334–6, and FO/414/248. Although Washington's attitude was clarified, a flurry of charges and counter-charges between the participants continued to complicate the scene. Geddes accused Hughes of a monstrous breach of conduct and of sending inaccurate reports to Harvey, and felt that both Harding and Hughes welcomed the opportunity to embarrass their own ambassador; Harvey complained of Geddes's report of 6 July to Hughes which suggested that the ambassador had misled Curzon.

41 This policy statement, Hughes envisaged, would seek to secure the territorial integrity of all Pacific states, to underwrite the Open Door and the principle of equal commercial and economic opportunity in China and the Pacific, and possibly to extend financial and development aid to Pacific states in addition to China.

42 On 8 July a truce was declared in Ireland and no doubt helped create a more favourable atmosphere.

43 Notes of meeting, E 20, 8 July 1921, Cab. 32/2. One curious point was Curzon's statement that Harvey had proposed that the United States call the Pacific conference to meet in Havana.

zon's alleged misrepresentation of their views, but this was a calculated outburst to secure an unequivocal assurance on the self-perpetuating nature of the alliance. Meighen defended Curzon, despite the fact that he personally had really opposed and had acquiesced only reluctantly in the instructions given the Foreign Secretary on 1 July. Hughes, however, succeeded in reinforcing his tactical position, for the meeting reconfirmed that the alliance would continue if the Pacific conference failed. On this crucial point, contemporary opinion and historical judgments led by J.B. Brebner have misinterpreted the will of the Imperial Conference.[44] The meeting had not abrogated the Anglo-Japanese alliance and Hughes rather than Meighen had won an immediate tactical victory, as Lloyd George confirmed officially on at least two subsequent occasions.[45]

This meeting had taken place on the Friday afternoon, that weekend the premiers retired to Chequers, and by Monday, 11 July, Secretary of State Hughes and Lloyd George had laid the basis for the Washington Conference amid an unseemly Anglo-American scramble to secure the initiative, further charges of bad faith, and more confusion. The evidence is not entirely consistent. From the British side, Curzon noted his conversation with Harvey of 5 July, where he had urged the Ambassador to approach Washington without delay on the Pacific conference proposal, but made no reference to a second meeting on 7 July.[46] Harvey, failing to report to Hughes until the evening of 8 July, noted a conversation with Curzon on 5 July but claimed that Curzon had denied the need for urgency, and that only at a second meeting on 7 July, with Lloyd George facing parliamentary scrutiny, had Curzon pressed the matter.[47] Lloyd George's

44 Gratton O'Leary, *MacLeans*, 1 Sept. 1921, and Brebner, 'Canada, the Anglo-Japanese Alliance and the Washington Conference,' 52. Both Borden and Meighen assured Brebner that his article was accurate but, Canadian nationalists not withstanding, Hughes's own account seems stronger on this particular issue (Hughes, *The Splendid Adventure*, 126–31).

45 Minutes of informal meetings of prime ministers, E 31 B, 12 July 1921, Cab. 32/4, and Lloyd George, statement, House of Commons, 18 August 1921, *Debates*, 5 ser., CXLVI (1921), 1697–1708

46 See note 39. Surely Curzon would have reported a significant, subsequent meeting to Geddes or to the Imperial Conference; Harvey in fact met Lloyd George and Curzon for dinner on Friday, 8 July, immediately prior to the weekend at Chequers; see note 55.

47 Harvey to Hughes; 8:00 pm, 8 July 1921, FR, 1921, I, 19–21

generally worded statement in the House of Commons on 7 July and an interpretative report in *The Times* on the following day seemed to arouse American suspicions. Harvey, viewing the matter as one of prestige and kudos, advised that Harding forestall Lloyd George, avoid any appearance of acting at Britain's instigation, and secure instead a situation where London acquiesced in Washington's leadership.[48]

Secretary of State Hughes, flooded with rumours but without word from Harvey, and even though he had just insisted that initiatives on the question of the Anglo-Japanese alliance and a Pacific conference must come from London, decided to act to ensure that the United States would issue the call for the disarmament conference which Congress demanded. Four hours before Harvey reported from London, Hughes cabled his principal ambassadors inquiring whether the powers would accept an invitation to a disarmament conference.[49] On 9 July, Hughes proposed to broaden the scope of the conference to include Pacific and Far Eastern problems and urged Harvey to secure British approval before Harding issued a public statement on 11 July.[50] Harvey carried out this mission on 10 July with some success, Lloyd George and the Foreign Office reluctantly and publicly surrendering the initiative, but the magnitude of Harvey's task is difficult to assess especially as a personal victory would seem all the greater if the struggle at Chequers with Lloyd George were exaggerated. Harvey claimed to have enlisted the support of King George v to assert pressure through Curzon[51] and told H. Wickham Steed of *The Times* that his delivery of Hughes's note to Chequers on 10 July

48 Lloyd George, statement, House of Commons, 7 July 1921, *Debates*, 5 ser., CXLVI (1921), 621–3; Harvey to Hughes, 9 July 1921, FR, 1921, I, 22–3. Confusion arose as to whether Lloyd George had suggested that Britain awaited replies from the United States, Japan, and China to a Pacific conference proposal. Lloyd George was scheduled to speak to parliament on 11 July and Harvey hoped to secure recognition of United States initiative before then.

49 Hughes to Harvey, 4:00 pm, 8 July 1921, FR, 1921, I, 18, and Hughes's memorandum on the calling of the Washington Conference, Hughes Papers, box 169, folder 3

50 Hughes to Harding, 9 July 1921, and Hughes to Harvey, 9 July 1921, FR, 1921, I, 21–4

51 Johnson, *George Harvey*, 323–4. Geddes dismissed this claim as absurd. Geddes to Curzon, 31 July 1921, BD, 1st ser., XIV, no 347, 361–2

forestalled a plot to issue invitations to a conference from London.[52] Wickham Steed, clearly better informed by Harvey than was the Foreign Office by Geddes of Hughes's intentions, told A.W.A. Leeper that the party at Chequers and Lord Riddell had bombarded him on 10 July with claims that credit for the proposed conference should be awarded to Lloyd George.[53] Whatever the details, clearly a squabble over prestige and leadership had ensued, Hughes had out-manoeuvred the British government, and contentment reigned in Washington as the world acclaimed Harding.

Irritation was more in evidence, however, in London, where Lloyd George reported to parliament on 11 July and the Imperial Conference reconvened at noon that day to assess the new situation.[54] Confusion mounted on irritation, more charges of bad faith were levelled and, significantly, at the very moment of public agreement a new bout of Anglo-American friction developed over the question of a preliminary conference. Lloyd George, stating that Harvey had agreed to a Pacific conference meeting prior to and at a different location from the disarmament conference and having a different composition, initiated the fracas, and assumed that adequate Japanese representation at the preliminary conference was the major problem, not United States agreement.[55] Obviously the British government, perhaps misled by Harvey, piqued, or merely confused, sought to elevate political over armaments questions and the imperial meet-

52 Steed, *Through Thirty Years, 1892–1922*, II, 362–4. Harvey had dinner at Chequers on 10 July along with the dominion premiers.

53 Leeper to Curzon, 10 and 11 July 1921, FO/800/329. The Foreign Office did not know whether Lloyd George had approached Harvey personally or whether Geddes had reported direct to Lloyd George, for they had received nothing from Geddes since 8 July. Vansittart minuted that, strangely enough, Geddes had sent nothing to them at that time.

54 Notes of meeting, E 21, 11 July 1921, Cab. 32/2

55 Hughes had specifically broadened the scope of his proposed conference on 9 July and yet both Lloyd George and Curzon, pointing to Harvey's assurances given on 8 July at dinner, assumed that Washington was merely concerned over the question of initiative. Lloyd George wanted the Pacific conference, comprising the empire, Japan, China, and the United States to meet in London before the dominion leaders dispersed and he expected the disarmament conference to meet later that year in Washington, with France and Italy replacing China.

ing debated the time and place of a preliminary Pacific conference, deciding on London before the end of August.[56]

The Imperial Conference also approved a draft of Lloyd George's statement to the House of Commons which, important for its tone and somewhat misleading in its content, publicly launched the controversy over the preliminary conference proposal.[57] The details of this controversy are much less important than the immediate damage to Anglo-American relations, just when the Irish issue was abating somewhat and should have resulted in a diminution of scepticism and hostility on both sides of the Atlantic. Curzon attempted to insist on the preliminary Pacific conference as vital to the success of any disarmament talks, raising his expectations to the point of hoping that Hughes or Harding might travel to London. Hughes, however, would entertain no such prospect, insisting that Pacific, Far Eastern, and disarmament questions were an integrated whole and must be discussed as such, and his suspicions reached the level of suggesting that Britain's preliminary conference proposal was a mere device to postpone the disarmament conference.[58] Hughes, therefore, remained

56 In a somewhat unreal and even frivolous atmosphere the dominion leaders discussed London, various places in the United States, Canada, Hawaii, Bermuda, Panama, and Cuba as possible locations, and even explored the idea of a Pacific conference in Washington followed by a disarmament conference in Europe.

57 Lloyd George, statement, House of Commons, 11 July 1921, *Debates*, 5 ser., cxlvi (1921), 914–19. The Premier emphasised the role of the Imperial Conference in initiating the steps leading to Harding's invitation and pointed out that Britain retained her alliance with Japan in the absence of any denunciation.

58 Curzon to Geddes, 14 and 16 July 1921, BD, 1st ser., xiv, no 335, 342–6, Cab. 32/6, and King Papers, file 1176; Curzon memorandum, 24 July 1921, on the situation re proposed conference at Washington, BD, 1st ser., xiv, no 337, 345–51, Cab. 32/6, King Papers, file 1176 and Lloyd George papers, F/210/2/12; minutes of inner cabinet meeting, 25 July 1921, Cab. 23/26; Curzon to Geddes, 27 July 1921, King Papers, file 1176; Geddes to Curzon, 27 July 1921, BD, 1st ser., xiv, no 340, 353–4; Geddes to Curzon, 28 July 1921, FO/414/248; Curzon to Geddes, 30 July 1921, King Papers, file 1176, Lloyd George Papers, F/60/4/19, and Cab. 32/6. Curzon offered several concessions; eg the decisions of the preliminary conference would require ratification by the Washington Conference and the latter meeting could reopen any issue, but Hughes was unmoved.

unmoved by arguments that neither British nor dominion leaders could afford to attend a prolonged conference in Washington. In addition, Japan did not support the preliminary conference,[59] some in London expected France to utilize the dispute to secure advantages in Europe,[60] Billy Hughes feared the undermining of his position on the alliance,[61] and Churchill expressed deep concern lest Britain sacrifice the prospects for a naval agreement and a settlement of war debts on the altar of the preliminary conference.[62] Churchill's solution, preliminary *à trois* conversations at the highest level with Japan and the United States, whatever the venue, attracted Lloyd George and both tended to blame Curzon for the imbroglio. Lloyd George also condemned American amateurishness and inexperience in international affairs and feared the hostile British press would seize upon the issue, with Northcliffe to the fore. 'However the British Empire must not be given away in order to secure a good reception (in the United States) for the Pilgrim of Printing House Square.'[63]

Churchill's idea of prior conversations in Washington, however, proved just as elusive as Curzon's preliminary conference in London. Hughes was lukewarm even to the idea of informal meetings in either capital and again he outmanoeuvred the British government. Lloyd George, with his domestic and imperial colleagues, attempted to repair the position in the last days of July but they were trapped by circumstance and conflicting desiderata.[64] The British cabinet, still

59 Eliot to Curzon, 14 and 20 July 1921, BD, 1st ser., XIV, no 334, 341–2, and King Papers, file 1176; notes of interview between Crowe and Hayashi, 25 July 1921, Cab. 32/6

60 Sir M. Cheetham (Paris) to Curzon, 17 July 1921, King Papers, file 1176

61 Hughes to Lloyd George, 18 July 1921 and nd, Lloyd George Papers, F/28/3/50 and 51

62 Churchill to Lloyd George, 18 July 1921, Lloyd George Papers, F/9/3/68; Churchill memorandum, 'Anglo-Japanese-American negotiations,' 23 July 1921, Grigg Papers, reel 8

63 Lloyd George to Churchill, 18 July 1921, Lloyd George Papers, F/9/3/69. Lloyd George viewed the Washington disarmament and Far Eastern conference as a potential mob scene, prolonged and anarchical, where France and Italy would threaten Britain's imperial interests.

64 Conclusions of inner cabinet, 25 July 1921, Cab. 23/26; Draft memorandum to the United States, E 46, 24 July 1921, Cab 32/6 and King Papers, file 1176; notes of imperial meetings, E 29, 26 July 1921, E 30, 26 July 1921, and E 31, 27 July 1921, Cab. 32/2

hoping for an agreement by which the United States would abandon her naval building programme, regarded a preliminary conference or prior conversations on the Pacific and the Anglo-Japanese alliance as the 'indispensable basis' for a disarmament conference. The imperial meeting tended rather to emphasise the need to retain the link with Japan, to avoid any rebuff to their ally and any hint that Britain would sell Japan short in China to court the United States and close the ranks of the white races. The need to promote understanding with the United States, however, suggested as graceful an acquiescence as possible to the idea of one inclusive conference, but the appeal of a preliminary meeting seemed virtually irresistible. Lloyd George even justified the obsession as necessary to establish rapport with the enigmatic Hughes and with America's elite for

The people who govern in America are our people. They are our kith and kin. The other breeds are not on top. It is the men of our race who govern America. I do not know whether they are in the minority or not but in the main they are on top. The only exception is General Smuts's race. He is very much the same. We all come from Holland.

Therefore, despite protests from Billy Hughes and Massey who were concerned to secure reaffirmation of the executive power of the Imperial Conference and confirmation of the decision to retain the Anglo-Japanese alliance, the imperial meeting decided on 27 July to press the United States for preliminary conversations. They suggested the inclusion of Japan and the dominions and that the talks should investigate the agenda of the main conference and attempt to achieve an understanding on the broad principles of Far Eastern policy.[65]

Geddes duly delivered this offer but Hughes was unmoved[66] and, after further attempts to press the case, Curzon, in a flurry of indignant self-righteousness, washed his hands of the affair and of all preparations for the Washington Conference, somewhat to Hughes's dismay.[67] In the final analysis, of course, in view of leftwing opinion, Lloyd George could not risk the indictment that he was willing to jeopardise the disarmament conference. The fracas ended as it began, fruitless and damaging, and Japan was suspicious and even bitter

65 Curzon to Geddes, 27 July 1921, King Papers, file 1176. This proposal suggested a site other than Washington in the United States.

66 Geddes to Curzon, 27 and 28 July 1921, BD, 1st ser., XIV, no 340, 353–4, and FO/414/248

67 Curzon to Geddes, 1 Aug. 1921, BD, 1st ser., XIV, no 349, 363 and FO/800/329

that Britain had not stood her ground in support of their alliance.[68] Geddes blamed Harvey and Harvey blamed Lloyd George, and the principal casualty was Atlantic accord. Inter-elite confidence, trust, and rapport between Britain and the United States were damaged, mutual public respect was shown to be fragile, and Geddes merely offered more words of wisdom on the abnormal mental state of American officialdom.[69] Lloyd George for his part was left to ponder the fact that in the discussions on imperial security Meighen offered nothing but advice whereas Hughes and Massey offered financial and naval assistance.[70]

The Imperial Conference never returned to this question except to confirm that they would not press further for preliminary negotiations lest they endanger the disarmament conference itself,[71] and Curzon turned to rebuild his fences with Japan which he did with some success.[72] Neither Lloyd George nor Curzon, however, could view the events of July 1921 with much satisfaction. They faced the Washington Conference without prior negotiations. Japan's attitude was less than clear, and, in view of Geddes's reports, Secretary of State Hughes remained a contradictory and somewhat obscure figure. In such circumstances there were scant grounds for optimism, especially as domestic, Irish, and European problems remained unsolved.

Certain conclusions seem permissible. During the discussions with the dominion premiers on 27 July, an exasperated Lloyd George, under pressure from Hughes, reaffirmed that the alliance with Japan would continue if the Pacific conference failed and until the allies

68 Nish, *Japan and the Ending of the Anglo-Japanese Alliance,* 379–80

69 Willert to Grigg, 19 July 1921, Grigg Papers, reel 7; Curzon to Grigg, 27 Sept. 1921, Grigg Papers, reel 9; and Geddes to Curzon, 31 July 1921, FO/800/329

70 Notes of meetings, E 26 A, 19 July 1921, E 26 B, 20 July 1921, E 26 C, 22 July 1921, and E 31 A, 27 July 1921, Cab. 32/4

71 Notes of meeting, E 32 B, 1 Aug. 1921, Cab. 32/4

72 Curzon to Eliot, 5 Aug. 1921, and Eliot to Curzon, 12 Aug. 1921, BD, 1st ser., XIV, no 355, 369–71, and no 357, 372–3. Curzon insisted that Britain had always worked to retain close links with Japan, to secure Japan's inclusion in any negotiations with the United States, and regarded a tripartite agreement as a vital prior condition to ensure the success of the disarmament conference. Japan welcomed the repeated assurance that the alliance would continue until they negotiated an adequate substitute.

gave one year's notice of termination. He suggested that Meighen rather than Hughes had cause to complain, for unless the Pacific conference agreed on a superior substitute in the form of a triple agreement, the alliance remained operative. Lloyd George's assessment was sound. Hughes had fortified his position, he had no need to indulge in public protests, and his case, dedicated to the theme of imperial security in the Pacific, was reasonable. Should the Atlanticist hypothesis prove tenable, he would welcome any steps by the disarmament and Pacific conference which secured the involvement of the United States, guaranteed the security of the Pacific, and yet retained a link with Japan.

Meighen's success was less tangible and could prove elusive, and he had little basis from which to sound the alarm publicly. The decisions to convene a Pacific and disarmament conference, to renew attempts to secure co-operation with the United States, to test the validity of the 'North Atlantic triangle,' and to seek to replace the Anglo-Japanese alliance with a tripartite entente were to a large degree tributes to Atlanticism. But the harvest remained to be gathered, the Pacific must yield its 'living and its dead,' and although Meighen could draw comfort from the encouraging indications that Harding's administration would participate in a tripartite accord, the preliminary conference affair must have seemed menacing. There also seemed to be a cumulative factor involved. The sceptics were willing to test Atlanticism again, but a further rebuff could be disastrous, for the 'special relationship' was already a sickly adolescent.

As an exercise in imperial relations the London conference had proved to be a significant point on the path to maturing relationships and interlocking and compensating influences. The British leaders could still tend to dominate, but less as a central hierarchy receiving petitions and suggestions, and more as the most powerful and important members of an imperial elite exploring the same alternative policies, subject to the same linear and plural influences, and viewing problems in global terms. National demarcations were not irrelevant but they were diminishing, and more is to be gained by viewing the controversy over the Anglo-Japanese alliance from the viewpoint of the Atlanticists and their critics than from that of dominion influences on British foreign policy expressed in simple, interstate relationships. Meighen, playing a forceful and creative role, had opened the official debate in February 1921. Canada's Atlanticist views met with some sympathetic response in London and the concept of a triple agreement received wide support as an ideal solution, though its practicability remained in doubt. Smuts reinforced the Atlanticist position during the Imperial Conference, even assuming the leadership on occasions. Indeed, one might view Meighen as being in support of Smuts rather than the reverse at certain stages. The South African premier was the more senior and the more prestigious, and, though his influence with Lloyd George had declined since the early weeks of the peace conference, he retained great accumulated prestige and Hughes could not treat him as lightly or as violently as he did Meighen. Meighen after all was the freshman and who but the inexperienced would meddle with imperial security or flirt with the dangers and immorality of the Lodge-Gardiner policy!

Atlanticists lurked or functioned in Lloyd George's government, in the Foreign Office, in the diplomatic service, and at the Board of Trade, and flourished in some of the dominions. While fighting for survival, they could call on sentiments favourable to the League and opposed to 'old diplomacy,' and, to sustain their thesis, point to the opinions of British commercial interests in the Orient and the views of Peking and Washington. The sceptics and the hostile, however, were a formidable group entrenched in the War Office, the Admiralty, the higher echelons of the Foreign Office, in the diplomatic service, and in the British and certain dominion cabinets. The priorities demanded by Hughes of Australia received sustained support, no public outcry emerged to alter them, and the verdict of the imperial meeting reflected this situation. The sceptics had the substance and the Atlanticists retained their faith.

Finally, the summer of 1921 had seen America's 'amateur statesmen' outwit Britain's professionals, and the victory irritated and secreted new problems. The United States suspected both Britain's motives and the long-term aims of her policy, for diplomacy had fostered confusion not clarity, and few could hold out their hands across the Atlantic with confidence. Clearly public expectations about the disarmament conference exceeded the level of mutual respect between the governments in London and Washington. Both administrations, for similar domestic and international reasons, saw the significance of the forthcoming congress but neither could view it with calm nerves and without traces of pessimism.

FOUR

The Washington Conference

Whatever the judgments of historians, to contemporary opinion the Washington Conference was a meeting of the utmost importance. Some looked to the gathering to produce a new order in the Pacific and Far East. Others expected a major contribution to peace by way of a limitation of armaments, and even the less sanguine regarded it as the most significant international conference to meet on American soil, the Portsmouth deliberations seeming trivial in comparison. To the Atlanticists the conference was the culminating phase of the opportunities presented in 1921 to secure Anglo-American co-operation on specific issues and to create a permanent working agreement between the empire and the United States. Not surprisingly, with the British representatives conducting detailed negotiations, the Canadian delegate was prominent in pursuit of this broader theme.

The most urgent political problem was still the Anglo-Japanese alliance. To Christie, the conference must replace the alliance with a broader multilateral agreement embodying mutually acceptable principles of policy, and, viewing the relevant agreements reached since 1907, he did not feel that a solution should elude them.[1] United States preparations, however, directed by Hughes, were devoted principally to naval questions, and the State Department produced no draft formula providing for the abrogation of the alliance prior to the conference. In London the situation seemed complicated by the rebuff received over the preliminary conference question and the resulting uncertainty about Japanese and United States attitudes. In

1 Christie, memorandum, 29 Oct. 1921, 'Substitution of inclusive agreement or understanding for Anglo-Japanese alliance,' King Papers, file 1176. Borden was Canada's chief delegate and Christie supervised the detailed preparations.

fact, restoration of normal relations with Tokyo proved far less difficult than Curzon feared.[2] After briefly hinting at prior Anglo-Japanese
negotiations to secure a preliminary understanding on their alliance
and then welcoming Britain's assurances that she would not relinquish the alliance without good cause and an adequate substitute,
Japan became a model of reasonableness. The Hara government
clearly preferred retention of the alliance, however amended, but
they would accept a tripartite agreement and were willing to join in
private à trois negotiations involving the United States to secure a
new understanding.

Curzon's doubts about the United States, while never erased, were
possibly reduced somewhat by mildly encouraging reports from
Washington, which, however, were themselves tainted by his lack of
faith in both Geddes and Harvey.[3] Curzon obviously expected continued United States opposition to the Anglo-Japanese alliance, the
misunderstanding over the preliminary conference had been real
enough, and the American press, reporting rumours of Britain's intent
to retain the essence of the alliance in a triple treaty, seemed
hostile.[4] By late September, however, Geddes announced that a new
atmosphere prevailed in Washington, that the recent 'soreness' and
suspicion had evaporated, and that Hughes sincerely regretted the
probable absence of Lloyd George from the conference.[5] In more
detailed reports Geddes noted a slump in Sinn Fein activity, an increase in anglophil sympathies helped by the publication of Walter

2 Eliot to Curzon, 15 Aug. and 11 and 15 Oct. 1921, FO/414/248; Eliot to
   Curzon, 23 Aug. 1921, BD, 1st ser. XIV, no 365, 382–3; Dugdale,
   Balfour, II, 328; Nish, Japan and the Ending of the Anglo-Japanese Alliance,
   379–81; Asada, 'Japan's "Special Interests" and the Washington Conference,
   1921–1922.' Asada shows that the Japanese delegation arrived at Washington
   with a 'blueprint of an Anglo-Japanese-American entente,' combining the
   advantages of earlier agreements and seeking to secure United States recognition of Japan's 'special interests' in China.
3 Curzon to Lloyd George, 28 Aug. 1921, Lloyd George Papers, F/13/2/42;
   Curzon to Grigg, 27 Sept. 1921, Grigg Papers, reel 9. Curzon accused Harvey
   of duplicity and, willing to reopen the circus of representation in Washington,
   suggested Milner as a replacement for Geddes. He noted that Lloyd George
   had spoken to Meighen about repatriating Geddes to Canada.
4 Geddes to Curzon, 20 Aug. 1921, FO/414/248
5 Geddes to Curzon, 21 Sept. 1921, FO/414/248 and BD, 1st ser., XIV, no 379,
   399–400; no 380, 400–01; and no 381, 401–5

Hines Page's correspondence and by Geddes's own speeches, and signs that American public opinion, impressed by the imperial conference, was attracted by the romantic appeal of co-operation between the English-speaking peoples. Moreover, American industrial and financial leaders agreed with Secretary of State Hughes that prospects for economic growth were tied closely to future Anglo-American co-operation.

Hughes personally, Geddes felt, despite a legalistic mind and a tendency to lose control of his feelings, and despite being saddled with a mediocre and suspicious State Department and the unfortunate Harvey, was a changed man. The Secretary of State, in the course of frank and friendly conversations, seemed less inclined to blame Britain for the problems he faced and had expressed a keen desire to secure Anglo-American accord. He now looked, according to Geddes, for a tripartite agreement on the Pacific and East Asia, emanating from private à trois conversations rather than from conference debate, and he wanted to avoid any arrangement that might seem hostile to Japan. Moreover, in Geddes's view, Hughes would not work with France or Italy at Britain's expense and unless an unfortunate incident occurred to disturb the status quo, the Washington Conference, in a 'poignantly religious atmosphere,' would open on a note of cordial Anglo-American co-operation. In addition, with Harding and his cabinet sympathetic, with delegates Elihu Root and Democratic Senator Underwood sincerely seeking Britain's friendship, and with Lodge prepared to acquiesce in what seemed wise politically, Geddes expected the Washington Conference to be a great success. In any event, Geddes assured Curzon, failure would not stem from a lack of American sincerity and determination to work for meaningful agreements. In contrast to these optimistic predictions, however, Geddes also reported that the Harding administration was arming itself with tariff legislation and debt collecting procedures to exert pressure on Britain and force acceptance of a tripartite agreement which safeguarded United States interests in the Pacific and the Far East. Finally, and surely of concern in London, Geddes concluded that most policies would be forfeit to the demands of the 1922 congressional elections.

Curzon's response was ambiguous but not idiosyncratic. In private, nursing his wounds over the preliminary conference, he berated Harvey for his duplicity and ineptness and Hughes for his party spirit, ignorance, and refusal to meet in advance with Britain and Japan.[6] In formal response to Hughes, however, Curzon was either warm and cordial, promising co-operation to secure a tripartite agreement, or at least moderate and guarded, deriving some satisfaction from the fact that Hughes conceded the need for quiet negotiations to secure a triple understanding prior to the conference.[7] Moreover, Curzon professed to see little difficulty in securing a three-power agreement to replace the Anglo-Japanese alliance, but he was concerned that its terms would in all probability be mere platitudes. In addition, he expected deadlock over China and feared protracted and fruitless debate over an impossibly broad set of issues unless the Americans learned the arts of diplomacy and the ways of conducting an international conference. Indeed, as neither he nor Lloyd George would be present to help educate their American counterparts, Curzon viewed the future both with detached concern and aristocratic contempt.

Clearly Curzon regarded the situation as less than satisfactory, especially as other sources of information reported continued suspicion of British policy in the United States, American fears that Britain would sabotage the disarmament negotiations unless Far Eastern problems were settled satisfactorily beforehand, and continuing anti-British propaganda.[8] One source of comfort was news of a virtual cessation of naval construction in the United States, but Lloyd George's illness and periodic absence from London, the prolonged debate over the composition of Britain's delegation, the question of dominion representation, and concern over the agenda added to Curzon's woes. Indeed, pressed as they were over Ireland, Egypt, Silesia, and domestic problems, one might sympathise greatly with Curzon and Lloyd George, but for the Premier's avoidance of the Washington Conference lest it be a fiasco, and Curzon's suggestion that, in view of the probable failure at Washington, they should take a leaf from President Harding's book and include a member of the official opposition in the British delegation. Obviously some Americans had learned at least some of the tricks of the trade and Curzon was not averse to distributing the blame for any lack of success.[9]

6 Curzon to Grigg, 27 Sept. 1921, Grigg Papers, reel 9

7 Curzon to Geddes, 25 and 28 Sept. 1921, BD, 1st ser., XIV, no 384, 407–8 and no 387, 416

8 F. Guest to Lloyd George, 4 Oct. 1921, Lloyd George Papers, F/22/3/29; Geddes to Curzon, 29 Sept. 1921, BD, 1st ser., XIV, no 388, 416

9 Minutes of cabinet meetings, 7 and 17 Oct. 1921, Cab. 23/27; Grigg to Curzon, 14 Sept. 1921, and Curzon to Lloyd George, 28 Sept. 1921, Lloyd

Finally, laconic advice from Churchill that Lloyd George should visit Washington briefly, court Hughes and Harding, establish an informal understanding with the United States and Japan, and demonstrate to the United States both the sincerity of Britain's motives and the determination to retain her world position; along with Henry Wilson's dismissal of the conference as diplomatic bankruptcy, was scarcely helpful.[10]

Initially the Foreign Office seemed unsure whether the Anglo-Japanese alliance should be discussed specifically at the Washington Conference, what role the United States should play in any such negotiations, and what precise relationship existed between the alliance and a tripartite agreement.[11] Curzon appealed to Lloyd George and, somewhat surprisingly, received prompt and categorical instructions.[12] The Prime Minister wanted close co-operation and consultation with Japan on all Far Eastern issues and Britain must refuse to discuss either the alliance or any Pacific problem with powers other than Japan and the United States, and at any level other than between principals. In Lloyd George's opinion, Britain could not discuss issues affecting imperial security at a conference of five or eight powers when two of the five had neither comparable interests and responsibilities nor adequate forces in the Orient. In sum, Britain's interests and policies were not for open and general discussion, and Geddes and the dominions were duly informed.[13]

Lloyd George had dictated the ground rules for negotiations on the Anglo-Japanese alliance and Curzon and Hughes, with acquiescence from Tokyo, had agreed to seek a tripartite arrangement in

George Papers, F/13/2/45 and 50; Curzon to Grigg, 11 Sept. 1921, and Grigg to Curzon, 14 Sept. 1921, Grigg Papers, reel 1; Fry, 'Anglo-American-Canadian Relations,' 425. After many exchanges, reminiscent of the debates over who should be sent to Washington as ambassador, Balfour, Lee, Geddes, Beatty, Hankey, and Riddell were chosen to attend the conference. However, no one could be sure whether Lloyd George was needed or whether he might arrive at a moment of crisis to save the day.

10 Churchill to Lloyd George, 8 Oct. 1921, Lloyd George Papers, F/10/1/10; Callwell, *Sir Henry Wilson*, II, 306–10, and Collier, Brasshat, 321

11 Lampson memorandum, 18 Aug. 1921, BD, 1st ser., XIV, no 363, 380–2

12 Curzon to Grigg, 11 Sept. 1921, Grigg to Curzon, 14 Sept. 1921, Grigg Papers, reel 1; and Grigg to Curzon, 14 Sept. 1921, Lloyd George Papers, F/13/2/45

13 Curzon to Geddes, 18 Sept. 1921, FO/414/248; Colonial Secretary to Governors General, 3 Oct. 1921, Lloyd George Papers, F/10/1/5

informal negotiations outside but parallel to the main conference. One basic assumption was, however, always maintained in London; although the search for a wider agreement would be sincere and sustained, should these negotiations fail, Britain would retain a modified alliance with Japan. Preparations in London covered a broad range of Far Eastern, Pacific, and naval problems and only one memorandum dealt specifically with the alliance question.[14] This Foreign Office paper noted that, while both the United States and Japan favoured or would accept a tripartite agreement, the new treaty must contain no military clauses and must be confined to a mere declaration of policy, accepting general principles and adopting a 'somewhat anodyne nature' to satisfy Washington. Two formulae existed; one reported by Geddes on 7 July, reflecting the views and interests of the United States,[15] and the other drawn up by Sir John Jordan. The American formula provoked little response, but Jordan's draft received more detailed scrutiny and, as its author participated in the preparations for and accompanied Balfour to the Washington Conference, it remains historically more significant.[16] Jordan suggested a declaration of policy to secure respect for the territorial possessions of the signatories and to promote peace and stability in East Asia and the Pacific. Secondly, the draft sought to preserve the common interests of all powers in China by supporting her independence and integrity and the principle of equal opportunity for the commerce and

14 Hankey to Lloyd George, 1 Nov. 1921, Grigg Papers, reel 9; Washington
Conference memoranda and index, ibid., reels 10 and 11; Ashton-Gwatkin
memorandum, 10 Oct. 1921, FO/414/248; Foreign Office memorandum, 10
Oct. 1921, 'Respecting a Tripartite Agreement,' FO/414/248 and BD, 1st ser.,
XIV, no 405, 448–50 (in this latter source the memorandum is dated 22 Oct.);
Wellesley memorandum, 20 Oct. 1921, FO/414/248 and BD, 1st ser., XIV, no
404, 434–48. From the pen of an Atlanticist, this last paper strongly criticised
Japanese policies and emphasised the need to create harmony and solidarity
between the white, Anglo-Saxon races.

15 Geddes to Curzon, 7 July 1921, BD, 1st ser. XIV, no 326, 328–9. This formula
sought to guarantee the territorial integrity of the Pacific states, including
Britain's dominions and colonies facing the Pacific, to confirm the policy of the
Open Door in China and to expand it to secure equality of commercial and
economic opportunity in the whole area covered by the prospective agreement,
and to offer financial and development aid to all Pacific states as well as China.

16 Appendix B to Foreign Office memorandum, 10 Oct. 1921, 'Respecting a
Tripartite Agreement'; see note 14

industry of all nations in China. Finally, in a third article, if these aims were endangered, the signatories would communicate fully and frankly and consider measures necessary to remedy the situation. Jordan's formula also suggested that they should invite China to adhere to these principles.

The Foreign Office memorandum suggested that the third clause could offer something substantial, for it seemed to be practically an undertaking to take common action and precluded independent steps by any signatory contrary to the principles of the agreement. Consequently, Jordan's draft could become a modest substitute for the Anglo-Japanese alliance. In addition, because all three powers feared the formation of hostile combinations in the future, Britain worrying lest Japan join Russia and Germany, Japan being anxious to avoid an Anglo-American grouping, and the United States being opposed to an Anglo-Japanese combination, the Foreign Office memorandum speculated on the value of a fourth clause. It stated that all three powers would agree not to join any arrangement or political combination inimical to any other signatory. The question of China's adherence remained unsettled, but the Foreign Office rejected any idea of a multilateral pact not including the United States as a worthless substitute for the Anglo-Japanese alliance. Curzon's reaction, however, was less than enthusiastic, for although he accepted the principles involved and welcomed any removal of American suspicions, he did not regard Jordan's formula as an adequate substitute for the alliance. Curzon still regarded the value of compensations offered 'by a temporary conquest of the *beaux yeux* of America' as scarcely adequate.

On the question of tactics the Foreign Office paper urged that the British delegation let the United States suggest a formula and only produce a British draft if and when the American attempt proved to be impracticable. This advice pointed to two conclusions; that Balfour did not leave England with an official draft and that consequently he enjoyed wide scope for personal initiative. Little evidence exists, however, of Balfour's concept of a tripartite agreement, although perhaps he and Lloyd George, while accepting the need to transform the alliance into a triple arrangement, were possibly reluctant to see the alliance ended.[17] Perhaps Balfour would seek to retain as much as possible of the value and essence of the Anglo-Japanese alliance in a broader agreement, so as to secure an adequate substitute, safe-

17 Dugdale, *Balfour*, II, 317–20

Balfour and Lloyd George in 1922

guard the empire's interests, avoid alienating either Japan or the United States, and fulfil the desiderata laid down by the Imperial Conference.

Balfour, in fact, reclining in bed and taking refuge from sea-sickness, crossed to Quebec City on board the *Empress of France* and, closeted with Jordan, Hankey, and Lampson, gave sustained attention to the problem. With their expert help, but without further consultation with London, Balfour concluded that two treaties were required; one to replace the alliance, dealing with the preservation of peace and the maintenance of the territorial status quo in and bordering on the Pacific, and the other devoted specifically to China.[18] Moreover, Balfour insisted that they must settle the political questions relating to the Pacific and China before entering into naval negotiations.

Balfour's draft three-power treaty, while omitting all reference to China, in fact owed something to Jordan's formula. His first clause contained the substance of Jordan's first and third articles, but it went further. In Balfour's proposed treaty the three powers would agree, in order to preserve peace and protect existing territorial rights in the Pacific islands and in the territories bordering on the Pacific, to respect those rights and consult on how to protect them whenever they were imperilled by the action of another power. Under the second article, if any two of the signatories wished to bind themselves to aid each other to defend those rights by force of arms they were permitted to do so, providing they acted defensively and kept the third signatory fully informed. The third clause stated that this tripartite treaty would replace any relevant existing agreements.

Clearly the second clause was the most significant, and the problem is to interpret Balfour's intent and estimate his level of optimism and expectations about United States and Japanese reactions. Articles one and three were gestures to the United States, suggesting a consultative pact and the termination of the Anglo-Japanese alliance. Clause two, offering the prospect of renewing the essence of that alliance or creating a similar defensive military arrangement, was a source of comfort to Japan, assuring her of Britain's good faith and determination to retain their special relationship. Balfour's draft triple treaty

18 Balfour memorandum, Nov. 1921, Balfour Papers, 49749; Hankey to Lloyd George, 11 Nov. and 12 Dec. 1921, Lloyd George Papers, F/62/1/1 and 9; Balfour to Lloyd George, 11 Nov. 1921, and Hankey memorandum, 11 Nov. 1921, BD, 1st ser., XIV, no 415, 466–70, and no 416, 470–1

was a compromise, attempting to balance between Washington and Tokyo and acknowledging the existence of new circumstances. Balfour and his expert advisers had accepted on the one hand the fact that Britain could not retain the original alliance with Japan at the cost of Anglo-American relations and at the risk of wrecking the disarmament conference. A tendency to regard the alliance as somewhat of an anachronism reinforced this assumption. On the other hand, however, Balfour would neither dismiss the possibility of a future Russo-German menace nor rebuff a valuable ally. Moreover, he could not ignore the decisions of the imperial meeting and especially the weight of Australasian opinion. The solution lay, therefore, in a tripartite agreement which included the United States but did not commit her to military obligations, which terminated the alliance in its original form without a rebuff to Japan, and which left open the option of recreating a defensive alliance in the face of a Russo-German menace. In this way Britain would reassure her Pacific dominions and remove North American fears that the Anglo-Japanese alliance would force Britain to be neutral in the event of a threatened or actual rupture between the United States and Japan. Both the Atlanticists and their opponents might applaud and Balfour would test dominion, United States, and Japanese reactions and weigh their suggested amendments. In the last resort, should the negotiations fail, the British government could, with varying degrees of reluctance in London, fall back on a modified alliance with Japan.[19]

When Balfour arrived in Washington from Quebec City his first task was to secure the agreement of the British Empire Delegation. Lee and Borden, canvassing old friends, and Geddes confirmed that the United States delegation was determined to secure the termination of the alliance, and that Root at least was confident that they could agree on a new arrangement for the Pacific. This information was relayed to the Empire Delegation at dinner on 10 November and Balfour, in splendid form and playing his hand with great skill according to Hankey, encouraged and secured a degree of harmony and good will to the point where he could safely launch his proposals. He

19 Interestingly, although clearly he did not understand all the implications of Balfour's draft, Churchill praised the United States naval limitation plan as fair and honest, and even generous in view of the fact that as far as Washington knew, Britain meant to retain the alliance. 149th meeting of CID, 14 Nov. 1921, Cab. 2/3

circulated his draft treaty, along with his formula dealing with China, and, again according to Hankey, the dominion representatives, flattered by Balfour's court, weighing the information on American attitudes and listening to Borden's advocacy of an entente to include the United States, accepted 'this ingenious draft.' On the assumption that everyone understood the implications of Balfour's proposal, clearly the compromise seemed to offer something to all points of view.[20]

Balfour had carried the Empire Delegation with ease in the course of one dinner and dissent never emerged, but Hankey regarded the next step, the approach to the United States, as a more formidable obstacle.[21] Hughes impressed him personally and the United States government was apparently prepared to work with Britain, but many in Washington, including Hughes, still seemed to fear a devious British scheme to retain the alliance with Japan and did not 'appreciate our intense desire for a Triple Agreement if it is possible.' Rumours of French and Italian intrigue against Britain were circulating and Hankey feared that the price of American acceptance of Balfour's proposals would be the inclusion of France and Holland. On the whole, however, Hankey expected Balfour to convince Hughes and secure acceptance of the substance of his scheme. Surprisingly enough, Hankey praised Geddes for his great help, his mastery of the issues, and for his successful cultivation of Harding's administration, and Hankey concluded that whether due to Geddes or not, Anglo-American relations were significantly improved and were more cordial than at any time since the peace conference.

The conversation between Balfour and Hughes on the evening of 11 November was cordial and frank enough, but immediately Balfour must have realised that his 'ingenious draft' would not carry the State

20 Hankey to Lloyd George, 11 Nov. 1921, Lloyd George Papers, F/62/1/1; Balfour to Lloyd George, 11 Nov. 1921, BD, 1st ser., XIV, no 415, 466–70; 'Notes by Sir R. Borden upon the Disarmament Conference at Washington which opened on 11 November 1921,' Borden Papers, memoir notes, vol. 8, 1921, 4600–993. (In effect these notes are a diary and will be cited as such. Hence for these developments, Borden diary, entries of 7, 9, and 10 Nov. 1921, 4604–9.) Hankey, mildly contemptuous, described Borden as 'the same as ever,' but in a most reasonable frame of mind; Pearce as 'a lightweight,' Salmond as 'garrulous,' and Sastri as 'little help.'
21 Hankey to Lloyd George, 11 Nov. 1921, Lloyd George Papers, F/62/1/1

Department, although he permitted Hughes to show it to his delega-tion.[22] In retrospect, Hughes's objections were hardly surprising. He feared lest any suggestion that they were negotiating an actual treaty should leak out, he did not want Balfour to approach the Japanese delegation with this draft, and he could not accept the word 'treaty' as such, whereupon Balfour promptly substituted the word 'arrange-ment.' Moreover, although Hughes wanted improved relations with Japan, he could not accept any commitment to recognise or defend the fruits of Japanese imperialism and he needed time to consider Balfour's draft as the preface to detailed negotiations. The inference was unmistakable; Hughes did not care for Balfour's formula and suspected that it would retain the essence of the Anglo-Japanese alliance.

Balfour in fact reported to Lloyd George that, although over-shadowed by the naval negotiations initiated through Hughes's mega-phone diplomacy, his informal talks with Hughes and then briefly with Prince Tokugawa were not unsatisfactory.[23] Nevertheless, faced with Hughes's initial objections, Balfour turned to the Japanese dele-gation. Ambassador Shidehara, fearing Anglo-American collusion and uneasy because of the Balfour-Hughes conversation, had ex-pected to negotiate for Japan, but illness impeded him and on 18 November Hankey met with Saburi, counsellor at the Japanese em-bassy.[24] Saburi assured Hankey that Japan, while preferring to retain their alliance, would accept an extension of the principles of the alliance into a tripartite agreement, but would oppose the inclusion of China or any European power in a new arrangement. Hankey, in response, and speculating on a resurgent Russo-German threat, won-dered whether, within a triple understanding, they could retain 'the power of reconstituting the alliance in case the old circumstances

22 Hankey memorandum on conversation between Balfour and Hughes, 11 Nov. 1921, Cab. 30/27 and BD, 1st ser., XIV, no 416, 470–1; Hughes memorandum on this conversation, FR, 1922, I, 1–2; Pusey, *Charles Evans Hughes*, II, 494–5 and Glad, *Charles Evans Hughes*, 298. Hankey was not present and his memorandum was based on Balfour's verbal account. Hughes's notes were a summary and neither memorandum is really satisfactory.

23 Balfour to Lloyd George, 14 Nov. 1921, Cab. 30/5; Hankey to Lloyd George, 17 Nov. 1921, Lloyd George Papers, F/62/1/3; Dugdale, *Balfour*, II, 328–9

24 Hankey to Balfour, memorandum, 18 Nov. 1921, Cab. 30/27; Balfour to Lloyd George, 24 Nov. 1921, Cab. 30/5 and BD, 1st ser., XIV, no 449, 505–11; Nish, *Japan and the Ending of the Anglo-Japanese Alliance*, 381

should recur.' Both agreed, however, that the attitude of the United States was pivotal and that the negotiations could make little progress until Shidehara recovered sufficiently to meet Balfour. Clearly both were prepared to engage in a thinly disguised pursuit of the essence of the Anglo-Japanese alliance.

Conversations between Balfour and Baron Kato, on 18 November and again on 23 November, with Hankey, Lampson, and Hanihara present on the second occasion, were either unproductive or merely a repetition of the meeting between Hankey and Saburi.[25] Significantly, however, Balfour, without further contacts with Hughes since their conversation of 11th November, confirmed that he wished to retain the right to renew the alliance should circumstances demand such a step. Britain and Japan would communicate fully with the United States on any such renewal which would not violate Article Eighteen of the League Covenant. Finally, Balfour handed Kato his draft triple agreement and their discussion concluded understandably on a very cordial note.[26] Shidehara, however, still indisposed, did not see how the United States could accept Balfour's proposals containing provision for the resurrection of a defensive military alliance. He began work, therefore, on a new tripartite agreement which offered the United States a consultative pact, but also sought protection for the 'vital interests' of the signatories in 'the Pacific and the Far East.' Here was a compromise of a different kind, the second prepared from a sick-bed for American consumption and justifiably described as a 'furtive attempt to salvage the remnants of the Lansing-Ishii agreement' of 1917.[27] In some ways Shidehara's draft was more promising than Balfour's or any that came from the United States delegation, but it required close scrutiny and amendment.

Although Anglo-American exchanges had not proceeded beyond the original conversation between Hughes and Balfour, the American delegation, with Root, Lodge, and Chandler P. Anderson of the State Department prominent, produced a draft agreement by 22 November. Hughes rejected their formula because it neither specifically cancelled the Anglo-Japanese alliance nor specified the number of

25 See note 24

26 Despite minor verbal changes, Balfour showed Kato substantially what he had offered to Hughes.

27 Asada, 'Japan's "Special Interests" and the Washington Conference,' 66; Nish, *Japan and the Ending of the Anglo-Japanese Alliance*, 382. In several respects Nish's interpretation of these negotiations is difficult to accept.

signatories.[28] Anderson then produced an amended version on 26 November for Lodge's scrutiny, and by 28 November their joint efforts resulted in a projected four-power agreement over Lodge's signature.[29] Despite certain acceptable features, such as limiting the scope of the agreement to 'insular possessions and dominions' and excluding China, Hughes rejected even this draft, and in any case it faced the competition of Shidehara's formula, which Saburi had presented to Balfour and Hankey on 26 November.[30] Shidehara's tripartite agreement stated that if their territorial rights or vital interests in the Pacific and the Far East were threatened, the signatories would communicate fully and frankly to decide on the most efficient measures to be taken jointly or separately to remedy the situation. Furthermore, if a controversy developed between two of the signatories, they could, in mutual agreement, invite the third power to a conference to adjust their disagreement. Finally, in the third clause, this agreement would provide for the termination of the Anglo-Japanese alliance.

Significantly, whatever else Shidehara intended, he had, understanding and anticipating Hughes's opposition, omitted any provision to retain the possibility of resurrecting the Anglo-Japanese alliance. Oddly enough, therefore, both Japan and the United States had rebuffed Balfour's proposal and he fought no rearguard action to reverse the trend.[31] Instead, working with Saburi, Balfour made one signifi-

28 Lodge Papers, file 'Washington conference 1922'; Pusey, *Charles Evans Hughes*, II, 495; Vinson, *The Parchment Peace*, 154–5

29 Lodge Papers, file 'Washington Conference 1922.' This agreement aimed to preserve peace and maintain the rights of the four powers in their insular possessions and dominions in the Pacific. The signatories would agree to respect these rights and, if peace were threatened or their rights endangered, they would communicate with each other to find a solution. Moreover, they would agree not to enter separate arrangements with any power which might prejudice these rights or the integrity of their insular possessions and dominions, or threaten the peace. Finally, this four-power treaty would supercede any earlier relevant treaty.

30 Memorandum of Balfour-Saburi conversation, 26 Nov. 1921, Cab. 30/27; Balfour to Curzon, 28 Nov. 1921, Cab. 30/5; Balfour to Lloyd George, 29 Nov. 1921, Cab. 30/5 and King Papers, file 1176. Shidehara's draft had been accepted by the Japanese delegation but had not yet received Tokyo's approval.

31 Balfour may have expected and even welcomed this outcome because of

cant amendment to Shidehara's proposals, removing the phrase 'vital interests.' He also inserted several verbal changes to clarify the meaning and intent of agreement.[32] Balfour, however, did not narrow the scope of the pact, permitting the retention of the phrase 'Pacific and Far East,' despite the fact that originally he had proposed separate treaties for the Pacific region and for China.

Later that same day Saburi showed the amended Shidehara draft to Hughes,[33] and Balfour handed it to Root and Lodge.[34] Despite insisting on the inclusion of France and the need to settle beforehand the Shantung controversy, both Lodge and Root were impressed with the formula. Hughes, however, meeting with Balfour on 28 November, recognised the merits of Shidehara's proposals but insisted on an additional amendment to that providing for the inclusion of France.[35] He wished the four power agreement to apply only to the islands of the Pacific region and to exclude all reference to mainland Asia. In this way, Hughes suggested to Balfour, they would isolate the difficult question of Shantung and secure a suitable and facile alternative to the Anglo-Japanese alliance. The move to include France Hughes described as necessary to eliminate senatorial and public suspicion, and he was not impressed with the problem of excluding the Netherlands or Italy. Moreover, Hughes did not regard the insertion of France as an excessive dilution of the agreement and indeed saw it as an intrinsically advantageous move.

Balfour agreed to approach the Japanese delegation, and Saburi, consulted by Hankey, expressed concern about the exclusion of the

United States opposition, but he can scarcely have foreseen that Shidehara would reject his gesture to Japan. Balfour reported to London, however, that he was satisfied with Shidehara's proposals as amended.

32 See note 30. Balfour's verbal changes focussed attention exclusively on territorial rights and removed the possibility of one of the two disputants preventing the calling of a conference with the third signatory to settle the disagreement.

33 Memorandum of Hughes-Saburi conversation, 26 Nov. 1921, FR, 1922, I, 3–4; Lodge Papers, file 'Washington Conference 1922'

34 Note of conversation between Balfour, Lodge, and Root, 26 Nov. 1921, Cab. 30/27 and BD, 1st ser., XIV, no 451, 512–13; Balfour to Lloyd George, 29 Nov. 1921, Cab. 30/5 and King Papers, file 1176

35 Balfour to Lloyd George, 29 Nov. 1921, Cab. 30/5 and King Papers, file 1176; Balfour to Curzon, 29 Nov. 1921, BD, 1st ser., XIV, no 458, 522–3; Asada, 'Japan's "Special Interests" and the Washington Conference,' 66

mainland. Hankey attempted to comfort Saburi on this point and concluded in his report to Lloyd George that prospects for an agreement seemed extremely bright, and that relations between the British and American delegations were very cordial and profitable.[36] The Japanese delegation, however, having dismissed the idea of providing for the future resurrection of the alliance with Britain, having accepted Balfour's removal of the phrase 'vital interests,' and now being faced with the omission of China from the scope of a four-power consultative agreement, was forced to consult Tokyo. Baron Kato, still without specific instructions on 2 December, assured Hughes and Balfour that the Japanese delegation accepted the proposed changes and expected its government to acquiesce, and Hughes, anxious to appease the sensitive French and to precipitate the negotiations, drew up a revised agreement between 2 and 7 December.[37] Balfour, for his part, assured the cabinet in London that China and the Asian mainland would be excluded from the scope of the agreement, that he would insist on the inclusion of Australia and New Zealand, and, in the absence of instructions to the contrary, he assumed he could proceed with the negotiations.[38]

Progress now depended on the content of Hughes's draft four-power agreement and its reception by Britain and Japan. Hughes's proposals, owing more to the amended Shidehara scheme than to Balfour's original formula, looked to the preservation of peace and the maintenance of the signatories' rights in their insular possessions and dominions in the Pacific. The four powers agreed to respect these rights and, in the event of a controversy between two of them, they would summon a quadruple conference to settle the disagreement. As in the Root-Takahira agreement, if their rights were threatened by the aggression of a non-signatory power, they would communicate

36 Hankey to Lloyd George, 29 Nov. 1921, Lloyd George Papers, f/62/1/6
37 Balfour to Lloyd George, 2 Dec. 1921, King Papers, file 1176; Balfour to Curzon, 3 Dec. 1921, bd, 1st ser., xiv, no 471, 535; notes of Balfour-Hughes-Kato conversation, 2 Dec. 1921, fr, 1922, i, 5 and 7–8; Pusey, *Charles Evans Hughes*, ii, 495–6 and Vinson, *The Parchment Peace*, 156–7. These negotiations ran parallel to the naval negotiations where Japan, if she were to accept the naval ratios proposed, expected a 'non-fortification agreement' and an acceptable treaty on the Pacific.
38 Curzon to Balfour, 2 Dec. 1921, Cab. 30/5 and bd, 1st ser., xiv, no 468, 532; Balfour to Curzon, 3 Dec. 1921, Cab. 30/5 and bd, 1st ser., xiv, nos 471 and 472, 535

fully to find the most suitable remedy, to be applied jointly or separately. The agreement would last for ten years and would continue
in force unless terminated on six months' notice. The fourth article
provided specifically for the abrogation of the Anglo-Japanese
alliance.[39]

After receiving news that Japan accepted the inclusion of France,
Hughes, with the approval of President Harding,[40] presented his draft
to Balfour on 7 December. Both agreed to change the six-months'
notice of intent to terminate the treaty to one of twelve months, and
then Balfour and Hughes met with Baron Kato. Kato tabled an alternative arrangement received from Tokyo, the principal amendment
being the inclusion of commercial interests along with territorial
rights, but Balfour and Hughes summarily rejected it. Hughes emphasised that he assumed that Japan would agree to a settlement of their
differences over the Pacific mandate islands, and, apart from the
problem of whether or not to include the Japanese main islands, all
three accepted the American formula in principle. Hughes would see
Viviani to secure French agreement, which he accomplished with
ease, and Balfour turned to the much neglected Empire Delegation
that afternoon.[41]

Balfour, claiming that Hughes's proposals were based virtually on
his own scheme, reported the success of the recent negotiations. He
emphasised both the narrow geographical scope of the arrangement,
relating exclusively to the Pacific islands, and the fact that the agreement was a treaty requiring ratification by the Senate. Should the
Senate reject the treaty, Britain would retain her alliance with Japan.
Balfour then confirmed, after an additional hurried conversation with
Hughes and Kato, that the Japanese main islands, Canada, the United
States, China, and Korea were excluded, but that Australia, New
Zealand, and all mandate islands were included in the agreement
under the term 'insular possessions and dominions.' Balfour also as-
sured the meeting that the treaty was merely a mutual agreement not
to disturb each other's rights, and noted that its approval depended

39 FR, 1922, I, 7–8; Balfour to Curzon, 7 Dec. 1921, BD, 1st ser., XIV, no 481,
    541–2
40 Balfour to Curzon, 7 Dec. 1921, Cab. 30/5, Cab. 30/27 and BD, 1st ser., XIV,
    no 480, 540–1; Balfour to Lloyd George, 9 Dec. 1921, King Papers, file 1176
41 Notes of 11th meeting of BED, 7 Dec. 1921, Cab. 30/1A; Borden diary, entry of
    7 Dec. 1921, 4670; Borden to Meighen, 8 and 12 Dec. 1921, Borden Papers,
    OC no 611; Balfour to Curzon, 7 Dec. 1921, BD, 1st ser., XIV, no 482, 542–3

on Japan and the United States reaching a settlement on Yap and agreeing to the extension of their commercial treaty to the mandate islands. The Empire Delegation made certain verbal amendments and ensured that minor disagreements between the signatories would not require a full four-power conference to achieve a settlement, but beyond that they made no challenge. As accepted on 7 December, Hughes's draft differed from the amended Shidehara proposals by the addition of a preamble, by inverting articles one and two, by adding the time limit in article three, and by the insertion of the fourth clause. Balfour applauded the last article because it would force the Senate to approve the four-power treaty if it wished to destroy the Anglo-Japanese alliance.

Each member of the Empire Delegation required time to consult his own government, but Balfour anticipated little difficulty from this source or from the somewhat superfluous expressions of concern then received from London.[42] In any case the British cabinet accepted the inclusion of France even though they expected Japan to regard the move as a serious diminution of the value of the agreement, and applauded the prospect of the two treaties dealing with the Pacific and China separately. The four-power treaty, Curzon noted, was confined to the relevant major powers and superceded the Anglo-Japanese alliance in a satisfactory manner, and the treaty on China would show the other powers at the conference that they were neither forgotten nor ignored.

As anticipated, the news from dominion capitals was encouraging. Pearce and Salmond reported Australian and New Zealand approval on 9 December and Borden secured Meighen's agreement by the following day, after assuring him that the treaty conformed with Canada's proposals to the imperial meeting.[43] The

42 Curzon to Balfour, 7 Dec. 1921, Cab. 30/5, Lloyd George Papers, F/141 and BD, 1st ser., XIV, no 478, 539–40 and no 479, 540. Curzon was particularly concerned to avoid the inclusion of Italy, regarding it as an unacceptable act of dilution, and to ensure that Britain and Japan forced the United States to reject Italian pretensions. In fact the problem of Italy's inclusion was settled easily.

43 Notes of 12th meeting of BED, 9 Dec. 1921, Cab. 30/1A; Borden diary, entry of 9 Dec. 1921, 4673 (a); Borden to Meighen, 8 and 10 Dec. 1921, and Meighen to Borden, 8 Dec 1921, King Papers, file 1176. Borden emphasised that the treaty was not a military alliance, imposed no warlike obligations, and looked to consultation and conference diplomacy, with public opinion asserting a

four-power treaty, therefore, bridged or papered over the divisions evident at the Imperial Conference, but further negotiations on 8 and 9 December produced new difficulties and two further drafts by the United States delegation.[44] Shidehara presented the major problem by demanding that they exclude the Japanese main islands from the scope of the treaty, as inclusion would be inappropriate, inconsistent, and disturbing to Japanese opinion. Balfour countered by pointing to the problem raised by excluding Japan while still including Australia and New Zealand; it might suggest differing status. He also raised the issue of possible public fear that sinister motives underlay Japan's demand and reminded Shidehara that Japan would receive no protection from a revived Russia should Tokyo insist on her exclusion. Whether convinced by Balfour or not, Shidehara withdrew the objection at the meeting on 9 December and verbal amendments were accepted to make categorical Japan's inclusion.

A further amendment by Shidehara, to enable a signatory to prevent the calling of a conference in case of a dispute between two of the contracting parties, suggesting that the conference should meet only if both disputants agreed, was also defeated. The delegates, however, accepted a move to exclude domestic issues from the scope of the treaty. Hughes's insistence that they recognise that the United States' acceptance of the four-power treaty did not jeopardise her rights and interests in all c class mandate areas in the Pacific proved contentious. Both Balfour and the Japanese acquiesced, however, further brief delays ensued while the French and Japanese delegations awaited instructions from home, Balfour carried the amendments through the Empire Delegation with ease, and by 10 December the negotiations were virtually complete. On that day, with Root and Underwood prominent and with the Senate in mind, Lodge, at his oratorical worst and parading his literary accomplishments, presented the four-power treaty to the fourth plenary session.[45]

benign influence to settle international disputes. As a model Borden regarded the treaty as admirable, but he was contemptuous of its practical value because of being confined in scope to the Pacific islands.

44 Balfour to Curzon, 9 Dec. 1921, Cab. 30/5 and BD, 1st ser., XIV, no 486, no 487, 546–7; and no 488, 547; Balfour to Lloyd George, 9 Dec. 1921, Cab. 30/6; FR, 1922, II, 8–29; Hankey to Lloyd George, 9 Dec. 1921, Lloyd George Papers, F/62/1/8; Lodge Papers, file 'Washington Conference 1922.'

45 Notes of 12th and 13th meetings of BED, 9 and 10 Dec. 1921, Cab. 30/1A; FR, 1922, I, 30–1; Conferences on the Limitation of Armaments, Washington,

The delegates signed the treaty on 13 December, Balfour receiving well deserved applause, but he and Hankey had been forced to reject Riddell's proposal that they postpone signing until negotiations for the naval treaty were complete.[46] Riddell viewed the four-power treaty as a success for the United States because it terminated the Anglo-Japanese alliance. Balfour and Hankey disagreed, feeling that the treaty would help the naval negotiations, and that even without a naval agreement Britain's position was not weakened. In their opinion, Anglo-Japanese relations were still cordial, they were rid of an 'unpleasant liability,' and Anglo-American relations were 'immeasurably strengthened.' Hankey's 'unpleasant liability' was obviously the Anglo-Japanese alliance, but both Curzon and Balfour paid homage to its historical value, saluted Japan's loyalty, and expressed hope that the long-standing friendship between Britain and Japan would continue.[47] Although a funereal oration, these were neither idle words nor empty sentiments and who could predict the effect of the four-power treaty?

There remained an epilogue of some significance. The protracted negotiations over Shantung, the delays on China, a blunder by Harding, the nagging doubt that Balfour had outwitted Hughes in the negotiations, and a revival of the question of whether Japan's main islands were included in the scope of the four-power treaty made its passage through the Senate perilous enough to raise the possibility of non-ratification.[48] Hankey feared that failure to secure a settlement on Shantung could provoke a rejection of the four-power treaty, which in turn would prevent Japan from accepting the naval agreement. Then President Harding, without consulting the State Department, told the press on 20 December that the four-power treaty did not apply to Japan's main islands. He retracted and Hughes corrected the error, but hostile sections of the press seized on the discrepancy,

November 12, 1921–February 6, 1922, 1612–18. Hughes subsequently asked for an additional document to show that the four-power treaty applied to the mandate islands.

46 Hankey to Lloyd George, 12 Dec. 1921, Lloyd George Papers, F/62/1/9
47 Curzon to Eliot, 13 Dec. 1921, and Balfour to Curzon, 19 Dec. 1921, BD, 1st ser., XIV, no 498, 555 and no 512, 566–7
48 Hankey to Lloyd George, Dec. 1921, Lloyd George Papers, F/62/1/11 and BD, 1st ser., no 517, 569–73; FR, 1922, I, 38–9; Vinson, *The Parchment Peace*, 163–5

accused Lodge of deceit, and received applause from the treaty's opponents in the Senate.[49]

Repercussions in Japan were unavoidable and Shidehara, fearing a Senate demand for an amendment excluding Japan's main islands, told Balfour that Japanese opinion had adopted the complex position of opposing both the inclusion of the main islands and their exclusion at the bidding of the United States Senate. They regarded the former as injury and the latter as insult and Balfour, providing they protected the status of Australia and New Zealand, agreed to accept any settlement satisfactory to Hughes and Shidehara.[50] Finally, Balfour and Hughes accepted Japan's specific request that they exclude the main islands, Hughes concluding that this amendment should aid acceptance of the treaty by the Senate.[51] The Empire Delegation was less optimistic and the British government, mindful of Wilson's fate, decided not to ratify until the Senate had sent the treaty to the President. However, on 24 March the Senate approved the four-power treaty with a reservation that there was no commitment to armed force, no alliance, and no obligation to join in any act of defence. With this reservation, emotionally satisfying to the isolationists but somewhat superfluous, the debate ended.[52]

The negotiations from 11 November to 13 December had dealt rather unpredictably with predictable problems, resulting finally in the four-power treaty. Balfour had suggested a tripartite treaty relating exclusively to the Pacific region, which offered something both to Japan and the United States and satisfied the demands of the Imperial Conference. Particularly significant was the clause providing

---

49 Minutes of 14th meeting of the BED, 19 Dec. 1921, Cab. 30/1A. Papers such as the *Washington Herald* spread suspicion about the origins and intent of the four-power treaty.

50 Balfour to Curzon, 25 Dec. 1921, Cab. 30/6 and BD, 1st ser., no 521, 576–7

51 Note of Balfour-Kato conversation, 4 Jan. 1922, Cab. 30/27 and BD, 1st ser., no 532, 585–7; minutes of BED meeting, 31 Jan. 1922, Cab. 30/1A; Hughes memoranda of conversations with Shidehara, 19 Dec. 1921 and 14 Jan. 1922, FR, 1922, I, 37–8 and 42–3; Hughes to Shidehara, 6 Feb. 1922, ibid., 45–6. The exclusion of Japan's main islands was contained in a supplementary agreement.

52 Curzon to Geddes, 2 March, and Geddes to Curzon, 14 March 1922, FO/414/ 249; Borden to King, 19 Jan. and Borden to Foster, 22 Jan. 1922, Borden Papers, OC no 611

for the possible resurrection of a defensive military alliance between Britain and Japan and, of course, if the negotiations failed Britain would retain a modified alliance with her Asian ally. At the same time, and logically, Balfour and his advisers were seeking the most suitable way to end Britain's exclusive arrangement with Japan and to achieve a meaningful reconciliation with the United States. Hughes, however, with the Senate in mind, could not accept Balfour's triple alliance, preferring a statement of principles to supersede all existing agreements. He looked for a consultative pact without military obligations and with generalised responsibilities. Implicit in Hughes's position was a determination specifically to terminate the Anglo-Japanese alliance and to prevent both its extension to include the United States and the possibility of its revival. Moreover, with Balfour's support, Hughes was determined to expand the tripartite into a quadruple agreement by securing the inclusion of France, and also, with British and Japanese support, to prevent further dilution by the exclusion of Italy and other pretenders. In sum, Hughes sought a four-power consultative treaty which restated the relevant principles of the Root-Takahira agreement, suggested involvement and not commitment, and avoided any hint of a machiavellian scheme to place the United States in an untenable minority position.

The Japanese delegation, although welcoming Balfour's initial gesture, recognised that they could neither retain the essence of the old alliance nor provide for its renewal in the future. Shidehara, therefore, turned to securing the recognition of Japan's vital interests not only in the Pacific region but also in China, in a consultative pact acceptable to the United States. Balfour, however, removed the phrase 'vital interests,' Hughes insisted that the agreement relate only to insular possessions and dominions, Tokyo's attempt to insert 'commercial interests' received no support, and consequently neither Britain nor the United States conceded Japan's claim to a special position on the Asian mainland.

The way was open for the United States delegation, guided by the Shidehara draft as amended by Balfour, to draw up a four-power consultative treaty providing for conference diplomacy, terminating specifically the Anglo-Japanese alliance, and relating exclusively to territorial rights in the Pacific. Therefore, after Hughes's initial opposition, the Japanese delegation in an attempt to court the United States had turned its back on the twenty-year alliance and had set the negotiations on the path to a more generalised agreement. Balfour, having established cordial relations with Hughes and being anxious to avoid any disruption of the naval negotiations, acquiesced and again carried the Empire Delegation with relative ease. As a result, the four-power treaty emerged as a compromise constructed finally by Hughes, but initiated by Shidehara and Balfour, and yet satisfying the United States and then Britain rather more than Japan.

From the British viewpoint they were rid of an alliance which, despite the arguments of Curzon and his group, was of diminished value and out of harmony with postwar circumstances. As Balfour reported to Lloyd George, the alliance had become a 'source of misunderstanding rather than a guarantee of peace' and, despite the compromises accepted, he felt able to applaud the results of his negotiations.[53] Balfour could point at one and the same time to the fact that he had helped improve Anglo-American relations, avoided a rebuff to Japan by following Shidehara's lead, retained some form of connection with Tokyo, and preserved imperial unity. The four-power treaty, in Balfour's opinion, was an acceptable and even masterly compromise which bridged the chasm between Japan and the United States, narrowed the differences between Australia and Canada, and gave comfort in descending order to Atlanticists, sceptics, and more antagonistic critics. Moreover, when viewed with the other results of the Washington Conference, Britain had participated in a comprehensive attempt to achieve disarmament and peace, she need not begin construction of a Pacific fleet, and she could hope for a new atmosphere of co-operation and conciliation in the Far East. At worst Britain faced uncertainty. Would the United States co-operate in a sustained and practical way, had Britain retained Japan's friendship, could she still exercise restraint on Japan, and were Britain's imperial interests better served and protected? Moreover, who could be optimistic about the future of China whatever the value of the nine-power treaty? Answers in the affirmative were likely to breed unfounded illusions of stability and optimism, but few were prepared to condemn the work of the Washington Conference because of inscrutable and unpredictable factors. Rather, contemporaries felt that the conference marked a significant if limited advance away from the troubles of the immediate postwar period.

Moreover, Borden and other enthusiastic Atlanticists could view the four-power treaty as a step forward in the history of the empire's relations with the United States. Britain had renounced her alliance

53 Balfour to Lloyd George, 6 Feb. 1922, Cab. 30/7 and BD, 1st ser., no 585, 643-5

with Japan and Borden expressed hopes that just as the 1817 Convention dealing with the Great Lakes had grown to include the whole border, so the spirit of the four-power treaty would extend to other issues and other areas.[54] In sum, the Atlanticists dared hope that the Anglo-Japanese alliance question would become a catalyst, permitting progress toward a new era of co-operation between the empire and the United States. This would reverse the dismal trends of recent years, secure American involvement in international affairs, and create a new wave of moral leadership by the English-speaking peoples.

Borden in fact was unwilling merely to wait on events and viewed the Washington Conference as an opportunity to pursue the Atlanticist thesis, using two means of approach. First, drawing on his personal contacts and friendships, but failing to appreciate the political and tactical problems facing Hughes, he made direct approaches to the United States delegation and to other prominent political figures.[55] In general, Borden found the American delegation encouraging and both Root and Lodge accepted the urgent need to secure a close understanding between the empire and the United States.[56] Former Secretary of State W.J. Bryan also encouraged Borden, agreeing that the powers should create an international tribunal with the United States as a member.[57] This organisation would, in times of crisis, investigate and judge the incident, the powers having agreed not to resort to hostilities pending these arbitration pro-

54 Borden to Meighen, 8 Dec. and Borden to H. Wrong, 30 Dec. 1921, Borden Papers, oc no 611 and post-1921 series, folder 246

55 Borden to Wrong, 30 Dec. 1921, Borden Papers, post-1921 series, folder 253; Vinson, *The Parchment Peace*, 127–8 and 140–8. American public opinion expected positive policies and the disarmament conference provided an opportunity for a declaration favouring association with an international organisation, but Hughes was forced to weigh irreconcilable isolationist opinion. He was also forced to avoid moves which might create controversies and endanger the conference, and, therefore, while paying lip service to the idea, he counselled delay and avoidance of any positive moves toward the League.

56 Borden dairy, entries of 9 and 10 Nov. 1921, 4606–9; Borden to Governor-General, 2 March 1922, Borden Papers, post-1921 series, folder 116; Lodge to Lord Charnwood, 18 Nov. 1921, Lodge Papers, file 1921, Sept.–Dec.

57 Borden diary, entry of 18 Nov. 1921, 4623; Bryan to Borden, 23 Nov. and Borden to Bryan, 26 Nov. 1921, Borden Papers, post-1921 series, folder 149

cedures. To both Borden and Bryan, this process was a viable preventive check to the outbreak of any war, and was especially
attractive because it would ensure that governments experienced
the salutary influence of peace-loving public opinion. Borden told
Bryan that such an organisation would have prevented the escala-
tion of the July 1914 crisis, that he would devote his major effort at
the conference to securing acceptance of the international tribunal,
and that the Anglo-Saxon powers would be its core and its source
of inspiration.

Although Bryan was scarcely a representative figure, Borden
seemed encouraged and on 23 November he approached Hughes,
choosing the period immediately following the clash with Briand
on the question of land armaments.[58] Borden put forward the idea
of a permanent international tribunal, likening its procedures to
those of the arbitration treaties in which the United States had participated between 1914 and 1916, and emphasising that no nation
would be committed to any specific action in the last analysis. The
United States would avoid, therefore, the embarrassing pitfalls of
the League Covenant. Less justifiably, Borden argued that France
would find comfort in her quest for security since, in his view, the
tribunal would fulfil the role intended in the abortive Anglo-
American Guarantee Treaty of 1919. Consequently, Borden suggested, with France soothed and encouraged, Hughes could expect
an amelioration of the conference's current problems.

Hughes, in reply, seemed sympathetic toward Borden's general
aims but was understandably sceptical about his predictions of
France's reaction. In any case, Hughes would not act until the conference had dealt with the immediate Pacific and Far Eastern problems. In other words, the time was not ripe. Not discouraged,
however, Borden urged that the principal representatives take up
the question and he then turned back to his second avenue of approach, the British Empire Delegation.

Hughes's dramatic naval disarmament proposals of 12 November
had already provided Borden with an appropriate issue, which he
raised in his discussions with the United States representatives and
in the debates of the Empire Delegation.[59] Borden feared that the
British naval experts would attempt to wreck Hughes's proposals and

---

58 Borden diary, entry of 23 Nov. 1921, 4634; Borden to Meighen, 23 Nov. 1921,
   Borden Papers, OC no 611 and King Papers, file 1921 (Mea-Mitchell)
59 Borden diary, entry of 15 Nov. 1921, 4617; Borden to Lougheed, 15 Nov.

he was determined to outmanœuvre them. This struggle, however, would be merely the first encounter in a broader campaign. After the disturbing discussions of 13 November, Borden prepared a memorandum in which he suggested that, while they should accept Hughes's plan in spirit and principle, the Empire Delegation could improve on it in two ways.[60] First, to achieve a greatly extended or even permanent holiday in capital ship construction rather than the ten-year holiday suggested by the United States, Borden advocated a series of disarmament conferences, held regularly every three or five years. Second, they should establish procedures, involving the United States, to ensure the peaceful settlement of international disputes, and Borden denounced the folly and futility of being satisfied merely with disarmament proposals. As he pointed out, the powers, once at war, would rearm rapidly and engage in total conflict. In sum, Borden urged that they pursue both his suggested amendments without appearing to challenge and without giving offence to the United States, and he suggested that his proposals would improve the prospects for disarmament and fill the vacuum left by America's failure to enter the League.

The Canadian government applauded Borden's memorandum, expressing the hope that his plans would ensure the entry of the United States into the League or at least into a concert of powers. Within the Empire Delegation, however, only Pearce of Australia gave full support and, although they discussed the idea of periodic disarmament conferences, Borden's second proposal for the peaceful settlement of international disputes was submerged beneath other business until mid-December.[61] The Foreign Office section of the delegation was even less encouraging and countered that although the United States was not a member of the League, Britain was satisfied with the Anglo-American Peace Commission treaty of Sep-

1921, Borden Papers, OC no 611. These discussions reflected Borden's position taken in the Empire Delegation.

60 Borden memorandum, 'American Proposal for the Limitation of Armament,' 14 Nov. 1921, Cab. 30/1B; Borden diary, entry of 14 Nov. 1921, 4614; Borden to Lougheed, 14 Nov. 1921, King Papers, file 1921 (L'heureux-Lyons)

61 Pearce, note on Borden memorandum, 14 Nov. 1921, Cab. 30/1B; Borden diary, entry of 16 Nov. 1921, 4618; Borden to Lougheed, 16 Nov. 1921, Borden Papers, OC no 611; Lougheed to Borden, 18 Nov 1921, Borden Papers, post-1921 series, folder 253 and Meighen to Borden, 6 Dec. 1921, Borden Papers, OC no 611

tember 1914. In their view, and hardly convincing, this treaty, referring disputes to a Permanent International Commission, went as far as possible toward averting hostilities and was perhaps a model for a more general agreement.[62] Borden dismissed this reply as 'hardly relevant,' pointing out that the treaty of September 1914 had not made United States membership of the League unnecessary and did not undermine the importance of establishing an international tribunal, in which the United States would participate. Clearly Borden and the members of the Foreign Office section were having difficulty in communicating with each other and the most Borden would concede was the possible value of the Anglo-American treaty as a model.[63]

This lack of progress and the submergence of his proposal to include the United States in machinery to prevent the outbreak of war prompted Borden to approach Hughes, and then to present his case directly to Balfour.[64] In a letter to Balfour, Borden adopted the procedures of the Permanent International Commission, created by the treaties signed between 1914 and 1916, as the model for his proposed international tribunal. He then reviewed his recent conversation with Hughes, faithfully reporting the mixed reactions of the Secretary of State. Undeterred, however, Borden pointed to Harding's statement of 25 November which seemed to favour internationalist policies and perhaps indicated that Harding favoured American entry into an association of nations created to avert war. In any case, Borden asserted, the power of public opinion rather than treaty obligations forced nations to aid each other, world opinion not legal commitments had defeated Germany, and he felt justified in pursuing a new international system. Borden acknowledged the danger of awakening recent controversies but he urged Balfour to accept the proposition that, while the United States remained outside the League, the British empire must secure her co-operation in some other effective association. Ultimately, Borden concluded, the United States might enter a League modified and amended to suit her international posture.

Harding's recent speech, neither an isolated event nor unaccompanied by private conversations, though lacking concrete proposals

62 Foreign Office section, note on Borden memorandum, 16 Nov. 1921, Cab. 30/1B

63 Borden memorandum, 19 Nov. 1921, Cab. 30/1B

64 Borden to Balfour, 26 Nov. 1921, Borden Papers, OC no 611

and appearing somewhat nebulous, nevertheless had aroused considerable interest. The President had provoked public speculation, discussion among pro-League Senators, and enquiries from the foreign delegates to the Washington Conference.[65] Borden was obviously involved in this response, but Balfour was less impressed.[66] He agreed with Borden that the Empire Delegation should discuss and give due consideration to the scheme for an international tribunal, but he was not anxious to duplicate the League's machinery unless that was the only way to secure American involvement, and providing the duplication was merely temporary. Balfour's reply reflected his preoccupation with detailed negotiations and doubtless Borden's proposal seemed not only marginal and premature but also an unwarranted intrusion into the work of securing actual American co-operation in the Pacific and the Far East.

Borden's response, sharp and touchy, scarcely improved matters.[67] He agreed that they should not duplicate the League's machinery, but he insisted that no institution by itself could prevent war nor remove suspicion of intended aggression. Borden's solution lay in the development of a sane, vigorous, and wholesome international public opinion, dedicated to the abolition of war by bringing peoples and nations into a system of permanent association and co-operation to settle disputes peacefully. He saw a world torn by economic disruption and political unrest, where anarchy ruled and permitted bankrupt nations to rearm, and allowed one supposedly friendly nation to increase her air force and submarine fleet. Of the great powers remaining outside the League, Borden viewed the United States as the most powerful, influential, advanced, and democratic, her international presence would provide a sustained, efficacious force to secure peace and stability, and, therefore, 'I should hope that we may not adopt an unheeding attitude or shrink from duplication of machinery if such a duplication would be of effective aid in that great purpose.' Borden did not seek to absolve the United States from error, and Wilson, who could not stoop to conquer, must accept some of the blame for America's absence from the League, but he claimed to perceive hopeful signs in Washington. Consequently, he suggested immediate overtures to restore America's participation in international affairs and to rebuild the Atlantic entente.

65 Vinson, *The Parchment Peace*, 141–6
66 Balfour to Borden, 29 Nov. 1921, Borden Papers, oc no 611
67 Borden to Balfour, 3 Dec. 1921, ibid., oc no 611

Robert Borden and Winston Churchill leave the Admiralty Office
in 1912

Apparently Balfour made no written reply and in any case Harding had already dampened down the speculation in Washington. In a press statement of 29 November the President carefully minimised the significance of his earlier comments on an association of nations, claiming that he envisaged little more than periodic conferences between the great powers.[68] Indeed, Geddes, reporting to Curzon, dismissed Harding's original comments as careless and misleading, and expressed fears that forces hostile to the League would denounce the whole affair as a British trick to ensnare the United States and embarrass the conference. Clearly, many tactical and long-term problems were involved, possibly threatening the Washington Conference itself and even the future of Anglo-American relations, and the Empire Delegation confined its response to a single and tardy debate on 17 December.[69] This discussion merely repeated the differences existing between Borden and Balfour, with the former suggesting both that American opinion was as advanced as any but that he saw little chance of the United States entering the League. Borden demanded, therefore, that they secure American participation in world affairs by means other than League membership. Balfour rejected this view, stating that the United States was more likely to co-operate on specific issues which aroused the idealism of her people, such as the trade in opium, than through any new international organisation. Balfour's arguments were accepted, the Empire Delegation decided that they would not raise the question of international organisations at the Washington Conference, and Borden acknowledged defeat.[70]

Borden's efforts, however, were both symbolic and intrinsically important as he pursued the interrelated themes of Atlanticism by way of Pacific and Asian problems, disarmament as a basis of security, and conference diplomacy and international organisations as the mechanism of stability and order. In the last analysis he believed in the force of an enlightened and mature world public opinion holding the future of peace in its hands, and despite the rebuff he was unrepentant: 'I am more and more convinced that the peace of the world can only be secured through the process of education, by which nations will be taught more and more to bring difficulties for

68 Geddes to Curzon, 30 Nov. 1921, FO/414/248
69 Borden diary, entry of 17 Dec. 1921, 4706
70 Similarly no moves were made by the United States. For an analysis of the
    reasons for this inaction see Vinson, *The Parchment Peace*, 143–8.

discussion and settlement around the council table.'[71] North American idealist, Atlanticist, and internationalist Borden searched for the enthronement of order, justice, and reason to preserve world peace, and he searched in vain, for in truth the opportunities were an illusion. Balfour, also an Atlanticist, preferred other means and approaches.

71 Borden to Rowell, 12 Jan. 1922, Borden Papers, post-1921 series, folder 253

FIVE

Prospects for Atlanticism

Inevitably, participants and politicians on both side of the Atlantic praised the work of the Washington Conference more readily than did professional naval and diplomatic opinion. To some degree this difference reflected the opposition of idealism and undue optimism to realism and cautious pessimism, although neither group had a monopoly of any one attitude or emotion. Governments and public opinion welcomed the apparent check on naval rivalry as consistent with the prevailing financial and political realities, recognizing that Britain and Japan had relinquished what they could not afford, and the Harding administration had surrendered merely what Congress would not permit. Naval experts, however, knew that the restraints placed on naval construction were temporary, that the five-power treaty legislated for potentially obsolescent forms of naval power, and that competition in the development of submarine and air forces and in classes of warships other than capital ships would proceed relatively unchecked. Moreover, British naval opinion deplored the surrendering of future primacy and their American counterpart lamented the lost opportunity to create a navy second to none. The political consequences of the Washington Conference seemed, however, more imprecise and speculative or even simply imponderable, and, consequently, with some significant exceptions, received both less intense condemnation and applause. Rather, observers spoke hopefully of a new era of peace and stability in the Far East and an atmosphere of co-operation which might spread rapidly to Europe and the Middle East.

More specifically, and distinguishing between oratory and analysis, what of the prospects of the Atlanticists and their critics? Initially at least, although not without reservations, most of British and

Canadian officialdom, including Curzon, felt that the Washington Conference had produced a beneficial effect on Anglo-American relations. By all accounts Hughes and Balfour had co-operated closely, each delegation had developed some confidence in the other, and their increasing rapport had not flourished at the cost of their relations with the Japanese. Moreover, the Irish settlement had helped the public atmosphere greatly and Hankey felt that Americans finally began to realize that Britain shared similar ideals with the United States.[1] Geddes hinted that the rise of Britain's popularity resulted from the impression that she had supported American policies, but on the whole he was optimistic and applauded Hughes's assessment that relations between London and Washington were more cordial than they had been for the last century and a half. Geddes also warned of French propagandists and Indian agitators and did not ignore the outstanding issues in Anglo-American relations, but he concluded that

... the sentiment is so much more favourable, the atmosphere is so much more genial that it is difficult to realise that this is the same country as that to which I came almost two years ago. Given wise and patient handling of our policy, I see no reason to doubt that we are at the beginning of a new and better epoch in Anglo-American relations.[2]

Significantly, Geddes had pointed to French propagandists and undoubtedly Britain had reaped a harvest of goodwill because the intriguing, petulant, gesticulating, and vaporous French had become the *bête-noir* of the conference. Indeed Hankey, revealing, like most members of Lloyd George's entourage, growing disillusionment with France, urged the Premier not to offer a guarantee treaty to Briand lest the United States object or take offence. The inference was clear. Hankey felt that prospects for improved relations with Washington would suffer if Britain involved herself further with the reactionary and militarist French.

The four-power treaty itself, while an uncertain and unpredictable arrangement, was from one viewpoint an extremely skilful compro-

---

1 Curzon to Balfour, 3 Feb. 1922. BD, 1st ser., XIV, no 578, 634; Hankey to Lloyd George, 29 Nov. 1921 and 13 Jan. 1922, Lloyd George Papers, F/62/1/6 and /13

2 Geddes to Curzon, 13 Jan. 1922, BD, 1st ser., XIV, no 547, 601–6; Geddes to Curzon, 13 Feb. 1922, FO/414/249

mise. It seemed to avoid an outright rebuff to Japan and yet offered the promise of Anglo-American co-operation. The Atlanticists could applaud and neither the sceptics nor more bitter critics could condemn it or mount a rearguard action against it, whatever their inner reservations. In sum, the policies advocated by the Atlanticists in 1921 seemed to be bearing fruit and relations between London and Washington seemed closer than at any time since the Peace Conference. In addition, many in London, including Lloyd George, Curzon, Hankey, and Balfour, began to hope that the rapport established at the Washington Conference would induce practical and immediate co-operation in other areas and over other problems. Again, however, they tended to demand a *beau geste* from the United States rather than to cultivate the new growth, and as a result they faced disappointment. In turn this disappointment reactivated the debate between the Atlanticists and their critics, and evidence of apostacy emerged.

Moreover, despite the actual and potential advances in Anglo-American relations achieved at the Washington Conference, the Atlanticists had met with some negative response, partly because their expectations were excessive and unrealistic. The discussions at Washington had not produced a broad working agreement between the United States and the empire, no entente involving the Atlantic powers had emerged, and Hughes had not committed the United States to future participation in any international organisation. As the Secretary of State's lukewarm response to Borden had indicated, the United States had not thrown off isolationism and could even lapse into continentalism. Moreover, Hughes would cautiously practise the art of the possible, guard against premature moves, avoid issues which might raise suspicion of entanglement in European affairs, and acknowledge that American foreign policy could not elude the grasp of domestic political and tactical considerations. Consequently, short-term advances in Anglo-American relations could not obscure the longrun uncertainties nor provide against a reversal of the more encouraging trends.

Rather, despite the Atlanticists' insistence that new opportunities were at hand and that agreement over Far Eastern problems had ushered in a new era of co-operation, Anglo-American relations would return to the less heady atmosphere of detailed negotiations on specific issues.[3] Most of the issues in 1922 were familiar ones, few

3 Hankey to Lloyd George, 13 Jan. 1922, Lloyd George Papers, F/62/1/13

of them were less pressing or difficult, and to the unconverted the path could still seem stern and even forbidding. Indeed, after the honeymoon of the Washington Conference, fundamental differences and incompatibilities could re-emerge which only the most dedicated Atlanticist could ignore or regard as surmountable. Long-standing irritants and sources of distrust remained and a British tendency to dismiss the United States policy-makers as amateurish and moralising was matched by American doubts about the long-term intent of British diplomacy. A gnawing suspicion persisted in the United States that somehow Britain and Japan had outwitted them and had gained more from the Washington Conference than they, and was matched by continued interservice naval rivalry. The great distance across the Atlantic made personal contacts difficult, and this fact seemed pivotal to those who, despite unhappy experiences with the French, thought salvation came by way of summit conferences. Moreover, in spite of Geddes's improved touch, Anglo-American relations were still not receiving the lubricants of sound representation. Finally, few disagreed with Hankey that the American press remained either hostile or indifferent to the fate of relations between the English-speaking peoples, and, if anything, the Washington Conference had emphasised the competition for moral leadership rather than demonstrating that either Britain or the United States would acquiesce in the leadership of the other.[4]

Of the issues in Anglo-American relations only the Irish tragedy and the question of oil exploration in the Middle East approached a satisfactory level. The Irish settlement was Lloyd George's triumph and, despite Curzon's instructions to Balfour to resist any American attempt to insert the oil problem into the agenda, progress toward a settlement was made outside the Washington Conference with the

Already in mid-January Hankey suggested that the Washington Conference was of less importance than the Cannes and Genoa meetings, than Europe's economic problems and the questions surrounding Russia and Turkey.

4 Hankey to Lloyd George, Dec. 1921 and 13 Jan. 1922, Lloyd George Papers, F/62/1/11 and 13. Hankey saw a fluctuating competition for moral leadership; the United States securing it through Hughes's naval disarmament proposals, Britain winning the leadership over the submarine question, the United States regaining it by proposing rules on submarine warfare, Britain countering by her alternate rules, and the United States then forging ahead on the issues of the use of poisonous gases and the framing of rules of warfare.

personal help of John Cadman, Britain's official oil expert.[5] Geddes had warned of persistent anti-British propaganda emanating from the Standard Oil Company, of continued suspicion that British policies were discriminatory and injurious to American national interests, and that H.P. Fletcher, while posing as a friend of Britain, was unscrupulously perpetuating the State Department's close co-operation with Standard Oil initiated by Colby. Geddes had concluded, therefore, that a serious obstacle to an Anglo-American agreement on oil policies would remain so long as Fletcher held sway in the State Department and he could only offer as comfort rumours that Fletcher would become ambassador to Belgium. Hankey, however, felt that a general improvement in Anglo-American relations would enable Hughes to handle forces hostile to Britain such as Standard Oil, and Cadman in fact was able to lay the basis for an agreement permitting American participation in the development of Mesopotamia's oil resources.[6] Cadman's work was valuable but other problems proved more difficult.

Naval rivalry persisted despite and in many cases because of the five-power treaty as experts and others debated its significance, impact and intent.[7] Geddes, for instance, quickly feared that Britain went precipitately too far in scrapping warships and might become a hostage to the United States and France. He warned that an element of risk existed not because of American malice but because of the irresponsibility of Congress, which amounted almost to frivolity and reflected an impenetrable ignorance of international affairs. Geddes reminded Curzon that Britain was dependent on the good faith of Harding and Hughes and on a vague and unorganised public sentiment favouring peace and disarmament, and he feared that, without Hughes, Harding would be unable to control Congress. Equally, economic and commercial rivalry and the connected questions of merchant marine strength and control of cable facilities were too fundamental to be affected seriously by the Washington Conference's results, despite the guidelines on China and the agreement on mandate islands in the Pacific.

5 Curzon to Balfour, 9 Nov. 1921, Balfour Papers, 49734; Rowland and Cadman, *Ambassador for Oil*, 100–4

6 Hankey to Lloyd George, 29 Nov. 1921, Lloyd George Papers, F/62/1/6; Geddes to Curzon, 20 Jan. 1922, FO/414/249

7 Curzon to Geddes, 16 Oct. 1922; Geddes to Curzon, 19 Oct. 1922, King Papers, file 1178

Looking beyond the Pacific and the Far East, both Lloyd George and Curzon had hoped that Balfour could use the opportunity of the negotiations in Washington to recreate American involvement in the Graeco-Turkish affair.[8] They looked for an officially sponsored prominent figure such as Root or Herbert Hoover to undertake arbitration as a way to restore allied unity, so disrupted by France's agreement with Kemal Ataturk, and to arrive at peace terms acceptable to the Angora government. Lloyd George assumed that he could dictate to Athens and that the United States, acting as a 'disinterested intermediary,' could join with Britain to restore peace and honour in the Middle East. Nothing came of the initiative and the absence of United States co-operation can hardly be equated with Britain's own errors and the duplicity of her allies as reasons why Lloyd George's government stumbled to Chanak. Yet those who expected so much from Anglo-American co-operation experienced further disappointment as they witnessed the sad confirmation rather than the reversal of a theme persisting since the Peace Conference.

The two principal problems in Anglo-American relations in 1922, however, were war debts and what Lloyd George identified as the whole question of European economic and political recovery. Atlanticism as a realistic policy would stand or fall on these two issues and they provided the crucial test of whether settlement of Far Eastern problems could produce broader and more generous co-operation. Initially the latter problem focussed on prospects for the Genoa Conference and Britain's attempt to secure United States participation, but to Lloyd George at least much more was involved. His endeavours to curb French extremism, check financial chaos, aid economic reconstruction, prevent the spread of Bolshevism, and secure a measure of military and air disarmament were parts of a broad policy to achieve European peace and security. Consequently, the Genoa Conference, regarded as a pivotal step forward toward these goals, took on excessive significance and American participation seemed vital.[9] One cannot ignore the suggestion of desperation or even obsession on Lloyd George's part over this question, for on the whole he had little evidence to encourage him.

Initially, Hughes would not permit either the Cannes discussions

8 Lloyd George to Balfour, 15 Nov. 1921, Lloyd George Papers, F/61/1/3;
   Grigg to Sir G. Thomas, 24 Nov. 1921, Grigg Papers, reel 1
9 Hankey to Lloyd George, 13 Jan. 1922, Lloyd George Papers, F/62/1/13;
   Grigg to Thomas, 19 and 24 Nov. 1921, Grigg Papers, reels 2 and 1

or prospects for the Genoa meeting to overshadow the Washington Conference, even though certain business groups applauded attempts to increase the tempo of economic advance in Europe. Subsequently, as the Washington Conference bore fruit, Hughes was unwilling to risk a congressional reaction against its results, just as he had been when confronted by Borden on the question of an international tribunal. Clearly, in Hughes's opinion, premature and precipitate steps toward further international co-operation could result in an isolationist backlash, especially if European problems were involved. In addition, Hughes sensed opposition to negotiations with the Bolsheviks, particular fear of reinvolvement in the reparations tangle, and even the disapproval of pro-League groups who disliked competitive schemes seeking to secure United States involvement abroad. Hughes argued, therefore, that timing was the essence and, to the dismay of the Atlanticists and the despair and anger of their critics, the United States placed Britain in a predicament. Delay in calling the Genoa Conference did not suit Lloyd George's political and diplomatic timetable, yet a premature request for American attendance would meet with a rebuff. Hence Lloyd George could either risk an invitation and its rejection or delay the urgent work of reconstruction.[10]

Despite Hughes's reluctance and Poincaré's obstruction, Lloyd George decided to gamble on the Genoa Conference, buoyed by faint wisps of encouragement that he somehow might secure American co-operation. Rebuff came in mid-May and Geddes delivered the brutal but hardly unexpected *coup de grâce*.[11] Hughes, Geddes reported, would not repent, he regarded the Genoa Conference as a grave error, and he would have no part of it. In Hughes's view, Bolshevism was crumbling and the Soviet government was ready to capitulate, but, repeating the impact of allied intervention in 1918, the Genoa Conference would play into Lenin's hands. The Bolshevik government now had a further opportunity to become the focus of national loyalty and of working class solidarity. Moreover, Hughes

10 Geddes to Curzon, 13 Jan. 1922, BD, 1st ser., xiv, no 547, 601–6; Hankey to Lloyd George, 20 Jan. 1922, Lloyd George Papers, F/62/1/15; Borden to King, 19 Jan. 1922, King Papers, file 1922 (Bennett-Bruce)

11 BED (Genoa) to Foreign Office, 15 and 16 May 1922, Lloyd George to Geddes, 16 May 1922 and Geddes to Lloyd George, 17 May 1922, Grigg Papers, reel 10. American Ambassador Child in Rome had somehow raised Lloyd George's hopes of Hughes repenting.

felt that the conference was fundamentally unsound because its success depended on the unlikely prospect of the Bolsheviks admitting error and relinquishing their doctrines, and also because it placed an exaggerated value on Russian trade. Consequently, Hughes expected the Bolsheviks to grow in confidence, successfully to demand new loans, gain a new lease on power, and even press for *de jure* recognition. Before the United States would join in discussions with Lenin's representatives, Russia must acknowledge her debts, concede foreign property rights, give just compensation, and refrain from pressing Harding's administration for loans. The most Hughes would offer, in order to help save Lloyd George's face, was possible American participation in conversations between economic experts, purely to gain information and only if Russia were not represented. Geddes concluded, therefore, that while Hughes held office the United States would not participate in the proposed discussions at The Hague, and he warned Lloyd George against any ambassador or 'globe-trotter' who offered advice to the contrary.

These were harsh words for Lloyd George to swallow and despair made digestion all the more difficult. As he told Harvey and Taft in July, the whole panorama of postwar problems became more difficult because of American withdrawal.[12] Austria was now on the point of collapse, Germany hovered on the brink of communism, and Russia trembled and wallowed in her troubles. If Germany turned to communism, Lloyd George warned, then Europe faced industrial and social upheaval, and the United States must not only give immediate financial and economic aid but also assert a detached, moral influence to help restore reason and cool Europe's passions. Lloyd George admitted that Britain could not give a moral lead because of her own involvement and he denounced France, being consumed by her hatred of Germany, as beyond any call to reason unless the appeal came from Washington. History, the Premier concluded, would damn the United States if she ignored this demand for responsible action. Harvey countered by enquiring why Lloyd George had failed to initiate negotiations on war debts, suggesting that Hughes intended first to settle with Britain and then, in unison with her as the other great creditor nation, turn to the task in Europe. But the United States would not co-operate in Europe until Britain

12 Notes of conversation, 5 July 1922, Grigg Papers, reel 10. Present were Lloyd George, Birkenhead, Churchill, Bonar Law, Grigg, Harvey, and Taft.

had settled her debts, and Harvey, therefore, in one gesture, reopened Pandora's box.

During the early days of the Washington Conference, Hankey had dared hope that new rapport in Anglo-American relations would lead to a settlement on debts, but by February 1922 Geddes offered little comfort.[13] He warned of preparations to begin collection of allied war debts through the Foreign Debt Refunding Act, and that Britain would be foolish to expect special treatment or any significant relief from the Harding administration.[14] Despite the obvious intent of United States policy, Lloyd George, involved with the Genoa Conference, delayed, and the cabinet did not decide until mid-July on measures which were eventually embodied in the Balfour Note of 1 August 1922, addressed to Britain's debtors in Europe.[15] This note offered cancellation of all allied debts owed to Britain and promised remittance of reparation payments received from Germany, providing Britain received reciprocal and generous treatment from the United States. Should the United States not reciprocate, Britain would collect from Europe only what America demanded of her, but obviously Britain preferred a multilateral cancellation of war debts as the preface to a combined effort to initiate economic recovery. Equally clearly Britain was placing the onus of rejection and failure on the United States.[16]

Whatever the economic and political merits of this policy, and Hankey subsequently endorsed it as an act of honesty, good faith, and firmness, the City opposed it, the government's own financial

13 Hankey to Lloyd George, 29 Nov. 1921, Lloyd George Papers, F/62/1/6; Geddes to Curzon, 6 Feb. 1922, FO/414/249

14 The latest date for maturity of obligations was June 1947; the interest rate would be not less than 4¼ per cent; no part of any debt could be cancelled despite any deferring of interest payments; the bonds of one government were not acceptable in exchange for those of another; and the Senate would scrutinise the whole refunding process.

15 Dugdale, *Balfour*, II, 350–1; Young, *Balfour*, 423–4; France, under Poincaré, reacted fiercely against the Balfour Note.

16 As on the question of the Anglo-Japanese alliance in 1921, Balfour seemed here to deny his Atlanticist beliefs. Again, however, this became a tactical question with Balfour believing that firmness was the path to Anglo-American co-operation and the preservation of Britain's interests. Alternatively, he may have opposed his colleagues but would not desert Lloyd George.

advisers warned against it, and the Atlanticists, with Grigg prominent and threatening resignation, denounced it. Sir B.P. Blackett, controller of finance at the Treasury, appealing directly to Lloyd George, described the policy as 'fraught with evil consequences' and as 'fundamentally insincere' since the government had rejected two practical alternatives.[17] Blackett argued that Britain could either fund and pay her debt to the United States, retaining a free hand in relation to European debts owed to her, or she could insist, as she had in the past, that Britain's debt to the United States was an indistinguishable part of the whole of intergovernment indebtedness. Instead, the cabinet professed to be ready to repay the United States but intended to collect from Europe what Washington demanded of her. In Blackett's view the cabinet, knowing full well that such a policy was impossible to implement, was acting insincerely, either merely pretending to be prepared to fund Britain's debt to the United States, or intending eventually to pay Washington, absolve Europe, but to grumble in public in order to indict American callousness. Britain could not collect from Europe what she owed to the United States, and Blackett urged a sincere attempt to fund the American debt, preparatory to an attempt to rescue Europe from financial chaos. Such a policy, he argued, might secure American co-operation and he asked 'If we really mean to try and save Europe and are merely venting our preliminary grumble before doing so, is it worth while to begin by pillorying American selfishness?'

Grigg's assault was more emotional.[18] Lloyd George must initiate heroic measures to save Europe and avoid the futile policy of attempting an act of salvation without the vital co-operation of the United States. Grigg laid down two axioms fundamental to Anglo-American relations. First, that all Americans regarded the British as a superior people because of their tradition, experience, skill, judgment, high standards, moral authority, and their soundness of mind and heart. Only this belief had prompted Americans to lend money to Britain rather than directly to the allies, and Grigg warned lest Britain slip from her pedestal and sink down to the level of the 'lesser tribes without the law' who inhabit the rest of Europe. Grigg

17 Blackett memorandum, 'Inter-Governmental Debt,' 12 July 1922, Lloyd George Papers, F/86/2/8
18 Grigg memorandum, 'Our debt to the U.S.A. and the European situation,' 6 July 1922, ibid., F/86/2/4

thanked God he was an Englishman. Second, he suggested that the United States was abnormally suspicious of British diplomacy just because of this recognition of superiority. Washington worried about being out-manœuvred in negotiation and could not be generous for fear of being trapped and defeated. Grigg urged, therefore, that Britain remove these suspicions, launch an effective appeal, and arouse the generous elements in American life.

With regard to war debts Grigg argued that failure to fund would deal a blow at Britain's credit, be a slur on her character, and reveal that she was no better than the pitiful European bankrupts. To deny her own superiority as a mere manœuvre in order to avoid paying her debts would be base, mean, and, moreover, futile as the United States would never believe that Britain was like the rest of Europe. American opinion, Grigg suggested, would denounce Britain for adopting a fraudulent position, pretending bankruptcy, and demeaning herself merely to discredit the United States. In sum, Grigg warned against adopting an ineffectual policy because Britain would be forced eventually to fund her debt; against alienating the Harding administration, retarding the rate of European recovery, and actually making the repayment of her own debt ultimately more difficult. Furthermore, he pointed out that the City preferred to repay than to risk the loss of credit and that Britain must repay to avoid the threat of a European collapse.

In Grigg's view, therefore, practical and moral considerations reinforced each other and he saw no alternative to funding and repaying the debt and disassociating Britain from general allied indebtedness. Lloyd George should provide moral leadership, cancel unilaterally the debts owed to Britain, and gather the harvest of American reciprocal generosity which Grigg felt sure would be forthcoming. Britain's declaration of policy should omit all reference to her obligations to the United States and should make a munificent offer to Europe as part of a settlement of German, Hungarian, and Bulgarian reparations, and as a gesture to promote the rescue of Austria. Then Lloyd George could, as the leader of one of the two great creditor nations, ask the United States to call another conference at Washington to implement an act of salvation. Here from Grigg was a classical statement of Atlanticism; Britain and the United States jointly were the hope of Europe and the world and were the source of moral leadership and disinterested vigour. He had no illusions about the 'manœuverers' in the cabinet who would oppose this policy but he exhorted Lloyd George to assert himself, stating 'That Winston is the protagonist of the bargaining policy deepens, if anything could, my suspicion of it.'

The cabinet, however, decided on this 'bargaining policy,' and for a government which had demanded much of the United States the Balfour Note was a sad denouement. American opinion regarded the note as a rebuke at least and even as an insult, or as an attempt by Britain to avoid her obligations. By October Ambassador Harvey warned Curzon of the alarmingly low level to which Anglo-American relations had fallen, suggesting that they had rarely been worse.[19] United States commentators had unanimously condemned the Balfour Note as a misrepresentation of the situation and as evidence of Britain's bad faith. Curzon disclaimed any personal responsibility, since he was recuperating abroad when the government drew up the document and Balfour had managed the Foreign Office in his absence. He merely suggested that Harvey surely exaggerated. Geddes, however, in reply and partly in defence of his own position, categorically denied Harvey's views.[20] He insisted that Britain was never more popular than at that moment, the American people and their government were friendly, the tone of the press was remarkably cordial, and even Congress's muted anti-British gestures owed less to malice than to irresponsibility, frivolity, ignorance, and a concern for a posture of 'America first.' Furthermore, Geddes denied that the Balfour Note had produced an uproar against Britain, even though A.W. Mellon had commented on its ambiguous language and a mild reaction of commercial rivalry had developed. Geddes dismissed Harvey's views as reflecting the influence of that section of the British press hostile to Lloyd George, or as a result of his fear that the United States would receive the odium of Europe. He even suggested that Harvey's words were a lever to force Britain's hand on the question of control of the Atlantic cable system. However, to substantiate his basic proposition, he emphasised Hughes's personal cordiality and the absence of 'tail-twisting' and anglophobia in the current American election campaigns.

The period had ended as it had begun with Geddes contradicting Harvey, and Curzon left to unravel their conflicting interpretations of the true state of Anglo-American relations. In retrospect, Harvey's assessment was clearly more accurate than that of Geddes, American

19 Curzon to Geddes, 12 Oct. 1922, King Papers, file 283
20 Geddes to Curzon, 25 Oct. 1922, ibid.

response to the Balfour Note was neither restrained nor cordial, and Atlanticism had either been flagrantly neglected and even undermined or found wanting. Given the weakness of their position in London and despite the salutory but brief impact of the Washington Conference, the Atlanticists should not have been surprised at this neglect and their critics could with ease resume a censorious role.

The problem was tragically cyclical, for Anglo-American relations rather than being 'special,' seemed enmeshed in exasperating contradictions. The Atlanticists felt that a fundamental and unique rapport existed between the British empire and the United States but sustained co-operation did not develop. Lloyd George's government would not base the future of British foreign policy on the good faith of the United States and successive American administrations did not make the expected response. On balance the Atlanticists tended to indict London more strongly than Washington and then in despair turned in varying degree to other themes and solutions.

The sceptics and the hostile, dominating Lloyd George's unbalanced and vulnerable coalition, had waited for a series of gestures from the United States and yet had frequently acted in such a way as to undermine cordiality between London and Washington. At one and the same time they had professed to expect little and yet had demanded much of the United States, and had failed both to encourage the desired reciprocal gestures and to refrain from bitter complaints when none was forthcoming. Curiously but not surprisingly they had conducted British foreign policy from a position of scepticism or worse but were disillusioned and angered when their fears were confirmed, and blamed the United States for their own frustration. Despite Atlanticist efforts, therefore, attempts to secure Anglo-American co-operation and a new entente had fared badly in the postwar years, and only because of the vast dimension of the problems involved can the participants escape censure. Those critical of Lloyd George may indict him for failure; those more sympathetic will acknowledge the difficulties of conducting global policy in a period of reconstruction.

Clearly the apparent advance in Anglo-American relations came during the Washington Conference, and the resulting Pacific treaty system was not devoid of value, but the promise of co-operation extending from Far Eastern and naval issues to encompass Europe, the Middle East, and financial problems failed to materialise. The Washington Conference stood virtually in isolation, and despite intermittent co-operation over such matters as reparations, and despite a period of rapport between Ramsay MacDonald and Roosevelt, the succeeding years brought only new irritants and disputes. The cruiser question reactivated naval rivalry in 1927 and Austen Chamberlain quarreled with Frank Kellogg. Economic and financial collapse and the Manchurian crisis revived misunderstanding. Neville Chamberlain and Roosevelt could never create a dialogue, and the years of American neutrality between September 1939 and December 1941 were a logical conclusion. The British empire and the United States were not competitive solitudes, but the Atlanticists were left to lament what they regarded as lost opportunities. In their view, the liberal-democratic powers were launched into the postwar decades fatally handicapped. In fact, as far as the interwar years were concerned, the Atlanticists reached for an illusion, but this did not deter elites in Britain and the United States, with a former sceptic oratorically prominent in London, from resurrecting the theme when faced with similar predicaments at the end of the second great war.

Bibliography

PRIMARY SOURCES

Unpublished Documents

The Records of the Cabinet Office, the Foreign Office, and the Committee of Imperial Defence in the Public Record Office, London

Private Papers – Great Britain

A. Balfour, British Museum, London; A. Bonar Law, Beaverbrook Memorial Library, London; Robert Cecil, British Museum, London; Austen Chamberlain, University of Birmingham Library; H.A.L. Fisher, Bodleian Library, Oxford; J.L Garvin, University of Texas Library, Austin; Edward Grey, Public Record Office; E. Grigg, Queen's University Library, Kingston; D. Lloyd George, Beaverbrook Memorial Library, London; Lord Lothian, Scottish Record Office, Edinburgh; Lord Milner, Bodleian Library, Oxford

Private Papers – United States

E. Denby, Burton Historical Division of the Detroit Public Library; E.L. Dressel, Houghton Library, Harvard University; W.H. Gardiner, Houghton Library, Harvard University; Charles Evans Hughes, Library of Congress, Washington; H.C. Lodge, Massachusetts Historical Association, Boston; W.H. Page, Houghton Library, Harvard University

Private Papers – Canada
Public Archives of Canada, Ottawa

C.C. Ballantyne; Sir R. Borden; J.W. Dafoe; Sir G. Foster; W.L.
Mackenzie King; A. Meighen; Sir G. Perley; N.W. Rowell; Sir C.
Sifton

Published Documents and Papers

Documents on British Foreign Policy, 1919–1939, E.L. Woodword,
R. Butler, and J.P.T. Bury, eds., 1st Series, i–xiv, London 1947–67
Papers Relating to the Foreign Relations of the United States: 1919,
i and ii, Washington 1934; 1920, i, ii, and iii, Washington 1935–6;
1921, i, and ii, Washington 1936; 1922, i, Washington 1937
Mantoux, P., *Les Délibérations du Conseil des Quatres (24 mars–
28 juin 1919)*, 2 vols., Paris 1955
Official Report, Great Britain, *Parliamentary Debates*, House of
Commons, 5th Series, 1919–22
Parliamentary Debates, Canada, House of Commons, 13th Parlia-
ment, 1919–21
British Foreign and State Papers, 1919–1922
Cmd. 1474 (1921), *Conference of prime ministers and representa-
tives of the United Kingdom, the Dominions and India, held in June,
July and August, 1921*
Cmd. 1627 (1922), *Conference on the Limitation of Armaments
1921–1922*
Sessional paper 47 (1922), *Conference on the Limitation of Arma-
ments*. Report of the Canadian Delegate including Treaties and
Resolutions, 15 March 1922
Sessional paper 61 (1920), *Jellicoe Report on the Naval Mission to
the Dominion of Canada, November–December 1919*
*Conference on the Limitation of Armaments, November 1921–
February 1922*. Washington 1922
Conference on the Limitation of Armaments, Sub-committees,
Washington 1922

Memoirs, Diaries, and Papers

Amery, L.S., *My Political Life*, 3 vols., London 1953–5
Barnes, G.N., *From Workshop to War Cabinet*, London 1924

Borden, H., ed., *Robert Laird Borden: His Memoirs*, 2 vols., Toronto 1938

Butler, N.M., *Across the Busy Years*, II, New York 1940

Cecil, R., *A Great Experiment*, London 1941

Cecil, Viscount, *All the Way*, London 1949

Chamberlain, Sir A., *Down the Years*, London 1935

Chatfield, Lord, *The Navy and Defence*, I, London 1942

Churchill, W.S., *The World Crisis*, IV, *The Aftermath*, London 1929

Daniels, J., *The Cabinet Diaries of Josephus Daniels, 1913–1921*, ed. J. Cronon, Lincoln, Nebraska 1963

Daniels, J., *The Wilson Era: Years of War and After, 1917–1923*, Chapel Hill, NC 1944

Geddes, Lord, *The Forging of a Family*, London 1952

– *The Truth About Reparations and War Debts*, London 1932

– *Where Are We Going*, New York 1923

Grey, Viscount, *Twenty-five Years*, 2 vols., London 1925

Haldane, R.B., *An Autobiography*, London 1929

Hankey, Lord, *The Supreme Command 1914–18*, II, London 1961

– *Diplomacy by Conference*, London 1946

Hardinge, Lord, *Old Diplomacy*, London 1947

Hoover, H.C., *The Memoirs of Herbert Hoover*, New York 1957

Houston, D.F., *Eight Years with Wilson's Cabinet*, 2 vols., New York 1926

Hughes, W.M., *The Splendid Adventure*, London 1929

Lloyd George, D., *Memoirs of the Peace Conference*, 2 vols., New Haven, Conn. 1939

Long, Viscount, *Memoirs*, London 1923

Meighen, A., *Unrevised and Unrepented: Debating Speeches and Others*, Toronto 1949

Pearce, G.F., *Carpenter to Cabinet: Thirty-seven Years of Parliament*, London 1951

Peterson, M.D., *Both Sides of the Curtain*, London 1950

Repington, C.A.C., *After the War: A Diary*, London 1922

Riddell, Lord, *Lord Riddell's Intimate Diary of the Peace Conference and After, 1918–23*, London 1933

Seymour, C., *Intimate Papers of Colonel House*, 4 vols., Boston 1926–8

Simpson, B.L., *An Indiscreet Chronicle From the Pacific*, New York 1922

Steed, H.W., *Through Thirty Years, 1892–1922*, 2 vols., London 1924

Vansittart, Lord, *The Mist Procession*, London 1958
Wallace, W.S., *Memoirs of Sir George Foster*, Toronto 1937
White, W.A., *The Autobiography of William Allen White*, New York 1946
Wilson, E.B., *My Memoirs*, New York 1938

SECONDARY SOURCES

Biographies

Adams, S.H., *Incredible Era: The Life and Times of W.G. Harding*, Boston 1939
Altham, E., *Jellicoe*, London 1938
Bacon, R.H., *The Life of John Rushworth: Earl Jellicoe*, London 1936
Baker, R. Stannard, *Woodrow Wilson and World Settlement*, III, London 1923
Birkenhead, Earl of, *The Life of F.E. Smith, First Earl of Birkenhead*, London 1960
Birkenhead, Lord, *Frederick Edwin, Earl of Birkenhead*, 2 vols., London 1933 and 1935
Blake, R., *The Unknown Prime Minister: The Life and Times of Andrew Bonar Law, 1858–1923*, London 1955
Bolitho, H., *Alfred Mond, First Lord Melchett*, New York 1933
Butler, J.R.M., *Lord Lothian (Philip Kerr), 1882–1940*, London 1960
Callwell, Sir C.E., *Field Marshal Sir Henry Wilson: His Life and Diaries*, 2 vols., London 1927
Chalmers, R.W.S., *The Life and Letters of David, Earl Beatty*, London 1951
Chapple, J.M., *The Life and Times of W.G. Harding: Our After War President*, Boston 1924
Collier, B., *Brasshat: A Biography of Field Marshal Sir Henry Wilson*, London 1961
Dugdale, B.E.C., *Arthur James Balfour*, 2 vols., London 1936–7
Edwards, J.H., *David Lloyd George*, 2 vols., London 1926
Garraty, J.A., *Henry Cabot Lodge*, New York 1953
Gollin, A. M., *Proconsul in Politics*, New York 1964
Glad, B., *Charles Evans Hughes and the Illusions of Innocence*, Urbana, Illinois 1967
Graham, W.R., *Arthur Meighen*, II, *And Fortune Fled*, Toronto 1964
Halperin, V., *Lord Milner and the Empire*, London 1952
Hancock, W.K., *Smuts*, I, *The Sanguine Years*, II, *The Fields of Force, 1919–1950*, London 1962, 1968

Hancock, W.K. and J. Van der Poel, eds., *Selections from the Smuts Papers*, III, *June 1910–November 1918*, IV, *November 1918–August 1919*, London 1966

Hendrick, B.J., *Life and Letters of Walter H. Page*, 3 vols., New York 1922–5

Hyde, H.M., *Lord Reading: The Life of Rufus Isaacs, First Marquess of Reading*, London 1967

Jessup, P.C., *Elihu Root*, 2 vols., New York 1938

Johnson, C.O., *Borah of Idaho*, New York 1936

Johnson, W.F., *The Life of Warren G. Harding*, Chicago 1923

– *George Harvey: A Passionate Patriot*, New York 1929

Jones, T., *Lloyd George*, Cambridge, Mass. 1951

Lloyd George, R., *My Father, Lloyd George*, New York 1961

Marjoribank, E., *The Life of Lord Curzon*, London 1932

Mallet, Sir Charles, *Mr. Lloyd George: A Study*, London 1930

Maurice, Sir F., *Haldane, 1915–1928*, London 1939

McKenna, M.C., *Borah*, Ann Arbor 1961

Millin, S.G., *General Smuts*, London 1936

Morrison, E.E., *Admiral Sims and the Modern American Navy*, Boston 1942

Mosley, L.O., *Curzon: The End of an Epoch*, London 1960

Nicolson, H., *Curzon: The Last Phase 1919–1925*, London 1934

Ogg, D., *Herbert Fisher*, London 1947

Owen, F., *Tempestuous Journey: Lloyd George His Life and Times*, London 1954

Perkins, D., *Charles Evans Hughes and American Democratic Statesmanship*, Boston 1956

Petrie, Sir C., *The Life and Letters of Sir Austen Chamberlain*, 2 vols., London 1939–40

– *Walter Long and His Times*, London 1936

Pound, R. and G. Harmsworth, *Northcliffe*, London 1959

Pusey, M.J., *Charles Evans Hughes*, 2 vols., New York 1951

Rawson, G., *Earl Beatty, Admiral of the Fleet*, London 1930

Ronaldshay, The Earl of, *The Life of Lord Curzon*, III, London 1928

Rowland, J. and Baron Cadman, *Ambassador for Oil: The Life of John, First Baron Cadman*, London 1960

Schriftgieser, K., *The Gentleman from Massachusetts: Henry Cabot Lodge*, Boston 1944

Sommer, D., *Haldane of Cloan*, London 1960

Thompson, M., *David Lloyd George*, London 1948

Trevelyan, G.M., *Grey of Fallodon*, London 1937

Waley, Sir L.D., *Edwin Montague*, London 1964
Wemyss, Lady, *The Life and Letters of Lord Wester Wemyss*, London 1935
Whyte, W.F., *William Morris Hughes: His Life and Times*, Sydney 1957
Wrench, J.E., *Alfred Lord Milner*, London 1958
Young, K., *Arthur James Balfour*, London 1963

Monographs

Albion, R.G., *Makers of Naval Policy, 1789–1947*, Washington 1950
Allen, H.C., *Great Britain and the United States*, New York 1955
Bagley, W.M., *The Road to Normalcy*, Baltimore 1962
Bailey, T.A., *Woodrow Wilson and the Lost Peace*, New York 1944
– *Woodrow Wilson and the Great Betrayal*, New York 1948
Beaverbrook, Lord, *Politicians and the War, 1914–16*, 2 vols., London 1928 and 1932
– *Men and Power, 1917–1918*, London 1956
– *The Decline and Fall of David Lloyd George*, London 1963
Borden, R.L., *Canada in the Commonwealth: From Conflict to Cooperation*, London, 1929
Bourne, K. and D.C. Watt, eds., *Studies in International History*, London 1967
Brebner, J.B., *North Atlantic Triangle: Interplay of Canada, the United States and Great Britain*, New Haven, Conn. 1945
Buell, R.L., *The Washington Conference*, New York 1922
Bywater, H.C., *Sea Power in the Pacific*, New York 1921
– *Navies and Nations*, New York 1927
Carter, G.M., *The British Commonwealth and International Security*, Toronto 1947
Chang, Chung-Fu, *The Anglo-Japanese Alliance*, Baltimore 1931
Chaput, R.A., *Disarmament in British Foreign Policy*, London 1935
de Conde, A., *Isolation and Security*, Durham, NC 1957
Davis, F., *The Atlantic System*, London 1941
Dennis, A.L.P., *The Anglo-Japanese Alliance*, Los Angeles 1923
De Novo, J. A., *American Interests and Policies in the Middle East, 1900–1939*, Minneapolis 1963
Ellis, L.E., *Republican Foreign Policy 1921–33*, New Brunswick, NJ 1968
Gardiner, W.H., *Writings on Sea Power and American Naval Policy*, private, nd

Gelber, L.M., *The Rise of Anglo-American Friendship*, London 1938

Gilbert, M., ed., *A Century of Conflict, 1850–1950*, London 1966

Graebner, N., *An Uncertain Tradition: American Secretaries of State in the Twentieth Century*, New York 1961

Griswold, A.W., *The Far Eastern Policy of the United States*, New York 1938

Hoag, C.L., *Preface to Preparedness: The Washington Disarmament Conference and Public Opinion*, Washington, DC 1941

Ichihashi, Y., *Washington Conference and After*, Stanford 1928

Johnson, F.A., *Defence by Committee: The British Committee of Imperial Defence, 1880–1959*, London 1960

Kenworthy, J. M. and G. Young, *Freedom of the Seas*, London 1928

Kerr, Philip et al., *Approaches to World Problems*, New Haven, Conn. 1924

Link, A., *President Wilson and his English Critics*, London 1959

Longrigg, S.H., *Oil in the Middle East*, London 1954

Lower, A.R.M., *Canada and the Far East*, New York 1940

Martin, L.W., *Peace Without Victory*, New Haven, Conn. 1950

Mayer, A.J., *Politics and Diplomacy of Peacemaking, 1918–1919*, New York 1967

Mott, F.L., *American Journalism*, New York 1950

Nish, I. H., *The Anglo-Japanese Alliance: The Diplomacy of the Two Island Empires, 1894–1907*, London 1966

Northedge, F.S., *The Troubled Giant*, London 1966

Ollivier, M., *The Colonial and Imperial Conferences 1887–1937*, Ottawa 1954

Rappaport, A., *The Navy League of the United States*, Detroit 1962

Roskill, S., *Naval Policy Between the Wars*, I, *The Period of Anglo-American Antagonism 1919–29*, London 1968

Russett, R., *Community and Contention: Britain and America in the Twentieth Century*, Cambridge, Mass. 1963

Sprout, H.M., *Toward a New Order of Sea Power*, Princeton 1946

Sullivan, M., *The Great Adventure at Washington*, New York 1922

Tate, M., *The Disarmament Illusion*, New York 1942

– *The United States and Armaments*, Cambridge, Mass. 1948

The History of the Times, IV, London 1952

Thompson, J.M., *Russia, Bolshevism and the Versailles Peace*, Princeton 1966

Toynbee, A. J., *Survey of International Affairs, 1920–23*, London 1927

– *The Conduct of British Empire Foreign Relations Since the Peace Settlement*, London 1928

Ullman, R.H., *Britain and the Russian Civil War November 1918 to February 1920*, Princeton 1968
Van Alstyne, R.W., *American Crisis Diplomacy*, Stanford 1952
Vinson, J.C., *The Parchment Peace: The United States Senate and the Washington Conference*, Athens, Georgia 1955
Watt, D.C., *Personalities and Policies*, London 1965
Wheeler, G.E., *Prelude to Pearl Harbour: The United States Navy and the Far East 1921–31*, Columbia, Missouri 1963
Willert, Sir A., *The Road to Safety: A Study in Anglo-American Relations*, London 1952
Young, E.J., *Powerful America*, New York 1936

Articles

Anon., 'The Victory that will End the War,' *Round Table*, viii, 30, March 1918, 221–37
Asada, S., 'Japan's "Special Interests" and the Washington Conference, 1921–22,' *American Historical Review*, lxvii, Oct. 1961, 62–70
Beloff, M., 'The Special Relationship: An Anglo-American Myth,' in M. Gilbert, ed., *A Century of Conflict, 1850–1950*, London, 1966, 151–71
Brebner, J.B., 'Canada, The Anglo-Japanese Alliance and the Washington Conference,' *Political Science Quarterly*, l, 1935, 45–57
Curtis, L., 'Windows of Freedom,' *Round Table*, ix, 33, Dec. 1918, 1–36
De Novo, J.A., 'The Movement for an Aggressive American Oil Policy Abroad, 1918–1920,' *American Historical Review*, lxi, July 1956, 854–76
Department of External Affairs (Ottawa), 'Christie Memorandum, 1 June 1921, "The Anglo-Japanese Alliance,"' *Monthly Bulletin*, xviii, Sept. 1966, 402–13
Fry, M.G., 'The Imperial War Cabinet, the United States and the Freedom of the Seas,' *Royal United Service Institution Journal*, cx, Nov. 1965, 353–62
– 'The North Atlantic Triangle and the Abrogation of the Anglo-Japanese Alliance,' *Journal of Modern History*, xxxix, March 1967, 46–64
– 'Britain, the Allies and the Problem of Russia, 1918–1919,' *Canadian Journal of History*, ii, Sept. 1967, 3, 62–84
Gardiner, W.H., 'Political and Naval Problems of the Pacific, 1921,'

March 1921, Pamphlet No 2-5061, Public Archives of Canada, Ottawa

Galbraith, J.S., 'The Imperial Conference of 1921 and the Washington Conference,' *Canadian Historical Review*, xxix, June 1948, 143–52

Hall, H. Duncan, 'The British Commonwealth and the Founding of the League Mandate System,' in Bourne, K. and D.C. Watt, eds., *Studies in International History*, London 1967, 345–68

Kerr, Philip, 'The Anglo-Japanese Alliance,' *Round Table*, xi, Dec. 1920, 87–97

– 'The British Empire, the League of Nations, and the United States,' *Round Table*, x, 38, March 1920, 221–53

– 'The End of War,' *Round Table*, v, 20, Sept. 1915, 772–96

– 'The Foundations of Peace,' *Round Table*, v, 19, June 1915, 589–625

– 'The Harvest of Victory,' *Round Table*, ix, 36, Sept. 1919, 645–71

– 'The Harvest of War,' *Round Table*, vi, 21, Dec. 1915, 1–32

– 'The Making of Peace,' *Round Table*, vii, 25, Dec. 1916, 1–13

– 'The Principle of Peace,' *Round Table*, vi, 23, June 1916, 391–429

– 'Walter Page,' *Round Table*, xiii, 50, March 1923, 289–99

– 'War Aims,' *Round Table*, vi, 24, Sept. 1916, 607–13

– 'The War for Public Right,' *Round Table*, vi, 22, March 1916, 193–231

Lower, A.R.M., 'Loring Christie and the Genesis of the Washington Conference of 1921–22,' *Canadian Historical Review*, xlvii, March 1966, 38–48

Nish, I.H., 'Japan and the Ending of the Anglo-Japanese Alliance,' in Bourne, K. and D. C. Watt, eds., *Studies in International History*, London 1967, 369–84

Tate, M. and F. Foy, 'More Light on the Abrogation of the Anglo-Japanese Alliance,' *Political Science Quarterly*, lxxiv, 1959, 532–53

Vinson, J.C., 'The Drafting of the Four Power Treaty of the Washington Conference,' *Journal of Modern History*, xxv, March 1953, 40–7

– 'The Imperial Conference of 1921 and the Anglo-Japanese Alliance,' *Pacific Historical Review*, xxxi, Aug. 1962, 257–66

Wheeler, G.E., 'The United States Navy and War in the Pacific,' *World Affairs Quarterly*, Oct. 1959, 199–207

– 'The United States Navy and the Japanese Enemy, 1919–1931,' *Military Affairs*, xxi, Aug. 1957, 61–74

Theses

Bowen, A.D., Jr, 'The Disarmament Movement 1918–35,' Columbia University 1956

Fry, M.G., 'Anglo-American-Canadian Relations with special reference to Far Eastern and Naval Issues, 1918–22,' London University 1963

Raffo, P.S., 'Robert Cecil and the League of Nations 1916–1927,' Liverpool University 1967

Smith, P.A., 'Lord Lothian and British Foreign Policy 1918–1939,' Carleton University 1968

Spinks, C.N., 'A History of the Anglo-Japanese Alliance, 1902–22,' Stanford University 1936

Index

This book

was designed by

WILLIAM RUETER

under the direction of

ALLAN FLEMING

University

of Toronto

Press